Lecture Notes in Economics and Mathematical Systems 486

Springer
Berlin
Heidelberg
New York
Barcelona
Hong Kong
London
Milan
Paris
Singapore
Tokyo

Michael Neugart

Nonlinear Labor Market Dynamics

Springer

Author
Dr. Michael Neugart
Freie Universität Berlin
Fachbereich Politik- und Sozialwissenschaften
Ihnestrasse 22
14195 Berlin, Germany

Cataloging-in-Publication Data applied for

Die Deutsche Bibliothek - CIP-Einheitsaufnahme

Neugart, Michael:
Nonlinear labor market dynamics / Michael Neugart. - Berlin ; Heidelberg ; New York ; Barcelona ; Budapest ; Hong Kong ; London ; Milan ; Paris ; Santa Clara ; Singapore ; Tokyo : Springer, 2000
(Lecture notes in economics and mathematical systems ; 486)
ISBN 3-540-67279-6

ISSN 0075-8442
ISBN 3-540-67279-7 Springer-Verlag Berlin Heidelberg New York

Springer-Verlag is a company in the BertelsmannSpringer publishing group.

Printed in Germany

Berlin, Freie Universität, Diss.; D188

Typesetting: Camera ready by author
Printed on acid-free paper SPIN: 10734376 42/3143/du-543210

To my parents

Acknowledgments

This work was inspired by Prof. Dr. Michael Bolle, who gave me the opportunity to conduct research and to teach at the Freie Universität Berlin. His support was manifold, contributing a great deal to my personal and intellectual development during the last three years. Michael Bolle has been an advisor that most doctoral students would wish to have.

My colleagues made a stimulating and friendly working environment possible. I had invaluable and interesting discussions with Dr. Ulrich Brückner, Dr. Martin Schulz, and Björn Rother. Bärbel Lehman was always genuinely concerned about my well being.

Prof. Dr. Richard Freeman gave me the opportunity to do research at Harvard University and at the National Bureau of Economic Research in Cambridge (U.S.A.) in autumn 1998. I am highly indebted to him. While staying there, many aspects of my work became clearer to me. Large parts were written in the PC room of the NBER. Thank you to all the nice people there who made it a pleasant stay. During that time, I met Dr. Erling Barth who was on leave from the Institute for Social Research in Oslo, Norway. I enjoyed having lunches with him and am grateful for his comments on my work.

At an early stage, Prof. Dr. Günther Schmid invited me to present parts of my work at the Wissenschaftszentrum Berlin. I am grateful for his support and the comments I received. While visiting conferences at the University in Cambridge U.K., the University of Porto, the London School of Economics, and the New York University, I received comments from several participants who cannot all be mentioned here. But I would like to say that PD Dr. Uwe Hassler gave helpful hints on technical aspects of my work. Most importantly, I met Prof. Dr. Willi Semmler through these occasions. Thank you for becoming the second advisor of the thesis.

I received financial support from the Nafög Kommission at Freie Universität Berlin, the Deutsche Akademische Austauschdienst, and from the funds of the Jean-Monnet-Chair of Dr. Ulrich Brückner. Thank you to all of them.

Berlin, 2000

Content

1 Introduction

Fasten your seat belts. This work is about endogenous and irregular labor market dynamics. Don't be scared. You will probably not get lost. As I will argue, labor markets might only be locally unstable. Those who do not rely on this preliminary note and need further orientation are referred to earlier works on nonlinear economic dynamics of such authors as Goodwin (1967) or Kaldor (1940), and on chaotic dynamics as introduced to economic theory by Benhabib and Day (1980), Stutzer (1980), or Day (1982) among the first.

In contrast to linear stochastic systems, the dynamic behavior of nonlinear deterministic models is rather rich. Cycles can become self-sustained, even erratic, although the underlying equations of motion are deterministic. Hence, incorporating nonlinear relationships opens the door for an endogenous explanation of economic dynamics – something that linear stochastic type models cannot achieve. Linear difference or differential equations only have a small range of time series behavior. In the case of global instability, trajectories are unbounded. The system explodes, which does not deal with what we observe on markets. At the margin, persistent cycles can occur which are, however, highly sensitive to the parameters of the system. Small perturbations of the parameters will either be followed by a convergence to a finite long run state or by infinitely increasing trajectories. A powerful explanation of persistent cycles fails. After all, global stability is the only category left within linear economic models from which to start. In that case, time paths converge to a single long run state - either monotonically or with damped oscillations. At best, cyclical behavior will be transitory until the system reaches its equilibrium. One arrives at enduring cycles only by adding a stochastic component. Exogenous shocks become the main ingredient that cause persistent deviations from a long run equilibrium. However, such an approach may be misleading.

Linear stochastic models imply that markets are stable, which may make a researcher feel comfortable and may explain why nonlinear approaches have been excluded for such a long time. Adelman and Adelman (1959), for example, tested a variant of the Klein-Goldberger model with U.S. data. They found from the solutions of impulse response studies, that if the Klein-Goldberger-Model is an appropriate description of the U.S. economy, the latter is inherently stable. When they added stochastic components, business cycles occurred that resembled real time series. Adelman and Adelman (1959, p. 620) concluded that their results tend to support the view of Frisch, alas that "...cyclical movements observed in a capitalistic society are actually due to random shocks...". Estimating parameters with the same data and simulating the same model with these parameters, Meissner (1971) derives different results. In particular, he concludes that not all solutions are stable. Did the intention that capitalist economies should be stable and well behaved drive the result of Adelman and Adelman (1959)? Maybe. At least it indicates that different tastes of researchers will have an important effect on the results, irrespectively of what the true underlying mechanisms are. Other reasons why nonlinear dynamical systems have been widely neglected have been put forward. It is certainly true that the analysis of nonlinear dynamical systems is more challenging from a technical point of view than that of linear differential or difference equations. To argue that it prohibited a more widely accepted nonlinear approach to economic dynamics is vague. A probably more prominent role is played by the emergence of powerful computers. An analytical treatment of nonlinear dynamical systems is often impossible. The only way to learn more about the dynamic properties is to simulate models which was impossible before, so that researchers who were aware of the potential impact of nonlinearities might have chosen to linearize the system in the end.

By choosing linear versions of intrinsically nonlinear economic systems, they may have excluded dynamic properties that would have made possible an endogenous explanation of economic dynamics. Since the work of Goodwin (1967), even though his model is structurally unstable and small perturbations may lead to explosive trajectories, and Kaldor's (1940) model on endogenous business cycles through nonlinear savings and investment functions, it is known that economic cycles can be self-sustained[1]. If it is true that nonlinear models give a better description of the underlying equations of motion, it follows that economies are neither inherently stable, nor do exogenous shocks alone cause cycles. It may be the case, that a linear fit to the data of a nonlinear economic process throws away valuable information about the true system behavior. A frequently cited experiment that strengthens that point was conducted by Blatt (1983, pp.224), who produced a time series along the lines of Hicks' model. The parameters implied an explosive second order difference equation. Hicks ceilings and floors bounded the fluctuations from above and below. Surprisingly, an AR(2) model fitted the generated time series 'very well'. Every proponent of a linear stochastic approach would have been happy about the result, although the AR(2) did not capture the structure of the true underlying system. Most importantly, the coefficients on the

---

1 Semmler (1986) gives a quick introduction into these early nonlinear business cylce models.

variables of the estimated equation implied a stable economy, whereas the underlying difference equation is unstable. One may conjecture that various other attempts to deliver an explanation of economic dynamics on the grounds of linear stochastic models actually failed in the past. The driving forces may have not been detected. Although the standard statistics were well behaved there might be more information in the data that is not exploited. Maybe even information that would imply a locally unstable economy.

Nonlinear models are certainly one step ahead of linear stochastic type models in terms of an endogenous explanation of economic dynamics. They will generate smooth cyclical paths for quite a range of parameter settings and initial conditions. No round off error will lead to either explosive or damped cycles, as would happen with cycles at the margin in linear models. But from a qualitative point of view, there is still a gap between the irregular behavior of real time series data and the smooth time paths of earlier nonlinear deterministic models (Kaldor 1940, Hicks 1950, or Goodwin 1967). That gap is closed by economic models with chaotic properties. These models, with the work of Benhabib and Day (1980), Stutzer (1980), or Day (1982) among the first, can generate aperiodic time paths on a finite attractor. There is qualitatively no difference to real time series data. They appear to be random but are deterministic. It is impossible to distinguish chaotic time series from stochastic processes simply by 'eyeball statistics'. Even standard techniques like frequency spectra fail, as a chaotic process incorporates frequencies of infinite order similar to a stochastic system.

The properties of chaotic time series bear important implications for economic policy. Besides endogenous aperiodic behavior, chaotic systems are characterized by sensitive dependence on initial conditions. This means that even the smallest error due to a misspecification of the initial state of a variable, or any parameter, will grow exponentially. Two trajectories that are very close at some point in time will diverge. After a while they pursue completely different paths. As the system is only locally unstable, which implies a finite attractor, these two trajectories might come close to each other again in the future. But they basically follow completely distinct paths. Insofar, forecasts of the long run are impossible as there are practical restrictions to pin down the exact state of an economy. If only it was possible to determine the exact parameter settings and values of the variables, one would be able to make a long run forecast. Where the economy will be in the near future is still possible to say, as long as the underlying equations of motion are known. If, however, one lacks a structural model of a chaotic economy, it is impossible to make predictions even in the short run. Chaotic time series are irregular and may incorporate structural breaks. Recently smooth behavior may abruptly be followed by wild oscillations, so that any technique that tries to extrapolate past behavior will utterly fail.

As causal relationships vanish, 'policy-matters' concepts have to be dropped. It is impossible to steer an economy from one point to another. This imposes quite some restrictions on economic policy. In fact, it would make it obsolete. An economic policy, for example, that tries to smooth business cycles, à la Keynes, is doomed to fail. The dose of any measure would always be too much or just not enough. If only it was possible to exactly hit the state that implies a trajectory that leads to the desired state, economic policy could achieve its goal. But this is, once more, infeasible from a practical point of view. Besides politicians or economic advisors would have to know the exact model of the economy.

It may also be noteworthy that deviations from a long run state of an economy do not necessarily come from political interventions. It is a popular argument that deficit spending and surplus saving policies destabilize an economy rather than create smooth cycles. However, even if the instruments were adequate to tackle economic fluctuations, timing the policy measures would still be a problem. Such policies may do the right thing, but always at the wrong time. Various lags, from the recognition of an upcoming depression, to the decision about measures that should be undertaken, and the time span until they become effective, would prohibit a fine tuning of the economy. To overcome the problem of stabilizing policies through fiscal programs, alternative, monetarist policies were proposed. Proponents like Milton Friedman argued that these kind of policies should be abandoned for those reasons, and be substituted by acclaimed growth rates for monetary aggregates. No lag problem would occur then. Needless to say that in a chaotic environment, any central bank will fail to find and implement the appropriate monetary growth rate to steer an economy to a certain point in the future. Monetarist views may as well be a misleading analysis and an ill born policy advice.

If exogenous shocks are not the driving force behind the fluctuations, then any policy that tries to dampen cycles by shielding the economy from outside influences will go wrong. Politicians, for example, might be inclined to 'decouple' their economy from others by cutting off trade flows. But, since it may not be the exogenous force that drives the cycles, the analysis of the problem is false and so would be the implication. A way out of the very narrow constraints that economic policy faces in a chaotic system are structural politics. If politics cannot steer an economy that is in a chaotic regime, it still has the possibility to remove the origins of chaotic behavior. Given that it knows the underlying equations of motion, economic policy could try to either adjust the parameters or to remove the essential nonlinearities. The economy would be back in a stable regime with clear cut causal relationships. Therefore, sensitive dependence on initial conditions would not make the achievement of long run economic goals infeasible.

If it should be possible to exclude chaotic dynamics in a nonlinear system, the narrow restrictions for economic policy widen. There is scope for pareto-efficient policies. Chaotic and nonlinear deterministic systems differ insofar as nonlinear deterministic relationships are a necessary, but not a sufficient, condition for chaos. A nonlinear deterministic system is chaotic only with sensitive dependence on initial conditions. Contrary to the point of view that any market intervention is detrimental, economic policies can improve welfare if the underlying equations of motion are nonlinear, but do not imply chaotic behavior. Nonlinear economic systems can have very rich landscapes with several locally stable equilibria. Thinking about a surface of a billiard-table that is not even, but has some sinks at different altitudes, illustrates the topic. The billiard ball might have become stuck at one of these sinks, say at one that has a higher altitude. If a high altitude means that it is a less desirable state in terms of welfare, it clearly would only take a small impulse to free the ball from the locally stable sink. Afterwards it would move to the more desirable state on its own. If such a landscape is a good description of long run labor market behavior, it bears important policy implications. It would, for example, only take a transitory fiscal impulse to leave a locally stable, high unemployment equilibrium. No permanent expenditures are needed, which eases expansionary fiscal policies (Pissarides 1986). Expectation formations cannot make the economic policy obsolete as it would do, for example, under Ricardian equivalence. Of course, the distribution of locally stable equilibria could just be the other way around, too. The high employment equilibrium could be the locally stable equilibrium that is abandoned by the policy measure (Manning 1990). In both examples, it would pay knowing the true underlying equations of motion, instead of a linear approximation that fits quite well in terms of standard statistics.

To investigate the importance of nonlinear relationships in economic systems, two paths have been followed. The econometric approach tries to detect the presence of information in the residuals left from linear fits to the data, which would indicate nonlinear dynamics. This strand of literature has made an important contribution, as researchers became aware of a nonlinear deterministic core that might be hidden in the data. But apart from problems related to specific tests, this approach has an important shortcoming. Even if it can be shown that linear, or even nonlinear, stochastic models do not fit the data adequately, hence, nonlinear deterministic or even chaotic dynamics play some role, one cannot pin down what kind of nonlinearity drives the result. Apart from general implications about what structural models should look like and what would follow for economic policy, no specific information is gained. One neither knows on what nonlinearity to focus, nor to what degree it would matter. This is why nonlinear models are so important. The analytical treatment or even simulations will show whether nonlinearities in standard economic models significantly alter the dynamics. It is possible that either a high or low degree of nonlinear structure can change the dynamic properties of a model, which enables one to draw more specific conclusions. This is a tedious approach but it is probably worthwhile to do. Some nonlinear relationships may be excluded from the beginning, since no good arguments exist to substitute a linear relationship. Others may be good candidates. We will try to find out whether there are important nonlinear relationships on labor markets, from which we can derive dynamic properties that can cope with time series data.

The following work takes standard labor market models and introduces specific nonlinear relationships. These nonlinearities are backed by, as we think, serious arguments, including empirical evidence on labor market behavior. Still, the models are highly stylized. For ease of analytical treatment and to highlight the role of a specific nonlinear relationship, only a few variables are incorporated. All examples are partial equilibrium models. Whether this is a too crude simplification and results would vanish in a general equilibrium context remains open.

Earlier models with nonlinear and chaotic dynamics are briefly discussed in chapter 2.1. The literature has been growing fast which makes a comprehensive survey nearly impossible. Alternatively, it tries to give insight into selected causes from which complex economic dynamics can arise. Besides these models, the most popular techniques for the study of nonlinear deterministic time series are sketched. The results from these approaches are reviewed before some of the methodological problems are discussed. To put our main concern on as broad a basis as possible, the following work tries to derive complex dynamics from various distinct approaches to model labor market behavior. The first two chapters ground on the neoclassical labor market model, where demand for labor is driven by the underlying production technology that generates a downward sloping function in real wages. Workers' preferences and the budget constraints are such that labor supply slopes upwards. It is the task of an auctioneer to find a real wage that clears the market. At the equilibrium, the real wage implies a demand for labor that exactly matches the supply decision of households. Chapter 3 discusses the implications that arise from the introduction of nonlinear supply curves. Demand follows a Cobb-Douglas production function with decreasing returns at a fixed capital stock. It is shown that a backward bending supply curve, as well as a nonlinear monotonous labor supply curve, can change the dynamics of the labor market completely. In particular, the equilibrium may become locally unstable. The real wage sequence that the auctioneer sets may even be chaotic. The robustness of these results is shown by studying the impact of a non-orthodox labor demand side within the same context, but assuming an upward sloping labor supply curve. Here, too, complex dynamics may arise. The dynamics enter the models as the auctioneer applies a proportional control rule to clear the market. He sets the real wage according to the disequilibrium quantities. This may cause objections against the observed market behavior. One may be inclined to argue that a rational auctioneer, who ever he is, would probably try to find another control rule if he constantly fails at clearing the market. In chapter 5, it is shown that an auctioneer who sticks to his adjustment rule, even in the light of his constant failure, behaves rational under certain conditions. In chapter 6, we switch to a different approach. It has been argued that stock models do not adequately capture important features of the labor market, as there can be large flows of workers from employment to unemployment, and vice versa, without changes in the level of unemployment. Flow models of the labor market would give a better picture by looking at the various possible transitions and their causes. We develop a simple worker flow model where the outflow rate from unemployment is an endogenous function of the level of unemployment. Under certain conditions, one can observe unemployment cycles of arbitrary order within a bounded range. The 'natural rate of unemployment' becomes a 'natural range of unemployment'. The third context that concerns us within local instability is a wage bargaining model. Wage bargaining models may deliver a better framework to think about labor market outcomes in economies where trade unions and employers' representatives bargain over some surplus of production. Contrary to the usually accepted upward sloping wage bargaining curve, we argue that the wage setting curve can become a non-monotonous function of the employment level. It may slope upwards when unemployment is low, but slope downwards when unemployment is high. We show that in a 'right-to-manage-model', endogenous employment cycles are possible. There may, once more, be a 'natural range of unemployment' instead of a natural rate. The last chapter tries to give an empirical assessment of nonlinear, possibly chaotic dynamics. It does not refer to one of the models developed before, but tries to find a nonlinear deterministic core in time series data of the German labor market. Whereas there is strong evidence for deterministic nonlinearities, there does not seem to be any hidden chaos. However, for several reasons, the empirical case against chaos is a weak one.

2 Nonlinear and chaotic economic dynamics

2.1 Earlier models revisited

The purpose of sketching some of the ideas and underlying mechanisms of nonlinear and deterministic models, is to show how these models can contribute to the understanding of complex economic phenomena. It is far from being complete. In fact, the literature in this field is growing fast and giving a comprehensive overview would be beyond the scope of this work[2].

Where erratic behavior cannot be explained within probabilistic approaches and is frequently labeled as error terms or unpredictable shocks, nonlinear deterministic models try to find an endogenous explanation. Thus exogenous forces may play a role in what we observe on markets but the driving forces would be specific nonlinear relationships. As linear stochastic models, nonlinear deterministic models have their shortcomings, though for different reasons. The conditions under which dynamics become irregular even in the absence of exogenous shocks might be viewed as unrealistic or of minor importance. Calibrated versions of nonlinear deterministic models sometimes incorporate parameters that are not backed by empirical estimates. But nonetheless, a rejection of nonlinear deterministic models on these grounds would be inadequate at this stage. These models can improve the understanding of economic dynamics. Attention is shifted to the role of nonlinear relationships that contribute to a consistent, endogenous explanation of irregularities and structural breaks in economic data. Nonlinear models might be able to exploit information that is left in the residuals of linear stochastic models, which these models render as stochastic and unexplainable.

---

2 For other surveys see i.e. Goodwin and Pacini (1992), Nishimura and Sorger (1996), Benhabib (1996), Lorenz (1997), Boldrin and Woodford (1990), or Kelsey (1988).

2.1.1 Interaction and irregular dynamics

The main concern of nonlinear models, where individual actions or economic aggregates are interrelated, is whether interdependency can destabilize market behavior, either on the macro or the micro level.

Interdependency of aggregated variables is given for open economies, or sectors within economies that are linked via trade or investment flows. Lorenz (1987a) shows that if the accelerator is a nonlinear function, autonomous sigmoid shaped investment can cause irregular behavior. Aggregate income in one country will vary erratically due to the economic activity imposed by another country. Such models capture the situation of a small open country that is dependent on the cyclical patterns of the world economy. They may serve as a qualitative explanation of the volatility to which small, open, and less developed countries are exposed. Smooth cyclical behavior of the world economy would be the forcing function that may be responsible for the erratic, but deterministic business cycles in the small and open economy. Extending the interaction to three countries will not extinguish the chaotic properties of interacting economic units at the macro level. Given there are nonlinear sigmoid investment and savings functions as proposed by Kaldor (1940) and, given countries are coupled via exports and imports, cycles can also become erratic (Lorenz 1987b). Furthermore, Lorenz (1987c) investigated the case of unidirectional investment within three countries finding strange attractors. Unidirectional investment captures asymmetries between developed and less developed countries in foreign direct investment. In such a framework, irregular cycles already occur if savings and investment functions are nonlinear in the country itself. Induced investment does not have to be a nonlinear function of income in the coupled country or sector.

On the microeconomic level, the impact of interaction on the dynamic behavior of certain variables has mostly been studied for consumption patterns. Consumption decisions are interrelated in many ways. One can think of markets where the number of buyers of a certain good depends on the amount of previous buyers. Such 'bandwagon effects' can have either sign. A positive feedback might occur if the utility that a person derives from the consumption of a specific good is dependent on the number of persons who also bought this particular good. Having an e-mail account will only pay if there are friends and colleagues who can receive e-mails. A powerful software tool will have less utility for its user, if service is sparsely available due to a low market penetration. Consumers, to give a further example, may wait to buy a certain good if information asymmetries are important. Then, a large amount of previous buyers will signal to them the quality of the good they intend to buy. Postponing the purchase of a good, until there is a certain fraction of buyers, may be an efficient behavior to overcome information asymmetries. Another reason why people delay consumption might be that they do not dare to buy a certain good as long as there are no other people who promote these goods as being fashionable. Of course, the latter effect can also be the other way around inducing a negative feedback mechanism. This might especially apply to status seeking consumers. The utility they derive from a good may decline the more widespread it is. They are snobs and they will not buy a cellular phone unless it has some features that distinguishes them from the masses.

Granovetter and Soong (1986) develop a threshold models with 'bandwagon effects' that generates irregular consumption cycles. They ground their model on distribution functions and do not explicitly apply utility functions. But this is not a crucial assumption. Even if preferences are derived from utility functions, interdependent consumer behavior can cause irregular dynamics. Incorporating 'bandwagon effects' or behavioral patterns like 'catching up with the Joneses' will yield preference functions that are dependent on socially relevant agents - 'My neighbor bought a larger car than I have, alas I want an even bigger one now'. Interrelated preferences and history dependence can easily be incorporated in the standard approach (Gaertner 1986, Gaertner and Jungeilges 1988), where agents maximize a Cobb Douglas utility function

$$U(x,y,a) = x^a \cdot y^{1-a} \tag{1}$$

under a budget constraint like

$$p_x \cdot x + p_y \cdot y = B\,. \tag{2}$$

If the coefficients in the utility function capture the various kinds of interdependency

$$a_{t+1} = h(x_t, y_t, x_t^n, y_t^n, \alpha) \tag{3}$$

consumption paths can become chaotic. In (3) the degree with which good x enters the utility function one period ahead, is dependent on the amount consumed today, the consumption bundle of a reference person n, and a parameter α. Of course, various specifications could be chosen to model the impact of the socially relevant person. But even for a simple linear feedback rule, dynamics become irregular. The amount of consuming x may not be stable in the long run. Agents prefer more units of x in one period compared to another. Nevertheless, the behavior is rational as the change in consumption bundles is caused by utility maximizing agents.

2.1.2 Overlapping generations and endogenous cycles

In the previous class of models, agents maximize present utility. This might be an unrealistic scenario as people will usually also care about their future. They probably maximize utility over a longer horizon by trading present for future consumption. It can be shown that even under such assumptions, chaotic cycles are possible. There is a whole range of utility functions and production technologies for which endogenous cycles will occur in models of overlapping generations.

In the common structure of overlapping generations models, each generation lives for two periods. Within each period there is a constant number[3] of young and old people consuming c_t^y and c_t^o, respectively. Each generation or individual (groups are homogeneous) maximizes utility with respect to his life time consumption $U(c^y_t, c^o_{t+1})$. Endowments are e_y when young and e_o when old. An intertemporal budget constraint restricts lifetime consumption. As consumption has to equal the sum of endowments, the maximum possible amount of consumption for the old generation is

$$c_{t+1}^o = e^o + \rho_t \cdot (e^y - c_t^y). \tag{4}$$

The old generation can spend the endowment of the second period of life, and an additional amount if they consumed less than their endowment when being young. ρ_t is an interest rate on these savings. The young save and lend money (or an imperishable good) to the old generation. Every unit of endowment not spent when young means a larger endowment for the second period of life, which increases consumption (Grandmont 1985). If, however, the young are impatient, they would spend more than their endowments and borrow from the old (Benhabib and Day 1982) - the second possible case in this setting. Which of both cases will hold depends on the endowments and the utility functions of the individuals. The aggregate market will be in equilibrium for $\{c_t^y, \rho_t\}^{\infty}_{t=0}$ if the consumption of the young and old generation is covered by the endowments of both generations in period t

$$c_t^y + c_t^o = e_t^y + e_t^o. \tag{5}$$

Maximizing utility under the restriction of a clearing market yields the first order condition

$$\frac{\dfrac{\partial U}{\partial c_y}}{\dfrac{\partial U}{\partial c_o}} = \rho_t. \tag{6}$$

The rate at which individuals trade present for future consumption is equal to the relative marginal utilities that these agents derive from consumption, while young and old. If, for example, the left hand side in (6) is smaller than the interest rate it would pay to a young individual to reduce consumption. Then he would spend the money when he becomes old. Should the left hand side be larger than the right hand side in (6), the individual would realize a welfare gain if he raises consumption now as additional utility in old age consumption is relatively low. A

---

3 In Benhabib and Day (1982) the population grows at a constant rate. This is, however, not significant for the basic result of the model. Hence, the following discussion refers to the case with a constant population (Goodwin and Pacini 1992).

convenient way to study the dynamics of such models is to draw an offer curve. Such an offer curve gives the loci at which the individuals trade present for future consumption for increasing interest rates. Thus it is a function in a space $\{c_t, c_{t+1}\}$ made out of points where the indifference curves touch the budget constraints for varying interest rates. Intersections of the offer curve with a 45° line are market equilibria.

If the young borrow from the old, irregular dynamics occur for a range of utility functions (Benhabib and Day 1982) as long as the isoquants of the utility map have a sufficient degree of curvature. Then, the offer curve will bend backwards and cross the equilibrium condition at an angle that causes an unstable equilibrium. Intuitively, the erratic behavior can be shown by of a period three cycle (Li and Yorke 1975). Suppose a first generation enters the world when the interest rate is high. To satisfy all their consumption desires, these young people have to borrow from the old. Due to the high interest rates, this will cost them a lot of future consumption in their second period of life. When it is old, the first generation will have to lend this amount to the young of the second generation. Hence, when the second generation is born, it will face a larger amount of consumption possibilities than the young people of the first generation. There is the endowment and the excess supply of the first old generation. This reduces the marginal utility of consumption when being young, and lowers the interest rate. It follows that the second generation will expand its old age excess supply compared to the first generation. It puts the third young generation in an even more comfortable position than the second young generation. Due to the comparably large excess supply of the second and now old generation, interest rates are very low now. But as the supply of money is large, and the marginal utility of consumption is already very low relative to the utility gain of an additional good that could be consumed when people are old, the third young generation will not borrow a lot. This reduces the excess supply of the third generation when they have become old and the fourth generation will be confronted with a small amount of consumption possibilities. They have their endowment to consume and only a little comes from the old generation. The interest rate signaling what the young would pay for an additional unit of consumption, in terms of future consumption, increases. If the interest rate switches back to an even higher level than what it was for the first young generation, a period three cycle is given, implying frequencies of infinite order.

The case where the young are savers (Grandmont 1985) follows basically the same mechanism. The underlying utility functions can cause some perverse interplay between substitution and income effects when agents face an increase in interest rates. Clearly, when the interest rate rises, present consumption becomes more expensive in terms of future consumption. Consequently, people will substitute present for future consumption. By the same time life income increases and if the consumption good is normal, this will trigger a further increase in old age consumption and present consumption. If the income effect on present consumption dominates the substitution effect, both present and old age consumption rise when the interest rate increases. Such an income effect implies that savings are a strongly *de*creasing function in the rate of return. Or, as the interest rate is the ratio of present to future prices in terms of the Grandmont model, savings have to increase with inflation (Blanchard and Fischer 1989, pp.251). This might be a dubious scenario. However, the agents' behavior causing the backward bending offer curve is rational. Agents maximize their utility. Benhabib and Day (1982) give some examples of utility functions that meet the conditions to generate a period three cycle. They are all separable in present and future consumption with utility in the second period of life being linear. The basic framework of the overlapping generations models has been widened to incorporate a production sector. This has given insight into the dependency of endogenous dynamics on the type of technology (Medio and Negroni 1996, Jullien 1988, Reichlin 1986). It could be shown, that irregular dynamics also occur as long as the elasticity of substitution between production factors is sufficiently small.

The main critique brought forward against models with endogenous dynamics and finitely living agents in an infinite economy, refers to the frequency of the cycles (Goodwin and Pacini 1992, p.270, Kelsey 1988, p.17, Boldrin and Woodford 1990, p.214, Reichlin 1997, p.177). As the length of a generation is shorter than the cycle, the explanation heads more toward the direction of Kondratiev waves. It would be less applicable to illuminate the causes of business cycles, as frequencies of the latter are generally lower than the life cycles of the people.

2.1.3 Growth models

Growth models with infinitely living agents try to respond to the critique that endogenous dynamics are solely caused by a maximization horizon that does not go beyond a life time of one generation. The main point against these models is that irregular dynamics would vanish if agents were able to optimize their behavior in a somehow longer time span. If there were any possibilities for intertemporal substitution over more than two periods, time paths would become regular. However, it can be shown that policy functions describing the path of optimal capital accumulation $k_{t+1}=f(k_t)$ may be chaotic even when agents live infinitely (Boldrin and Montrucchio 1986, Deneckere and Pelikan 1986). Whereas these approaches take an irregular policy function and prove the existence of an economy that can generate endogenous dynamics, Boldrin and Deneckere (1990) derive the dynamics from a specified economy. The structure of their model will be sketched to illustrate the underlying mechanism.

It is an economy with two sectors, one of which produces a consumption good and the other an investment good. There are two production factors. Whereas labor input is fixed, the capital stock varies with the production of investment goods. Consumers maximize the discounted value of consumption

$$\max_{l_t^k, l_t^c, k_t^c, k_t^k} \sum_{t=0}^{\infty} \delta^t U(c_t) \tag{7}$$

under the restrictions

$$\begin{aligned} c_t &\leq f(k_t^c, l_t^c) \\ k_{t+1} &\leq g(k_t^k, l_t^k) \\ l_t^c + l_t^k &\leq l \\ k_t^c + k_t^k &\leq k_t \end{aligned} \tag{8}$$

with some initial capital stock k_0. The constraints in maximizing discounted utility come from the production sector. Consumption cannot exceed the possible production of consumption goods that is determined by the capital and labor input in this sector. The social planner has to decide whether an investment good that is produced today should go to the consumption sector or to the production sector tomorrow. Raising the capital stock in the consumption sector will increase consumption, hence utility, in the near future. However, this increase is made at the cost of future capital accumulation and therefore future consumption. Assume the consumption sector has a Cobb Douglas production technology, and the investment sector is Leontief with a fixed factor input proportion γ. Labor is fully employed and normalized to one, so that γ is equal to the capital intensity. Thus, when the aggregate capital intensity is less than γ, the capital intensity in the consumption sector will be smaller than γ. The occurrence of a cycle can be explained starting with two consecutive aggregate capital intensities for which the inequality $k_1<k_2<\gamma$ holds. A capital intensity that is smaller than the production coefficient γ implies that output is raised in the investment sector even further. This follows from the Rybczinsky theorem, which says that an increase in capital production is efficient, if the capital intensity in the investment sector is higher than it is in the consumption sector[4]. Hence, the capital stock rises and the aggregate capital intensity eventually becomes larger than γ shifting the output from the investment sector to the consumption sector. No more capital will be added. Due to the capital depreciation aggregate capital intensity eventually falls below γ, initiating a new cycle.

Irregular and endogenous dynamics will arise if the production technologies support the switch in capital intensities. Furthermore, it requires a high degree of impatience, since otherwise the individuals would make use of the arbitrage opportunities that arise through the changes in the capital intensities. As the capital stock increases, the slope of the production possibility frontier changes, which implies large variations in the rates of returns or in the relative prices. If it was obvious that investing now will increase future consumption by a relatively

---

4 See i.e. Neumann (1991).

large amount, additional capital would be pushed into the investment sector. The capital stock would not decline as severely as it does with myopic behavior, which dampens the switching behavior. As a result, cycles would die out. Consequently, one might argue that shortly living agents of the overlapping generation models were replaced by infinitely living agents who heavily discount the future. The critique brought forward against the overlapping generation models, then, would still be applicable. However, when the production of investment and consumption goods is based on a Leontief technology, chaotic dynamics arise even at reasonable discount rates near to one (Nishimura and Yano 1995). Therefore, irregular dynamics are not necessarily caused by myopic utility maximization. Even if agents anticipate relative price changes, dynamics can become irregular. Although this result is achieved at the expense of fixed proportions of input factors for both production sectors, the main concern of this type of growth model holds. It is hard to rule out complex dynamics even under standard assumptions on production functions and preferences, and utility maximizing agents.

2.1.4 The role of expectations

Besides the local instability of economic systems that chaotic models try to illustrate they have also been used to respond to the critique of backward looking behavior. It was argued that backward looking agents would not act rationally, because they would make systematically wrong forecasts. By applying fixed rules based on previous experiences, they would always repeat the same mistakes. The questions arises as to why these agents do not change their behavior. Mainly criticized on these grounds were cobweb models generating permanent and regular cycles in prices and quantities (Muth 1961). With chaotic cobweb models, however, it is possible to show that backward looking behavior is consistent with rational behavior. Forecasting based on backward looking rules may yield results that are not systematically wrong.

Before going into a more detailed analysis of the conditions under which these results hold, it might be helpful to sketch the basic framework of cobweb models and to show under which conditions the dynamics become chaotic. There is a single good, and the market clears at a price p_t The demand for that good is a function of the current price

$$D_t = D(p_t). \tag{9}$$

The quantity to be supplied in this period is driven by an expected price p_t^e

$$S_t = S(p_t^e). \tag{10}$$

Agents do not know the price of that period, but have to make a guess, as a lag in production forces them to start producing the good they want to sell earlier. Such production lags are not important only for agricultural markets (Finkenstädt 1995), but also for labor markets where the time for education puts a wedge between the decision to become an electronic engineer, and the application for a position as a university graduate (Freeman 1976). Supply and demand at time t determine the market price p_t which can be written as

$$p_t = D^{-1}(S(p_t^e)). \tag{11}$$

The market clearing price p_t will be lower than p_t^e if for an expected price p_t^e supply exceeds demand. Conversely, if the amount of goods supplied at the expected price p_t^e falls short of the demand at this price, the market clearing price p_t will be higher than p_t^e. Hence, the market clears through price adjustment. Quantities can only be changed for the following period, which suppliers will do depending on their price expectations. Obviously, various kinds of expectation formations can be incorporated into the model and combined with linear and nonlinear supply curves. When agents have naïve expectations

$$p_t^e = p_{t-1} \tag{12}$$

and supply and demand are linear functions of the price, there are only three possible types of price adjustment dynamics. Depending on the relative slopes for demand and supply, the market price will either converge to an equilibrium, explode, or run into a period two cycle (the well known 'hog cycle'). Assume the slope of the supply curve is larger than the one of the demand curve in absolute terms, and supply exceeds demand. Then, the current price will be lower than the price that the suppliers expected. With naïve expectations, the current price will also be the expected price in the consecutive period. Then, the demand gap will be smaller than the supply gap was before. The upward pressure on the price will be lower than the downward pressure was in the proceeding period. The prices will converge to an equilibrium. For the same reasons, the market will become unstable if the slope of the supply curve is smaller than the slope of the demand curve in absolute terms. The dynamics change with nonlinear supply or demand functions. A nonlinear supply curve may arise when producers observe declining prices and fear a further decrease. In that case, they might be willing to increase supply, instead of reducing it (Artstein 1983 and Shaffer 1984). The threat of even smaller profits in the future may trigger further sales of stocks or launch government interventions for minimum prices, as is well known for agricultural products. In both cases, agents anticipate future events which yield a supply curve that is nonlinear and nonmonotonic. For comparably lower prices, supply slopes downward which folds back trajectories repelled from the market equilibrium. Prices will not rise forever, such as in the unstable case of a linear cobweb model, but will vary irregularly.

Substituting the assumption of naïve expectations for adaptive expectations widens the class of nonlinearities for which dynamics can become irregular. It requires a degree of nonlinearity that is 'smaller', opposed to nonmonotonic supply or demand curves to arrive at irregular market behavior. With adaptive expectations, the producer forecasts the price, based on a weighted average of the price that he expected for the previous period and of the price for which he could sell his products

$$p_t^e = (1-w) \cdot p_{t-1}^e + w \cdot p_{t-1}. \tag{13}$$

In (13) agents stick to their previous forecast, but also take into account that their prediction was not exactly right. The more they neglect the actual market price for their prediction of the price of the following period, the smaller w will be. If w is zero, and agents do not want to learn from their experiences, expectations are naïve again. Suppliers believe for w=0 more in their own expectations than in the actual market price of the preceding period. Self-fulfilling prophecies can drive the market to a stable equilibrium price. In the other extreme with w=1 and a nonlinear but monotonic supply curve, agents believe what happens today will also hold for tomorrow, and a stable period two cycle occurs. If, however, expectations are adaptive and neither of the extreme cases rules, a nonlinear and monotonic supply curve (Hommes 1991 and 1994, Chiarella 1988), or a nonlinear monotonous demand curve if supply is a linear function of the expected price (Finkenstädt and Kuhbier 1992), will suffice to generate irregular dynamics. Such an S-shaped supply curve may be grounded on set-up and fixed costs that dampen supply when prices are low. A capacity constraint flattens the supply curve when prices are comparably high. A monotonous and nonlinear demand curve follows from a standard approach, such as maximizing a Cobb Douglas utility function with respect to a budget constraint.

Although the assumption of adaptive expectations draws a richer picture of human behavior than naïve expectations, one might argue that agents make forecasts based on a somewhat longer record of previous experiences. Failures in price anticipations might be memorized and taken into account for following forecasts. A memory effect might stabilize the market even when supply and demand is nonlinear. This is somehow true and applies to the very long run (Holmes and Manning 1988). However, if agents anticipate the price of the following period by taking the average of all short run equilibrium prices, there will be sensitive dependence in the short run - even when the market is stable in the long run. It can take a considerably long time until the price fluctuations settle down. The market participants will have to tackle erratic price fluctuations for a rather long time, which weakens the point that irregular dynamics are of minor importance.

As mentioned at the beginning, the rational expectations approach claims that backward looking agents, even if they take account of the whole history, are an incorrect model of human behavior since they might imply that agents make systematic forecasting errors. Forecasters might be wrong all the time by applying fixed rules, and the question arises why these agents do not change their behavior when these rules cause losses. Rational agents would not make these failures for a longer time period. They might be wrong in their forecast once, but they will not make the same mistakes forever. Market participants, so to say, have a better knowledge about the underlying laws of motion. Strict versions of rational behavior would hypothesize that the agents know the model exactly. Thus, the rational expectation approach imposes a lot of 'computational power' on its agents, making it hard to believe that rational expectations are an adequate model for human behavior. One might be inclined to stick at least partly to some degree of adaptive behavior. Models with chaotic dynamics can build the bridge. Consistency of adaptive behavior with rational agents can be shown on the grounds of chaotic cobweb models under various forms of expectations. The approach assumes an agent that does not know the exact model, but is aware of some econometric tools. He applies these methods to extract information out of the time series. Calculating autocorrelation coefficients might be one such tool that he can apply. Under these assumptions, adaptive behavior has been called consistent with rational behavior if the errors of the actual and predicted variables are not autocorrelated, and weakly consistent if the coefficients of the autocorrelation function become zero for lags larger than one. As differences between the predicted and actual time series indicate information that could have been exploited by the adaptively behaving market participants, their behavior would not be rational. Changing the rules for forecasting, based on the information of the autocorrelation functions, would yield better results.

The chaotic time series of various models have been tested for consistency. Of course, results are dependent on the type of model that generates a chaotic time series so that general conclusions cannot be drawn. But still, they serve as examples that can strengthen the role of backward looking agents in economic theory. For cobweb models, weak consistency is more likely if the past is relatively unimportant for the prediction. The more agents memorize, the larger the degree of nonlinearity has to be to arrive at chaotic price fluctuations and weak consistency (Hommes 1998). An example of a cobweb model in which agents can learn from the past performance of their predictor and adjust it is discussed in Hommes and Sorger (1998). The econometric tool that the agent applies here, is a linear regression analysis of the generated time series. Price forecasts follow an AR(1) process, where the long run average price and the first order autocorrelation coefficient vary the more observations agents gather. For both cases, a monotonic and a nonmonotonic supply curve, backward looking, and learning agents will find a stable single long run equilibrium, without having exact knowledge about the underlying equations of motion. In another model Brock and Hommes (1997) analyze a situation where agents can choose between a simple predictor and a more powerful tool that grounds on rational expectations. It is assumed that the use of the latter imposes some costs, whereas the simple predictor is a rule of thumb and therefore free. Agents will switch forecasting rules, driven by profits they could make applying one of the rules. Hommes (1998) shows weakly consistent backward looking expectations for that model.

Although consistency is strongly dependent on the type of model that generates the time series, the underlying notion, that in a chaotic world backward looking expectations may not contradict to rational behavior, is a serious argument. Thus, nonlinearities do not only give insight into complex and endogenous price dynamics but are also able to integrate the concept of adaptive expectations in a world of rationally acting agents.

2.2 Evidence on chaos in economic dynamics

In the past, various tests have been developed to detect nonlinear deterministic and chaotic dynamics in time series. The most important tools are introduced briefly, as they will be applied to test for chaos in German labor market data in chapter 8. Further evidence is reviewed, and some problems of time series studies for a nonlinear deterministic core in economic data are discussed.

2.2.1 Tests for nonlinearities and chaos

Chaotic systems are characterized by sensitivity on initial conditions. Trajectories, that are nearby at a specific point in time, diverge exponentially as time evolves. When a system is chaotic, very small errors in the determination of the initial stage (i.e. due to measurement restrictions) will grow exponentially so that forecasts are impossible in the long run. Lyapunov exponents are a measure for this dynamic property. The higher a positive Lyapunov exponent, the less time passes by until the observations fill the entire defined space. The trajectory will eventually fold back as the system is bounded to a set *S* (attractor) but will never reach the initial value. A common algorithm to determine the rate by which trajectories diverge was proposed by Wolf et al. (1985). Wolf et al. define a fiducial trajectory that is made out of observations following an initial data point. A second point, that is next to the starting value in phase space, is then chosen to calculate the distance between these two trajectories until a threshold value is reached. If the threshold is exceeded, the development of the distance can no longer be regarded as a measurement of the local dynamic properties. Therefore, the fiducial trajectory will be compared to a new trajectory, starting from a point with a comparable phase space orientation. The dominant exponent is finally achieved by averaging the exponential growth rates of all the separating pairs of vectors.

Grassberger and Proccaccia (1983) propose the correlation dimension as another approach to distinguish random from deterministic systems. Here, a time series has to be transformed into a phase space representation. Vectors of length m located in a m-dimensional phase represent the time series. Under the transformation, a time series with N data points $\{x_1, x_2, \ldots, x_N\}$ becomes a matrix

$$X = \begin{pmatrix} X_1 \\ X_2 \\ \cdot \\ \cdot \\ X_{N-(m-1)\cdot T} \end{pmatrix}$$

with

$$X_i = (x_i \quad x_{i+T} \quad \ldots \quad x_{i+(m-1)T}).$$

The dimension of the reconstructed phase space is m (embedding dimension). This m has to be chosen large enough to capture the 'true' dynamics of the underlying system. It follows that large data sets are needed to achieve reliable results, given a comparably high dimensional process. T is called the reconstruction delay. As a rule of thumb, T is set equal to the value where the autocorrelation function becomes zero for the first time[5]. Two points in phase space are said to be correlated if they lie within a m-dimensional ball, with radius r centered around one of the two vectors in space. Counting these points for every vector in phase-space with a Heavyside function yields the correlation integral

$$C(r,m) = \lim_{T_m \to \infty} \frac{1}{T^2} \sum_{i,j=1}^{T_m} H(r - \|X_i^m - X_j^m\|) \tag{14}$$

with the Heavyside function defined as

$$H(y) = 1 \text{ if } y > 1 \tag{15}$$

and

$$H(y) = 0 \text{ otherwise.} \tag{16}$$

The ratio of the logarithm of the correlation integral and the logarithm of the radius of the ball is the correlation dimension:

$$D(m) = \lim_{r \to 0} \frac{\ln C(r,m)}{\ln r}. \tag{17}$$

Distinguishing between deterministic and stochastic processes is possible by calculating the correlation dimensions for various embedding dimensions m. A correlation dimension which grows with the embedding dimension means that the points of the state vector equally fill the space in which the time series was transformed. In this case, the underlying system is called stochastic. However, if the correlation dimension settles to a specific value and becomes independent for different values of the embedding dimension, the process under investigation is

---

5 Another method, based on a nonparametric test, is proposed by Mizrach (1996).

deterministic. This is due to a non-random structure underlying the system. Once the embedding dimension of the system is reached, increasing m will not yield another correlation of the vector points in space, because their position follows a deterministic rule. As opposed to a random process, points are not equally distributed in the phase space. To illustrate this, think about the well known quadratic iterator $x_{t+1}=a\cdot(1-x_t)$. If one generates a time series for this map with some parameter a in the chaotic regime, say a=4, then a plot of the time series in a space $\{x_t,x_{t+1}\}$ will yield a hump shaped graph (c.f. Figure 1). Calculating the correlation integral for a specific radius r of this system, will give some arbitrary number that is different from the correlation integral of a random system for the same r that fills $\{x_t,x_{t+1}\}$ with equally distributed points. Furthermore, one will get a higher increase in correlated points by raising r for the random system. The slope, and hence, the correlation dimension will be higher. What discriminates both systems in terms of whether they are stochastic or deterministic is the same exercise for higher embedding dimensions. Increasing the embedding dimension m by one will give a three dimensional space $\{x_t,x_{t+1},x_{t+2})$ that a random system would equally fill with vector points. Contrary, the points in that higher space for $x_{t+1}=4\cdot(1-x_t)$ still follow the deterministic rule. At the margin, there will be more correlated points for the stochastic system than for the quadratic map. This means that the correlation dimensions keep growing with the embedding dimension for the stochastic system, whereas it should settle to a specific value for any low dimensional deterministic process. Insofar, the correlation dimension delivers a tool that allows to discriminate between stochastic and deterministic behavior.

Testing time series with the BDS-statistics (Brock, Dechert, Scheinkman and LeBaron 1996) builds on the concept of reconstructing the dynamics of a system in space and calculating the correlation integrals. As a random time series of i.i.d. observations follows the rule

$$C_m \approx C_1(r)^m \tag{18}$$

a test statistic can be written as

$$B_{m,T}(r) = \frac{\sqrt{T}\cdot[C_{m,T}(r) - C_{1,T}(r)^m]}{\sigma_{m,T}(r)}. \tag{19}$$

Under the null hypothesis of an i.i.d. process, the BDS test follows a standard normal limiting distribution. Intuitively, the correlation integral can be interpreted as the probability that a vector in space lies within a m-dimensional ball, with a specific radius r centered around a reference point. If the process is i.i.d., the probability that two points in the m-dimensional space lie next to each other will be equal to the probability of the m-th moment of any two points being close together. In this case, the numerator will become null. Only if both probabilities differ, as the m-dimensional space is unequally filled with vector points, will the test statistic become different form zero. The null hypothesis is then rejected. This is consistent with some type of dependence in the data, such as frequently occurring patterns in the time series that result in a cluster. However, as will be pointed out later (chapter 8), the rejection of the null does not necessarily imply nonlinear deterministic dynamics.

2.2.2 Results

Hsieh (1989) investigated daily foreign exchange rates and found evidence for nonlinear dependence. Kugler and Lenz (1990) confirmed these results for weekly exchange rates of the US-Dollar versus the Swiss Franc, the French Franc, the German Mark, and the Yen from 1979 to 1989. Mizrach (1996) delivered evidence for nonlinearities in daily FF/DM exchange rates from 1987-1992. Cecen and Erkal (1996) tested exchange rates on an hourly basis from January to July 1986 of the British Pound, the German Mark, the Swiss Franc, and the Japanese Yen in terms of the US-Dollar. They argue that nonlinearities are important for the dynamic behavior of exchange rates, but find little evidence for low-dimensional chaos. Similar results were achieved by Brooks (1998) who tested ten daily Sterling denominated exchange rates over a period of twenty years. He excludes chaos, but argues for strong evidence on nonlinearity. Frank, Gencay and Stengos (1988) tested quarterly data of the GNP for West Germany, Italy, Japan and the U.K. The authors find no evidence for chaos, but reveal nonlinear structure for the data of Japan. However, due to a comparatively low number of observations, their results should be interpreted with caution. Scheinkman and LeBaron (1989a) searched for nonlinearities in yearly per capita GNP for the U.S. from 1872 to 1986. Nonlinearities, as they argue, may be due to changes in the variance. Both authors (Scheinkman and LeBaron 1989b) also discovered that, to a certain extent, variation in U.S. stock returns data come from nonlinearities as opposed to randomness. Hsieh (1991), testing stock returns, indicates that nonlinearities are important in terms of variance changes. However, chaotic dynamics do not apply. Barnett and Chen (1988) referred to monetary aggregates as a possible field of nonlinear or chaotic dynamics, and showed that highly aggregated monetary demand and supply series have chaotic attractors. Finally, Frank and Stengos (1988) examined Canadian aggregates including unemployment data. To their surprise, the hypothesis of randomness could not be rejected. However, as an uncommon algorithm was used by Frank and Stengos, doubts were raised by Medio (1992) about the validity of their results. Brock and Sayers (1987) found nonlinearities in U.S. quarterly employment and unemployment data from 1950 to 1983 and 1949 to 1982. Unemployment series for the US and the UK were tested by Alogoskoufis and Stengos (1991). Neither the UK sample from 1857 to 1987, nor the data for the US from 1892 to 1987 indicated chaotic dynamics. However, Alogoskoufis and Stengos argue for nonlinearities underlying the unemployment dynamics for the UK, while the US unemployment can best be described by a linear model with ARCH errors. In chapter 8, German labor market data is tested[6]. The results corroborate the view of Brock and Sayers (1987) and Alogoskoufis and Stengos (1991).. There is evidence for deterministic nonlinearities in German labor market data, but probably none for chaotic dynamics although Lyapunov exponents are slightly positive in three out of four cases.

Although evidence for chaos is still weak, and seems to be contradictory to the growing literature on economic models with chaotic dynamic properties, most of the authors find nonlinearities as an important source of complex economic processes. A rejection of chaotic dynamics in economic systems seems to be too early, even though there is only very little evidence. The methods might still be too weak to detect chaotic dynamics. Data sets impose further problems.

2.2.3 Some pitfalls and shortcomings

The vast amount of empirical studies on nonlinearities and chaos in economic time series cushions the problems that arise with the use of correlation integrals, the BDS test, or the estimation of Lyapunov exponents. In fact, these techniques can only more or less detect nonlinear structure in data sets. Therefore, results either way should be interpreted with caution.

As with every empirical study, the data set might incorporate noise for various reasons. The time series have to be comparably long to deliver reliable results when tested for a nonlinear deterministic core. For example, with quarterly data and 400 observations, the time span becomes a hundred years. Within such a long period, the criteria for data collecting can change. Definitions for the manufacturing or service sector might have altered. A person who would not have been employed when working less than 10 hours a week at the beginning of the observation period might be counted as employed a couple of years later. This clearly adds structure to the data that is not related to market dynamics, but to 'exogenous shocks' caused by the data mining organization. Adjusting the data sets to eliminate this misleading data will not circumvent the problem. It might just add another detrimental structure to the data. Then, the tests may detect nonlinearity in the data where there is none. It is obvious that these problems are less important for financial time series on an hourly basis that cover a few years and gather nevertheless a huge amount of observations. But, it is a serious problem when GDP or employment data is tested. From this point of view, evidence for nonlinearities or chaos is relatively stronger for comparably shorter time series than for studies that cover long intervals.

The need for large data sets rests on the 'algorithm' of the correlation integral and the BDS-test. They try to discriminate any kind of structure from equally distributed points for a space representation of a time series. If the system that

---

6 See also Neugart (1999).

underlies the time series is random, the likelihood at which a region in state space is visited would be the same all over the space. Given a process that is not white noise, some regions in state space will inherit more vector points than others. There will be clusters. Assuming that it takes at least 10 observations per embedding dimension (n+1) to detect a geometric shape as opposed to a random distribution, it would take 1000 observations to identify a two dimensional system (n=2). One would need 10.000 data points if the underlying system is three dimensional. Viewed the other way around, given there are 500 data points and the real system is three dimensional, less than 5 points per embedding dimension have to suffice to judge whether the process is random or not (Ramsey et al. 1990, p.992). Therefore, it is necessary to collect as many data points as possible to arrive at somehow reliable results. This is less difficult for financial time series, and hence, most of the economics studies focus on the latter. But for time series with quarterly or yearly observations, one will unlikely have many more than 500 observations.

Economic time series of that length are very often not stationary. GDP series usually have trends, so does European unemployment data of the last 30 years. As the BDS test is a test for linearity, trends have to be eliminated. Otherwise, a rejection of the null hypothesis could be due to nonstationarity. A conclusion that a time series has a nonlinear deterministic core would be impossible. In order to exclude a rejection due to a nonstationary data set, first differences are usually taken. As is well known, this adds additional noise to the data. The signal noise ratio deteriorates because high frequencies become relatively stronger than the lower frequencies of the underlying signal. Unfortunately, by the same time one would very much like to have low noise levels in the data. This would make the interpretation of positive but small Lyapunov exponents easier. If there is a significant level of noise in the data due to measurement errors, changing data mining techniques, people answering questions not honestly etc., no straightforward conclusion is possible from the calculation of the largest Lyapunov exponent. Noise biases the measure of how trajectories of similar pairs of state vectors diverge as random shocks hit these trajectories at different times and strength. Whether under such circumstances the divergence of nearby trajectories is due to sensitive dependence on initial conditions or noise is impossible to distinguish. The larger the impact of noise becomes, the larger the degree of stretching and folding in state space has to be to surpass the threshold given by the degree of noise in the data. All divergence that takes place under this threshold might be due to chaotic dynamics or random shocks, so that a small positive Lyapunov exponent does not necessarily imply chaos.

To illustrate the impact of various noise levels on a deterministic process, the quadratic map was iterated 400 times, dropping the first 100 iterations. Figure 1 shows the phase space representation of the transformed time series with a lag of one. Not surprisingly, it resembles the humped shaped form of the map $x_{t+1}=4\cdot(1-x_t)$. The impact of noise on the data was simulated by a randomly generated time series with a uniform distribution. For the noise level of 10% (Figure 2), the random numbers varied in the interval [-0.05;0.05], and for the other noise levels in Figure 3 and Figure 4 in the intervals [-0.10;0.10] and [-0.15;0.15], respectively. The random time series was added to the time series generated by the deterministic map. Thus, the quadratic map became a 'nonlinear stochastic process' that followed $x_{t+1}=4\cdot(1-x_t)+\varepsilon_t$ with ε_t as a uniformly distributed stochastic component. Obviously, such a simple structure like a quadratic function can still be recognized under rather high noise levels. But it is also clear that the scattered plots impose some restrictions on the calculation of Lyapunov exponents. If that measure is only slightly positive, it becomes hard to tell that this is due to an underlying deterministic core.

In addition to nonstationarities, several other processes are nested within the alternative hypothesis of the BDS test, so various filters have to be applied to find them. Besides nonstationary data, other possible causes for a rejection include linearities, stochastic nonlinearities like changing variances (ARCH or GARCH effects) or seasonalities. The latter are often removed with some sort of moving average process. However, what these filters do to the attractor of the time series in state space is pretty unclear. An ARMA model that is fitted to the generated time series of a Henon map yields, for example, a correlation dimension for the residuals that is different from the correlation dimension for the residuals of an AR filter. Equivalent biases occur for a generated time series of the logistic map (Chen 1993, p.229). Filtering high frequencies out of experimental data for the Belousov-Zhabotinskii reaction changes the shape of the attractor, but biases the estimate of the Lyapunov exponent only slightly down (Wolf et al. 1985, pp.304). The examples imply that the test results can be, but are not necessarily, sensitive to filters. Any filtering will change the state representation which it is supposed to do, but can also add structure to the data that a BDS test may falsely detect as a nonlinearity. As the impact of the filtering on the outcome of the tests varies due to unknown rules, the interpretation of the test statistics becomes tentative.

Given that the problems arising from noisy data and filtering could somehow be solved satisfactorily, the BDS test proved to be a powerful tool to detect nonlinear structure. It seems to react very sensitively to (unfortunately) any departure from linearity (Barnett et al. 1997, pp.180). Confronted with generated time series from a logistic map, a GARCH and an ARCH process, a nonlinear moving average process and an ARMA model, the BDS test was right for every time series with 2000 observations. The tests for the shorter time series (380 observations) showed once more how important the length of the time series is. Results became ambiguous for the GARCH data and linearity was also only weakly rejected for the nonlinear moving average process.

Additional tests are available with which it is possible to shed some more light onto the causes of the rejection of the linearity on the grounds of the BDS test. Residuals of ARCH and GARCH processes will show whether there is stochastic nonlinearity in the data arising from changes in the variance.

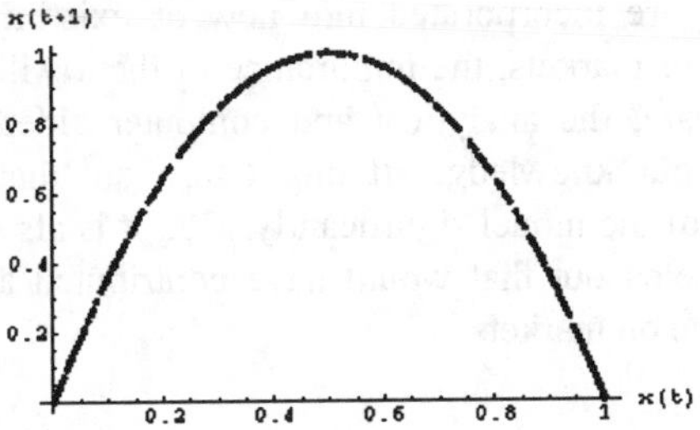

Figure 1: Simulation of the quadratic iterator x_{t+1}=4·(1-x_t) without noise.

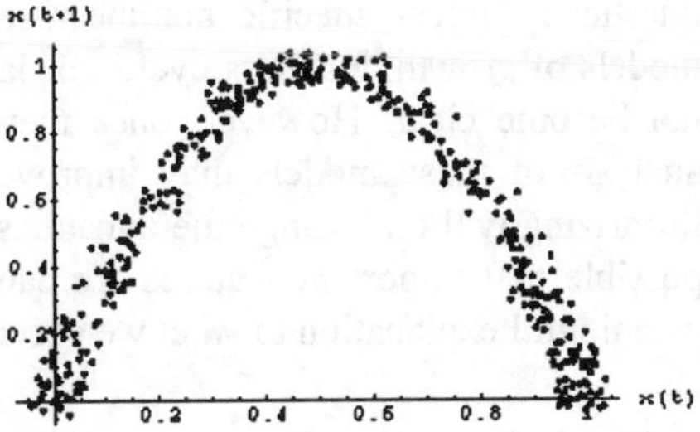

Figure 2: Simulation of the quadratic iterator with a noise level of 10%.

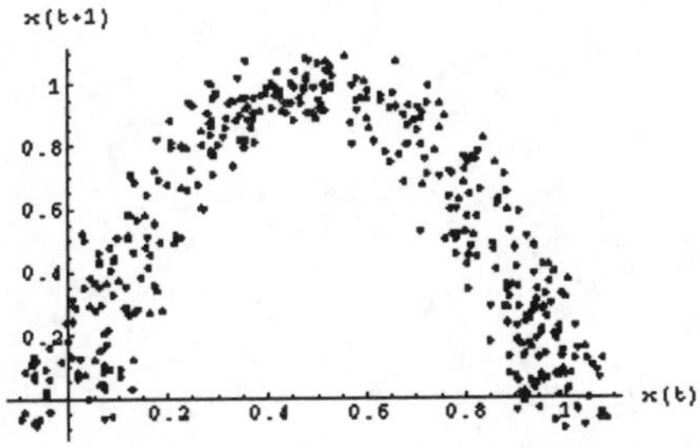

Figure 3: Simulation of the quadratic iterator with a noise level of 20%.

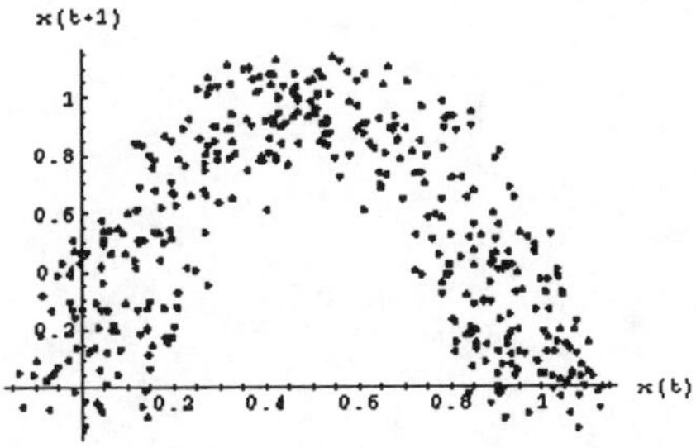

Figure 4: Simulation of the quadratic iterator with a noise level of 30%.

Other tests (c.f. Barnett et al. 1997) can be used to detect a nonlinearity in the mean. What is still missing is more specific information on the type and importance of the nonlinearity. For example, it is not possible to trace back the irregular behavior to increasing returns from an aggregate production function or a nonlinear savings function. Nor do the tests submit information on the importance of nonlinearites. Although a stronger rejection with rather high BDS values is likely to give some information on the significance of a nonlinear deterministic core, it does not give insight into whether any S-shaped savings function will generate endogenous business cycles, or only a rather strongly S-shaped function will do so. One would certainly like to know if it is the saving behavior, and if so, to which degree ups and downs of a business cycle are ruled by the curvature of a savings function. Unfortunately, the empirical methods cannot answer these questions. Unless specific nonlinearities are incorporated into new or existing models of growth, business cycles, or labor markets, the importance of them will not become clear. However, once they are, the analytical and computer aided analysis of these models may improve our knowledge. It might turn out that linearizing will not change the dynamics of the model significantly. But, it is also possible that important features are canceled out that would have contributed a meaningful explanation to what we observe on markets.

3 Nonlinear labor supply and real wage adjustment

In standard models of the labor market, supply slopes upwards and demand slopes downwards in a real wage employment space. Supply and demand schedules mostly intersect at rather steep slopes to assure stability, although the empirical evidence on labor supply and labor demand elasticities in equilibrium cannot be pinpointed to single values. Knowing that narrow bandwidths for labor supply and demand elasticities do not exist, there is surprisingly little concern about what would happen in these models from a dynamic perspective if labor demand and supply intersect at flat angles. What are the features of a labor market where the supply of labor and the demand for labor are very elastic? If a real wage increase induces a comparably large increase in the supply of labor, and by the same time a large decrease in the demand for labor, a deviation from equilibrium might destabilize the market or lead to very long adjustment paths. After a negative productivity shock, for example, it might take a very long time until real wages and employment reach the new equilibrium. If the shift of the demand curve yields a new equilibrium where supply and demand intersect at even flatter angles, the equilibrium might become unstable. Maybe it is the more likely unstable equilibrium that lead to a minor interest in labor markets that have flat supply and demand curves, since when these curves are linear, the labor market would become globally unstable. Of course, an explosive system is not a desirable outcome. It can hardly explain anything. Nonlinear supply and demand curves bring in some new aspects. A labor market equilibrium with flat supply and demand curves may only be locally unstable. Furthermore, nonmonotonous supply and demand curves can intersect at more than one employment level or may not intersect at all. Such labor market models open the door to 'fragile equilibria' (Blanchard and Summers 1988) that may cope well with some of the stylized facts on European unemployment. Besides long adjustment periods and locally unstable equilibria, dynamics can become irregular. Real wages may never find their way to the labor market equilibrium. Time series would appear to be random, even though the underlying labor market model is deterministic. Real wage and employment dynamics would be endogenous and cycles self-sustained.

Before turning to the dynamic aspects, topics will be discussed on why a linear specification of labor supply might be inadequate. The arguments ground on the standard static labor supply model but do also shed some light on habit formation and bandwaggon effects. The evidence on labor supply elasticities and intertemporal substitution effects is briefly surveyed. It follows that nonlinear monotonous and non-monotonous supply curves cannot be ruled out on theoretical and empirical grounds.

3.1 Beyond a linear and upward sloping labor supply

3.1.1 Stable preferences, budget constraints, and the supply of labor

The common framework to think about static labor supply rests on the assumptions of a utility maximizing agent, who faces restrictions in terms of a specific real wage that is offered to him and a maximum available time that he can either spend on leisure or work. A higher real wage makes leisure more expensive in terms of opportunity costs. As comparably more income is lost if the agent does not work, it would be too expensive to spend that much time not working. Leisure is substituted for work. Excluding the substitution effect, the agent also realizes a higher income without a change in working time from the fact that he will get a higher hourly real wage. Therefore, if leisure is a normal good, real wage increases will also trigger a higher demand for leisure. Hence, the income effect works into the opposite direction of the substitution effect. The degree to which labor supply slopes upwards or bends backwards for rising real wages depends on the relative strength of the substitution and income effects. When the substitution effect dominates, labor supply elasticities will be positive. Conversely, labor supply elasticities will be negative when the income effect is stronger. If both effects cancel out, labor supply is inelastic. Technically, it is possible to derive distinct slopes of the labor supply curve by assuming specific utility functions and budget constraints. One could, for example, model utility along the lines of a Cobb Douglas function. Then, with a linear budget constraint, labor supply would be inelastic. A CES utility function would generate a positively or a negatively sloped labor supply depending on the degree of substitution that is incorporated. Various other forms could be assumed depending on what one believes the agents' tastes are. It is therefore the question of what determines the tastes that will be put in the foreground next. Specific models will be discussed in Cases 1 and 2.

A backward bending labor supply curve is often associated with underdeveloped economies (Huang 1976). It is assumed that in such societies people offer work only to a certain amount, which is determined by their subsistence level. As real wages rise, people would reduce the number of working hours. Even though a considerably higher income would be feasible, no more work is offered. There is a certain level of income with which they can live a life along their preferences. Farmers, for example, might tend to supply labor until a minimum income will insure their living standards. From then on, it may be the case that the opportunity costs of not working are sufficiently small. The income effect dominates and households prefer leisure time. To conclude that this rules out negatively sloped labor supply curves in affluent societies would be wrong. The elasticity on labor supply might also be negative in more developed economies. This can be seen by taking particular consumption decisions into account. It is probably true, that individuals in a 'leisure-park' economy will demand leisure goods, since time off work can only be consumed with surfboards, sailing boats and the like. Otherwise, leisure would perhaps turn out to be a boring or even an empty experience. Labor supply would go up as these goods have to be bought. In this sense, consumption goods and leisure are complementary and the substitution effect would prevail over the income effect. A change of the sign of the slope of the supply curve would be less likely. However, this mechanism is twofold (Finegan 1962, Chichilnisky et al. 1995, p.283). There is no doubt about the complementarity of leisure time and leisure goods. But the argument holds also the other way around. Why buy a surfboard if there is no time for surfing? Having more leisure goods only pays if there is time to enjoy them. Insofar, an income effect may outweigh the substitution effect from a certain real wage level onwards, even in wealthy economies.

The inclusion of assets brings in some more aspects that can illuminate the likelihood of positive or negative signs on the labor supply curve. It is obvious that the wealth of a household will rule the decision to supply more or less labor when confronted with a rising or falling real wage level (Barzel and McDonald 1973). A wealthy person will not supply labor up to a certain real wage. Above this critical real wage, the supply curve will slope upwards at least for a while. Opportunity costs rise and labor is substituted for leisure. In that way, incorporating assets yields a discontinuous labor supply schedule with a positive real wage operating as a threshold. Such a discontinuous labor supply function may also capture the supply behavior of spouses where the income of one part stands for the assets, and the other part is only willing to work for a real wage level sufficiently high. In this framework, a negative elasticity would not make sense at the margin because a person would not choose to work more, but rather not to work at all when real wages fall. He or she would prefer to live from the assets. However, this does not exclude a reversal in the sign if real wages are considerably above the amount of assets that the person holds. In other words, decisions at the margin can differ from the behavior of individuals, once the real wage level in an economy is relatively high. Insofar, assets do not necessarily rule out a negatively sloped labor supply curve.

Besides assets, restrictions might differ from a linear budget constraint. The intuition that lies behind a linear budget constraint is that households are free to choose the amount of work they are willing to supply. In an economy where working time restrictions play a prominent role, this might be an inadequate procedure (Killingsworth 1983, p. 48). "Take it or leave it"- schemes head into the same direction. In both cases, finding the optimal solution of how to allocate working time is constrained by the preferences of the labor demand side. People might be restricted to working time schedules and prerequisites for production processes that do not allow firms to profitably expand or reduce daily working hours. Although it might be optimal for households to supply more labor or reduce it at the going real wage, they cannot[7]. For the purpose of illustration, consider the extreme case where daily working hours are fixed for a whole economy. Neglecting entry decisions to the labor market, this yields an inelastic labor supply function. Even when real wages rise, labor supply remains at one level due to the fixed working time arrangement. Relaxing the possible range of working hours widens the spectrum for optimization. A point expands to a segment on the budget line and the elasticity will not be zero anymore.

3.1.2 Labor supply and path dependent preferences

So far, labor supply models referred to utility functions with arguments in consumption and leisure. Both variables may be the driving forces of labor supply behavior. But there can also be some kind of path dependency. People may get addicted to past behavior so that habits enter the supply of labor. A high level of consumption in the past may prevent people from accepting a lower standard of living in the future. Long spells of unemployment or extended sabbaticals may hold back unemployed workers to apply for jobs. Tastes may change through the evolution of more convenient living conditions so that a backward sloping labor supply curve may be only transitory in underdeveloped countries (Vatter 1961). In addition to the effect from the own behavior in the past, spill-overs from other market participants (bandwaggon effects) can change preferences. Unemployed workers who live in areas with comparably high unemployment rates might be less stigmatized than elsewhere so that search intensities decline.

The examples imply that one might have to take into account that preferences as well as labor supply change over time. There have been various attempts to model and analyze the consequences from unstable preferences (Becker and Murphy 1988, Dockner and Feichtinger 1993). The point of these approaches is that preferences do not only rest on aggregates like consumption and weight (these are overeating dieting models) but also on stocks of habits. It is not hard to think about labor supply behavior within such models. Applied to the labor supply decisions of households, the longing for leisure will be larger, the longer the time spent not working as people get addicted to spending their time off work. This idea might be backed by empirical studies on the duration dependence of exit rates (c.f. chapter 7.1.2), which suggest that exit rates decline because of social security

---

7 Maybe they choose to work in the informal sector instead.

arrangements. With respect to the working time variable, workaholics are the flip side of the coin.

Consider path dependent preferences of the type

$$U = U(C, L, H) \tag{20}$$

where C stands for consumption, L for leisure, and H is a stock of habits variable that depends on the own past performance in habit models (Vendrik 1993), or on the behavior of reference persons if bandwaggon effects are modeled (Vendrik 1998). In such a framework, long run elasticities may differ from the short run. Long run supply schedules including a forward as well as a backward bending part may even become discontinuous functions. A certain real wage goes along with two different supply levels. The basic mechanism that underlies labor supply in models with habit formation is the following: if it is the short run perspective and one is on the forward sloping part of the labor supply curve, an increase in real wages will trigger a larger labor supply. People may get used to more working hours, the habit stock rises, and in a longer perspective even more labor is supplied for the same real wage. With addiction to work, a lower real wage level will induce the same amount of labor supply as a comparably higher real wage level would do without addiction. The increase in labor supply goes on until there is no additional effect from the stock of habits. In the long run equilibrium, the total increase in working hours is larger than the one induced by the initial rise in wages. For decreases in the real wage, the reverse holds true. Thus, the long run curve is flatter. Real wage changes induce larger changes in the supply of labor in the long run than in the short run. The consequences of a rise or fall of the real wage in the backward bending part are ambiguous. Whether the short or long run supply curve is flatter depends on the strength of the effect from the stocks of habits. When real wages increase in the backward bending part, leisure time and consumption increase. If the individual gets more addicted to consumption than leisure, the long run labor supply curve is steeper than in the short run. Contrary, if the demand for leisure outweighs consumption caused by the initial wage change, the long run backward bending part will be flatter than the short run relationship. To show how discontinuities enter the long run labor supply, one can think of a person with a certain reservation wage. At the margin, a small wage change will cause participation in the labor market. He or she will supply labor and get addicted to work. If real wages fall again, the person will remain in the labor market even if the wage rate falls below the former reservation wage. Hence, for a given real wage, labor supply is indeterminate. Which state is realized depends on the history, or in other words, on the employment record. Hysteresis rules the supply of labor. In any case, with habits included, labor supply can become a nonlinear function of the real wage level.

3.1.3 Empirical labor supply elasticities

Labor supply elasticities for static models have been estimated at length. Results are far from being conclusive (Franz 1991, p.82). There is no labor supply elasticity that would tell to what extent individuals increase or decrease their supply due to a wage change. It is even hard to give a fairly narrow interval. Compensated wage elasticities, as summarized in Killingsworth (1983), for what he calls second generation studies vary between -0.08 and 0.95 for men. Even if the largest and smallest values are omitted, the range is still -0.06 and 0.84. The estimates for women due to this survey vary even more. Here, the largest compensated wage elasticity is 15.35 and the second largest 14.79 going down to a smallest compensated elasticity of -1.06 and -0.26 respectively if the smallest estimate is skipped again. Hence, it is not only the size of the change in labor supply due to a wage increase that cannot be forecasted robustly. Even the sign indicating whether an increase will lead to a higher labor supply or a reduction is unclear. There is no clear-cut evidence from these studies that would tell whether labor demand slopes upward or bends backwards. This is corroborated by the survey in Pencavel (1986, p.69, p.73). There, labor supply elasticities range from -0.19 to 0.84 for tests with U.S. data and between -0.09 and 0.30 for British males. A more recent study on labor supply for men and women arrives at a compensated hours worked wage elasticity of 0.4 for men and 0.66 for women (Kimmel and Kniesner 1998).

Of course, a lot of the variation in these results grounds on different data sets and methodological issues. Severe obstacles arise when estimating labor supply elasticities, biasing the results (Heckman 1992). One of the biases arises by using samples that only include employed workers. This will regularly yield wrong estimates since decisions at the margin play a dominant role. A wage increase for working individuals might only slightly change the amount of work that is offered, but it will have a larger effect if it induces non working individuals to supply labor. Hence, wage changes that are somewhere at the reservation wage for quite a lot of people will significantly increase the estimates of the supply elasticity. The problem can be circumvented by including non-workers in the sample. The cost of doing this, in addition to the already existing problem that data sets only contain information on average productivity but not marginal returns, is that hypothetical wages for the non-workers have to be estimated. This can be done by calculating wages as a function of some personal characteristics like education, age, sex, or experience on the basis of the workers sample and applying the wage function to the non-workers. However, this might cause a bias in the wage function for the non-workers, since the relationship between characteristics and wages for the workers will not necessarily be the same for the non-workers. The groups might be heterogeneous to a degree that the wage regression does not capture.

Although, second generation studies deal with the problems arising from decisions at the margin, the estimates still vary considerably as was shown. The best to be said about estimates based on static labor supply is that compensated wage elasticities are usually higher for married women than for single women or men. Second, elasticities are certainly not zero at the margin where individuals enter or exit the labor market. Both results do not rule out a nonlinear monotonous nor a non-monotonous labor supply curve.

Besides estimates of static models, various attempts have been made to find out to what degree households allocate labor over time. Theories of intertemporal labor supply suggest that in addition to current wages, future values have to be included to explain variations in working hours. Tests of the intertemporal substitution hypothesis as surveyed by Card (1991), base on models where individuals maximize utility over their life thus causing employment cycles. It is assumed that people supply labor according to their real wages today and to expectations about real wages and interest rates for the rest of their life. Intertemporal substitution of labor supply between today and the future, or leisure between today and the future, drives the cycle. Unemployment is not caused by constraints from the labor demand side. Agents are free to choose, and if they decide to work less in the present there will be assets to live from. This gives the framework for the tests. The underlying model usually draws on an explicit utility function with arguments in consumption, leisure, and a taste variable. Discounted utility is maximized under a budget constraint where discounted excess consumption has to be covered by the individual's assets. The model gives first order conditions that can be tested. If the data rejects the intertemporal substitution model, this could mean, for example, that workers are constrained in their decision to supply labor. Labor supply might not only be the outcome of an interplay between income and substitution effects. Arguments on demand side restrictions would gather weight.

Lucas and Rapping (1969) tested one of the first models along these lines. They derive a labor supply schedule with different short- and long-run elasticities. In the long run labor supply is fairly inelastic, with an elasticity of 0.03, whereas labor supply reacts to wage changes in the short run with η=1.4. More recent studies usually do not favor the idea of large intertemporal substitution effects. Mankiw et al. (1985) arrive at estimates for the parameters of the utility function that are implausible, which rejects unconstrained utility maximization. Ham (1986) also gets a misspecified estimation equation via an intertemporal labor supply model. Furthermore, it was found that intertemporal substitution models fit better for workers who self reportedly do not face constraints. Dividing a sample into two groups, one which would like to adjust their labor supply but cannot and one which is unconstrained, yields evidence for the impact of constraints (Ball 1990) as the intertemporal model produced better results for the unconstrained group. Although Alogoskoufis (1987) finds evidence in favor of the intertemporal substitution hypothesis, it seems to be more likely that labor supply is constrained by some factors from the demand side. A more recent study by Zabel (1997) heads into the same direction. Most of his estimates derived from a life-cycle model of labor supply behavior are insignificant. The empirical evidence, or better to say, the lack of empirical evidence on intertemporal substitution strengthens the argument of demand side restrictions and supports models on labor supply where the budget constraint is not continuous. It furthermore indicates that estimates based on static labor supply models may not reflect the true preferences of the supply side. It seems that there is no coherent picture about labor supply behavior. Sticking to linearized versions of upward sloping supply curves might rule out some interesting properties that less conventional models of the labor market have to offer.

3.2 A bare-bones model and labor market equilibria

Before going into specific labor demand and supply functions, some general aspects of labor market equilibria and real wage adjustment will be discussed. For that purpose, a short run labor demand curve is assumed that follows from an aggregate production function with variable labor input and decreasing returns to scale

$$f = f(L) \text{ with } f'(L) > 0 \text{ and } f''(L) < 0. \tag{21}$$

The labor demand of firms that is based on this type of production function is only valid for the short run, as it implicitly assumes that capital is fixed. In the medium or long run, firms would consider adjusting the capital stock. But in the short run firms choose to vary their labor force if adjustment costs for capital are considerably high or adjusting the capital stock is infeasible due to investment lags, for example. By maximizing the profit function

$$\max_L \Pi = \max_L (p \cdot f(L) - W \cdot L) \text{ with } W>0 \tag{22}$$

the firm's demand for labor becomes a downward sloping function of the real wage $W/p=w$. To keep the problem as simple as possible, the product price is set equal to one so that $W=w$[8]. The higher the real wage is that firms have to pay, the higher the marginal product of labor has to be to meet the profit maximizing condition. With decreasing returns, a higher real wage induces a lower demand for labor and vice versa

$$L_D(w) > 0 \text{ with } L_D'(w) < 0. \tag{23}$$

The degree to which returns are decreasing controls the slope of the labor demand curve. If the economy operates at an employment level that coincides with low marginal returns, a small increase in the real wage will induce a comparably large

8 In chapter 4.1 the conditions will be shown, under which the price setting behavior of firms can change the slope of the labor demand curve.

decrease in the demand for labor. In other words, labor demand is very elastic if marginal returns are low.

In the standard model of the labor market, one would introduce a labor supply function where supply increases with higher real wages to arrive at the well known X-diagram in the real wage employment space. An upward sloping labor supply function grounds on the assumption that substitution effects prevail over income effects. Households expand their supply of labor when real wages rise. As there will usually be an upper bound to labor supply, it follows that

$$0 \leq L_S(w) \leq L_{\max} \text{ with } L_S'(w) \geq 0. \tag{24}$$

It was argued in chapter 3.1 that under certain conditions the income effect can also dominate the substitution effect. This may lead to an upward sloping labor supply curve when real wages are low, and a backward bending supply when real wages become larger. In the backward bending regime, a further real wage increase leads to a decline in labor supply. Assume w^c is the real wage level where the income effect outweighs the substitution effect. For real wages lower than w^c, labor supply will be upward sloping, while for real wages higher than w^c, it will be backward bending.

Depending on the shape of the labor supply curve, and given that demand slopes downward in the employment real wage space, there might be one, two, or even no equilibrium[9].

Whether these equilibria, should they exist, are stable crucially depends on the adjustment rule. Usually, it is assumed that there is upward pressure on (real) prices if the demand for labor exceeds the supply and, vice versa, downward pressure if demand for labor falls short of supply. An auctioneer who surveys the market would assure that prices adjust if quantities are in disequilibrium. If these assumptions capture the market behavior correctly, a first look at the labor market equilibria in Figure 5 shows that an upward sloping supply and a downward sloping demand coincide with a stable equilibrium as long as supply and demand intersect at a sufficiently steep angle. Real wages will rise when labor demand exceeds labor supply. The pressure on wages comes from the firm's optimality condition. At the going real wage it would rather employ more workers since marginal returns are higher than the marginal labor costs. But labor supply falls short of demand since households are not willing to supply the amount of labor that firms are willing to employ at the going real wage.

---

9 Real wages are now on the horizontal axis and quantities on the vertical axis. In such a space, an equilibrium, where supply and demand intersect at steep angles, is equivalent to flat angles in the real wage employment space. The change in the axis is more convenient for a graphical derivation of the real wage adjustment map. But still, the ongoing discussion will refer to a real wage employment space when flat angles are mentioned.

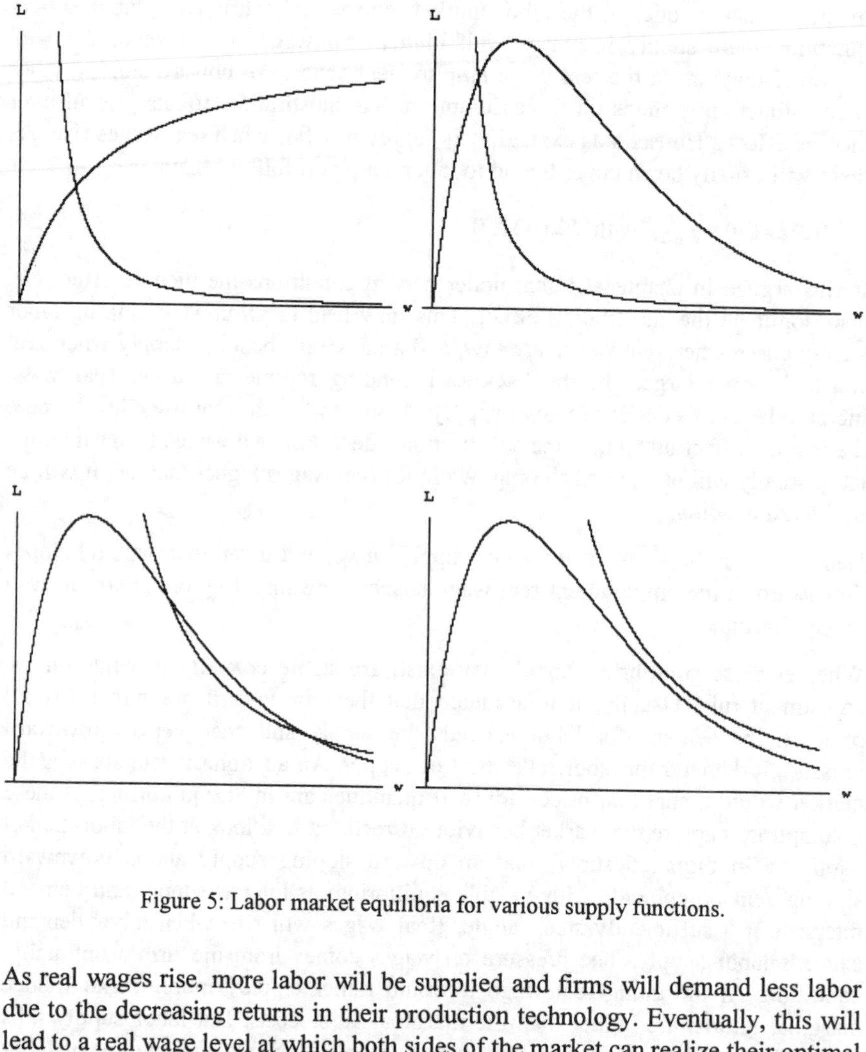

Figure 5: Labor market equilibria for various supply functions.

As real wages rise, more labor will be supplied and firms will demand less labor due to the decreasing returns in their production technology. Eventually, this will lead to a real wage level at which both sides of the market can realize their optimal supply and demand. The same mechanism holds for a real wage level that is initially higher than the equilibrium real wage. Here, the real wage induces a supply of labor that is larger than the demand for labor. If the excess supply produces sufficient downward pressure on the real wage, and real wages fall, less people will decide to work. Furthermore, labor demand increases. Again, the market eventually moves towards its equilibrium. At least there is a tendency to get back to the equilibrium. This also holds true for the low real wage equilibrium in a model where labor supply bends backwards. The signs on excess demand next to the equilibrium imply real wage pressure that forces the labor market back to the equilibrium. At the high real wage equilibrium demand exceeds supply if real wages deviate to the right of the equilibrium. The auctioneer will choose to increase real wages because this is the rule that proved to stabilize the market. As labor supply is downward sloping, this causes an even lower supply of labor. Labor demand declines too, but with a smaller margin, so that excess demand increases. Real wage pressure rises which causes real wage movements away from the high real wage equilibrium. As an initial real wage between the low real wage and high real wage equilibrium sparks falling real wages, the high real wage equilibrium is unstable. Finally, the demand curve may lie far to the right of the backward bending supply curve. Both curves do not intersect. There is no equilibrium at all. As demand exceeds supply at any real wage level real wages keep on rising[10].

Although it is possible to pinpoint the direction of real wage changes the stability analysis has to be vague as long as there is no explicit formalization of the underlying adjustment mechanisms. Which of various possible adjustment rules serve best is a difficult question to answer. There are different kind of plausible mechanism on which to ground a more formal stability analysis. Prices as well as quantities might adjust. Prices might react to differences in quantities, as was assumed above, but also on prices itself. The same, of course, might be true for quantities. Variables can change simultaneously and the speed to which prices vary might not only be dependent on the difference in the quantities' but also on past changes in the prices. Besides these proportional and derivative control rules, there are also integral control mechanisms. A survey of various adjustment rules is given in Flaschel, Semmler, and Franke (1997). The choice of a specific rule that brings the dynamics into static models can influence the properties of the model (c.f. Bolle 1971, 1973, and 1975). Therefore, it is crucial to find an adjustment mechanism that adequately describes the way in which markets behave in disequilibrium.

3.3 Adjustment dynamics

The following adjustment rule will simply recur to price adjustments that are driven by excess demand or supply. Furthermore, it is assumed that a change in real wages will be proportional to the amount at which demand and supply differ. Whereas the feedback from quantities on prices seems to be a reasonable

---

10 Manning (1990) conjectures that in a very sclerotic labor market with supply and demand curves that do not intersect, employment may follow a random walk. This is a more compelling outcome than explosive real wage trajectories, but it requires different assumptions on how markets adjust than the ones that underlie the approach here.

assumption, one might be inclined to argue that there is no proportionality for real wage changes. It might well be the case that a large excess demand causes a relatively larger change in real wages than a small one. Furthermore, and probably more important, there might be an asymmetry in the adjustment of real wages. A certain excess demand might induce a larger real wage change in absolute value than the same amount of excess supply does. Since the proportionality factor that ties the quantities to the price changes can also be interpreted as an adjustment speed, an asymmetric proportional adjustment rule would capture differing length of adjustment periods when employment is above or below its equilibrium. In fact, there is empirical evidence on real wage gaps for several European countries in the eighties (c.f. chapter 4.3) that would probably justify such an assumption. But not everything that is desirable is also feasible when it comes to an analytical treatment of the model. Especially, if supply and demand schedules are nonlinear. More sophisticated adjustment rules can make models intractable from an analytical point of view. At least, it will be very tedious to learn something on the properties with the help of simulations.

There is another important question about the behavior of the auctioneer. It relates to whether he observes the market continuously, or at discrete and fixed time intervals. This is crucial for the dynamics, as it is well known that in continuous time only three dimensional systems can become chaotic, whereas in discrete time even one dimensional systems can exhibit chaotic behavior (Lorenz 1993). In continuous time, the auctioneer would have to check whether there is excess demand or supply and decide on the real wage change every infinitely small second. It seems, however, more likely that agents collect information and make decisions from time to time. Of course, this aggregate model of homogenous agents implies that all agents act at fixed time intervals. This might be questionable. But once homogeneity is assumed, the latter argument makes no difference whether a model should be developed in continuous or discrete time. All agents act in the same way in every aspect. Even if continuous time models should prove to be more adequate approaches to explain economic dynamics, there would still be the problem that comes from discrete data sets. Every data is discrete and therefore a continuous model can never be tested capturing the intuition that lies behind it. When it is confronted with the data, every continuous time model becomes discrete, and one has to find arguments that justify the assumption that these data sets can give adequate information on the validity of a model in continuous time.

For all those reasons, but still being aware that this can be a crucial assumption that, once changed, would alter the results significantly, the dynamic analysis will be based on the following adjustment function

$$w_{t+1} - w_t = \lambda \cdot [L_D(w_t) - L_S(w_t)]\,. \qquad (25)$$

When demand exceeds supply, real wages will increase proportionally and, vice versa, will fall proportionally if for a given real wage labor supply is larger than demand. The proportionality factor λ can also be interpreted as an adjustment parameter that captures the speed with which real wage changes will (or, as will be shown later on, will not) clear the market. The adjustment time is the inverse of λ. Given there is a stable equilibrium, the larger the effect of an excess demand on the change in real wages is, the less time it takes to clear the market.

For a labor market such as in (25), at least three questions arise. If labor supply and demand intersect, can these equilibria become unstable? If so, is there a trapping area for trajectories that are repelled from the equilibrium? Can these trajectories become chaotic? All three issues will be addressed.

The stability condition for (25) is

$$\left|\frac{dw_{t+1}}{dw_t}\right|_{w^*} < 1 \tag{26}$$

which implies that the slope of the adjustment map has to be smaller than one in absolute value at the equilibrium real wage. If it is not, trajectories will be repelled from the equilibrium once latter is only slightly perturbed. The inequality in (26) can also be written as

$$-2 < \lambda \cdot \left(\left.\frac{dL_D}{dw_t}\right|_{w^*} - \left.\frac{dL_S}{dw_t}\right|_{w^*}\right) < 0\,. \tag{27}$$

As long as the product of the adjustment speed and the difference of the slopes for labor demand and labor supply is less than zero and larger than minus two, the equilibrium will be stable. As the bare-bones model assumed a downward sloping labor demand, the first term in the brackets is always negative. Two cases for the supply of labor were outlined: a monotonously increasing labor supply curve, and a labor supply that changes its sign. If substitution effects always prevail income effects, labor supply increases with higher real wages. In this case, the second term in the parenthesis is always positive, so that the sum of the slopes is always negative. Insofar, it cannot be excluded that the whole expression becomes smaller than minus two. Even if labor demand is downward sloping and labor supply slopes upward, there might be no stable equilibrium. An unstable equilibrium occurs if labor demand and supply intersect at small angels and the adjustment speed is high. Small angels are given if labor demand and labor supply are fairly elastic at the equilibrium. Then, a small positive change in real wages implies a considerable increase in labor supply, and a relatively large decrease in the demand for labor. If the auctioneer reacts very sensitively to deviations of labor demand from labor supply, he will translate it into a large wage increase or decrease in the following period. This might not be the equilibrium real wage, but even further away from it than the initial deviation so that the equilibrium becomes unstable.

If the demand curve crosses the supply curve in the backward bending regime, the second term within the parenthesis is negative as an increase in real wages would reduce labor supply. If, furthermore, the slope of the labor demand curve is smaller than the slope of the supply curve in absolute values, the equilibrium is always unstable no matter how fast real wages adjust. This can be seen from (27 as the difference between the slopes in labor demand and supply is always positive. If the real wage is slightly higher than in the equilibrium, the auctioneer will choose to increase real wages as he sees excess demand on the market. Higher real wages cause even larger excess demand. Real wages keep on rising. If the real wage is to the left of the equilibrium, he will lower real wages so that the high real wage equilibrium in the backward bending regime is unstable. If there is another equilibrium in the backward bending regime, where labor demand intersects supply from above, it will be locally stable for sufficiently low adjustment speeds that ensure that the lower bound of the stability equation is not violated. In fact, one would expect a more stable equilibrium as the expression within the parentheses is larger compared to an equilibrium in the upward sloping labor supply regime.

There might be a trapping area for those equilibria that are not structurally unstable if real wages are repelled from the equilibrium. To see this, one has to have a look at $w_{t+1}=f(w_t)$ and its slope for real wages that approach zero or infinity. Given the bare-bones model, the adjustment map will have the following properties:

$$\lim_{w_t \to 0} f(w_t) = \infty \tag{28}$$

and

$$\lim_{w_t \to \infty} f(w_t) = \infty . \tag{29}$$

f becomes infinite for real wages next to zero as well as to infinity. When real wages approach zero, labor is relatively cheap and there is a tremendous demand, but almost nobody is willing to work. The real wage set by the auctioneer for the following period will consequently be very high. For slightly higher real wages than zero, excess demand will be smaller so that the real wage of the following period will be smaller than it would be with an initial real wage that was almost zero. Hence, the slope of the adjustment map will be negative for real wage levels next to zero

$$\lim_{w_t \to 0} \frac{df(w_t)}{dw_t} < 0 . \tag{30}$$

As labor supply becomes either zero, or approaches a finite value for very high real wages, and furthermore, labor demand will almost be zero, an increase in real wages will actually not change excess demand. Tomorrows real wage level will be the one of today, at least at the border.

$$\lim_{w_t \to \infty} \frac{df(w_t)}{dw_t} = 1 . \tag{31}$$

The expressions (28) to (31) imply a fish hooked adjustment map. If it can be shown that these adjustment maps lie above the horizontal axis, trajectories repelled from the equilibrium will be bounded between an upper and a lower real wage level. This holds at least for the bare-bones model, where supply does not bend backwards. If, there is a second equilibrium, the upper bound of the real wage range must not exceed the high real wage level to assure that there is a set

$$\underline{w} < w_t < \overline{w}$$

that maps onto itself. Then, trajectories starting at real wage levels below $w^{*,\,high}$ will move to lower real wage levels and eventually enter the real wage regime $w_t < w^{*,\,low}$. Every trajectory in this regime will be thrown back to $w_t > w^{*,\,low}$ in the following iteration. As the smallest possible real wage level for $w_t < w^{*,\,low}$ is the first iterative of w^{min}, a trapping area is given if

$$f^2(w^{\min}) < w^{*,high} .$$

The boundaries of the real wage trapping area are then

$$\underline{w} = f(w^{\min}) \tag{32}$$

and

$$\overline{w} = f^2(w^{\min}) . \tag{33}$$

The single humped shape of the adjustment map implies that the dynamics within the trapping area might become chaotic in the sense of Li and Yorke (1975)[11]

Li and Yorke-theorem: If the adjustment function f is continuous on an interval I, maps onto itself and an initial real wage w_0 can be found within this interval that satisfies

$$f^3(w_0) \geq w_0 > f^1(w_0) > f^2(w_0)$$

then the one-dimensional map is chaotic. Trajectories starting from two points w_{01}, w_{02} in a subset S of I ($S \subset I$) will come arbitrarily close to each other and divert again as time goes on.

$$\limsup_{n \to \infty} \left| f^n(w_{01}) - f^n(w_{02}) \right| > 0$$

---

11 The theorem of Li and Yorke (1975) goes back to Sarkovski who found out that a period three cycle under the conditions above implies an infinite number of other cycles, c.f. Lorenz (1993).

$$\liminf_{n\to\infty}\left|f^n(w_{01})-f^n(w_{02})\right|=0$$

Furthermore, trajectories will not converge to any periodic cycle

$$\limsup_{n\to\infty}\left|f^n(w_{01})-f^n(w_{02})\right|>0$$

with w_{01} starting in S and w_{02} as an initial real wage of a periodic trajectory.

Such a period three cycle is likely to occur and is grounded on the nonlinearity of labor demand and supply, and the adjustment speed of the market. Start with a negative excess demand at an initial real wage w_0. Supply of labor is larger than the demand for w_0 and the auctioneer applies his market clearing rule lowering the real wage level. The real wage of the following period will be less than the initial one ($w_0 > w_1$). If there is still negative excess demand for w_1, because the auctioneer did not decrease real wages enough to clear the market, he will decide to lower the real wage level even further to w_2 ($w_0 > w_1 > w_2$). However, this time he might have overdone it and decreased real wages to a level w_2 where labor demand exceeds supply. Realizing this excess demand, he decides that an increase in real wages will surely clear the market. If the excess demand in period two was sufficiently high, w_3 may even be larger than or equal to w_0 ($w_3 \geq w_0 > w_1 > w_2$). As a period three cycle implies an infinite number of other frequencies (Li and Yorke 1975), there is scope for deterministic chaos. Although the auctioneer tries hard to set real wages in a way that the labor market clears, he constantly fails to do so. The sequence of the real wage levels he chooses to achieve his goal looks random, but is actually deterministic.

Whether the equilibrium becomes unstable, and whether there is a trapping area with chaotic oscillations, depends on the specific assumptions on the labor supply and labor demand side. To illustrate the possibility of such labor market dynamics, two models will be discussed. Both capture the properties of the bare-bones model and allow a more detailed analysis of the dynamics.

Case 1 - Labor supply bends backwards

For each of the two cases, labor demand will be derived from a Cobb-Douglas production function where capital is fixed

$$f(L) = A \cdot L^{\alpha} \text{ with } 0<\alpha<1 \text{ and } A>0. \tag{34}$$

Then labor demand becomes

$$L_D(w) = \left(\frac{w}{A\cdot\alpha}\right)^{\frac{1}{\alpha-1}}. \tag{35}$$

This is a downward sloping function in real wages. Labor demand will be combined with two different labor supply curves. One of which changes its sign to capture the feature of a backward bending supply. The other is upward sloping for all real wages and saturates at a maximum labor force L_{max}. A convenient way to model a labor supply function that slopes upwards for low real wages and bends backwards for higher real wages, is given by the function

$$L_S(w) = B \cdot w \cdot e^{-\delta \cdot w} \text{ with } B > 0 \text{ and } \delta \geq 0. \tag{36}$$

B may be restricted from above to normalize the maximal available labor supply to one. As can be shown easily, L_S in (36) has the properties required earlier

$$\lim_{w \to 0} L_S(w) = \lim_{w \to 0} \frac{B \cdot w}{e^{\delta \cdot w}} = 0 \tag{37}$$

$$\lim_{w \to \infty} L_S(w) = \lim_{w \to \infty} \frac{B \cdot w}{e^{\delta \cdot w}} \overset{l'H.}{=} \lim_{w \to \infty} \frac{B}{\delta \cdot e^{\delta \cdot w}} = 0. \tag{38}$$

With a production function (34) and a backward bending labor supply following (36), the real wage adjustment process becomes

$$w_{t+1} = w_t + \lambda \cdot [(\frac{w_t}{\alpha \cdot A})^{\frac{1}{\alpha - 1}} - B \cdot w_t \cdot e^{-\delta \cdot w_t}]. \tag{39}$$

Figure 6, Figure 7, and Figure 8 show the graphical derivation of the adjustment map (39) that follows from the labor demand and supply functions (35) and (36), respectively.

Subtracting demand from supply for given real wages yields Figure 7. The excess demand function is zero for the equilibrium real wage rate. For all other real wages, there is either a positive or negative excess demand for labor. Adjustment speeds that are larger than one stretch the excess demand function while it is compressed for $0<\lambda<1$. By adding w_t (a 45-degree line) to $\lambda \cdot e(w_t)$ one obtains the adjustment function $w_{t+1}=f(w_{t+1})$. The adjustment map crosses the diagonal at the low (and high) equilibrium real wage rate. It was already argued that the high real wage equilibrium is always unstable. The low real wage equilibrium in (39) may become locally unstable under certain conditions. If B is small enough, trajectories repelled from the unstable equilibrium are bounded from above and below. Real wage cycles can become chaotic within these boundaries. A proof of chaotic cycles along the lines of the Li and Yorke (1975) theorem seems to be infeasible due to the highly nonlinear structure of the adjustment map. But it is possible to derive some conditions under which a period three cycle will occur. By trying different parameters and initial conditions, one can find a period three cycle. There exists a real wage range for which (39) maps onto itself, as long as the parameters are chosen in a way that the upper bound does not exceed the high real wage equilibrium.

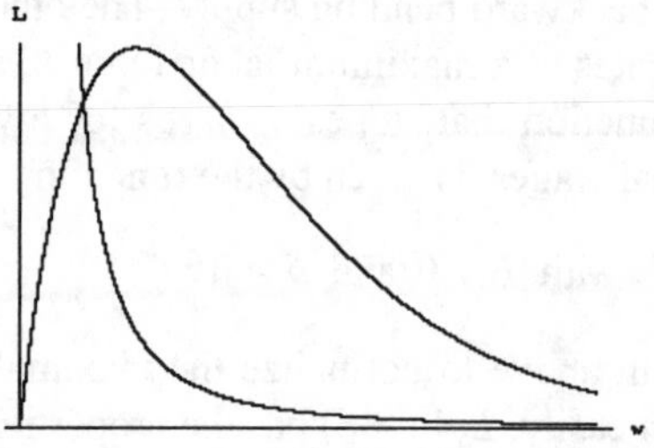

Figure 6: Labor demand and supply.

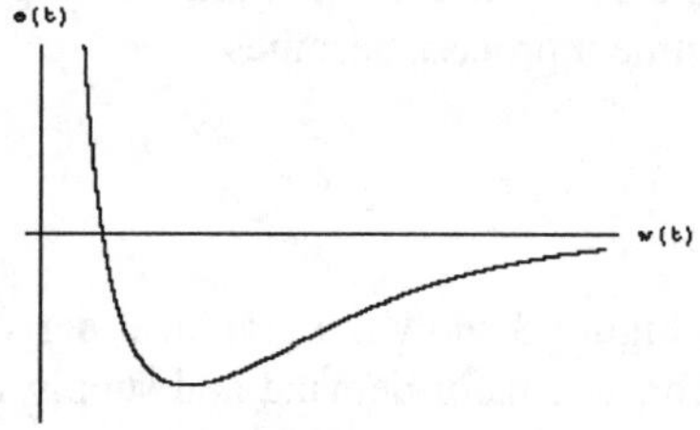

Figure 7: Excess demand function.

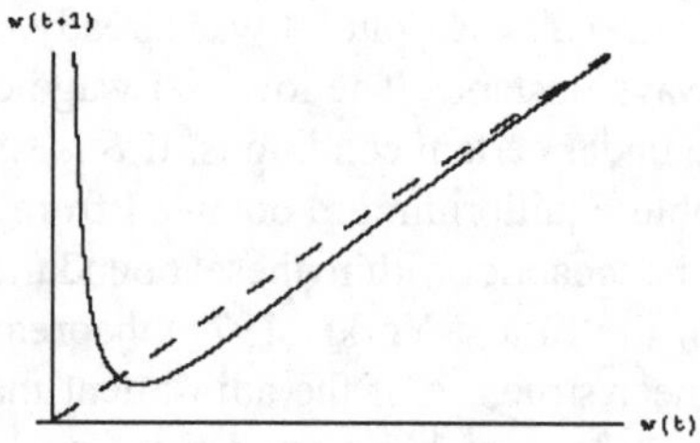

Figure 8: Adjustment map.

What remains to be shown is the existence of a period three cycle (c.f. Li and Yorke 1975). In a first step, a condition will be derived under which tuning B will shift the minimum of the fish hooked map f. Afterwards, it will be shown that there can exist a B for which

$$f^1(w_{\min}) < w_{\min} < f^3(w_{\min}) < f^2(w_{\min}) . \tag{40}$$

The second part of the approach is similar to the one in Hommes (1994), as a linear version approximates f.

Labor supply maximizes for

$$w_{\max,L_S} = \frac{1}{\delta} \tag{41}$$

and is independent from B. Tuning B would strengthen the hump-shaped form of the adjustment map if it was possible to find parameters, so that the real wage that minimizes the adjustment map is equal to (41). Then the minimum would always be given for $w_{min}=1/\delta$. A sufficient condition for this is that the slope of the adjustment map is zero for $w_{min}=1/\delta$

$$\left.\frac{dw_{t+1}}{dw_t}\right|_{\frac{1}{\delta}} = 1 + \lambda \cdot \frac{dL_D}{dw_t} = 0 . \tag{42}$$

An adjustment speed that satisfies (42) is given by

$$\lambda = \frac{1}{\alpha \cdot A \cdot (1-\alpha)} \cdot \left(\frac{1}{\alpha \cdot A \cdot \delta}\right)^{\frac{1-\alpha}{2-\alpha}} . \tag{43}$$

Now one can choose B so that the second iterate of w_{min} is slightly smaller than the high real wage equilibrium

$$f^2\left(\frac{1}{\delta}\right) \leq w^{*,high} - \zeta \text{ for } \zeta > 0 . \tag{44}$$

Furthermore,

$$F(w_t) = -\mu \cdot \left(w_t - \frac{1}{\delta}\right) + f\left(\frac{1}{\delta}\right) \text{ for } 0 < w_t \leq \frac{1}{\delta} \tag{45}$$

and

$$F(w_t) = \left(w_t - \frac{1}{\delta}\right) + f\left(\frac{1}{\delta}\right) \text{ for } \frac{1}{\delta} < w_t < \infty \tag{46}$$

with

$$\mu = \frac{f^2(\frac{1}{\delta}) - f(\frac{1}{\delta})}{\frac{1}{\delta} - f(\frac{1}{\delta})} \tag{47}$$

shall be a linear version of *f*. For *F* one can show that

$$F(\frac{1}{\delta}) < \frac{1}{\delta} < F^3(\frac{1}{\delta}) < F^2(\frac{1}{\delta}). \tag{48}$$

From the definition of *F* it immediately follows that

$$F(\frac{1}{\delta}) < \frac{1}{\delta},\ F(\frac{1}{\delta}) < F^2(\frac{1}{\delta}),\ \text{and}\ F^3(\frac{1}{\delta}) < F^2(\frac{1}{\delta}).$$

What remains to be shown is that

$$F^3(\frac{1}{\delta}) - \frac{1}{\delta} > \varepsilon \ \text{for}\ \varepsilon > 0. \tag{49}$$

Using (45) and (46), (49) can be written as

$$F^3(\frac{1}{\delta}) - \frac{1}{\delta} = \mu \cdot (\frac{1}{\delta} - f(\frac{1}{\delta})) + 2 \cdot (f(\frac{1}{\delta}) - \frac{1}{\delta}) > \varepsilon. \tag{50}$$

In order to fulfil (50) one has to increase *B* so that

$$\mu > \frac{\varepsilon}{\frac{1}{\delta} - f(\frac{1}{\delta})} + 2. \tag{51}$$

To assure that the second iterate of the minimum of the adjustment map does not exceed the high real wage equilibrium, there has to be an upper bound to μ that is determined by (44) and can be written as

$$\mu \le \frac{w^{high} - \zeta - f(\frac{1}{\delta})}{\frac{1}{\delta} - f(\frac{1}{\delta})}. \tag{52}$$

For such a μ, a period three cycle will occur implying real wage cycles with any other frequency. Basically, (52) states that the high real wage equilibrium has to be sufficiently far to the right in Figure 8. The derivation of a more specific parameter setting from the inequality in (52) would require an explicit solution of the high real equilibrium. However, one can show by trying that there are parameters that fulfill (51) and (52). For example, by setting λ=0.75, α=0.5, δ=1, A=1, B=2.8, and w_0=0.8 one gets the sequence w_1=0.3380, w_2=1.4720, and w_3=0.8492.

Figure 9 shows that if there is a single and stable long run low real wage equilibrium, it can take a considerably long time for such a labor market to move to a new equilibrium after a small shock. Consider, for example, a negative productivity shock that shifts the labor demand curve to the left. The old equilibrium real wage may have been at w=0.6, whereas the new one is approximately 0.55. Then, it will take more than thirty periods for the market to settle to its new equilibrium. As the real wages overshoot the new equilibrium real wage, one cannot call this persistence in its original meaning. But loosely speaking, this is persistent behavior as the current state of the labor market (at t=30) is driven to a large extent by a shock in the very past (at t=0).

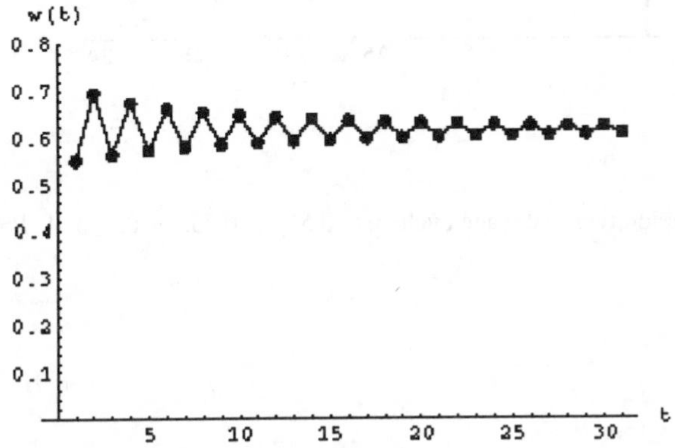

Figure 9: Real wage adjustment path after a small shock, w_0=0.55, λ=0.75, α=0.5, δ=1, B=2, A=1.

Increasing B generates a period two cycle (Figure 10). Now there are two long run real wage equilibria. The market switches from a high real wage level to a low one and back. The period two cycle is robust against variations of the initial real wage and the parameter B. As long as the second iterate of the minimum of the adjustment map is smaller than the high real wage equilibrium, all real wages that are smaller than the high real wage equilibrium and larger than zero will be attracted by it. Figure 11 shows a simulated real wage time series starting from a disequilibrium real wage level if the system is chaotic. As can be seen, real wages vary irregularly but do not exceed an upper and lower level. Without any exogenous shocks, real wages do not converge to an equilibrium level. There is a disequilibrium real wage range.

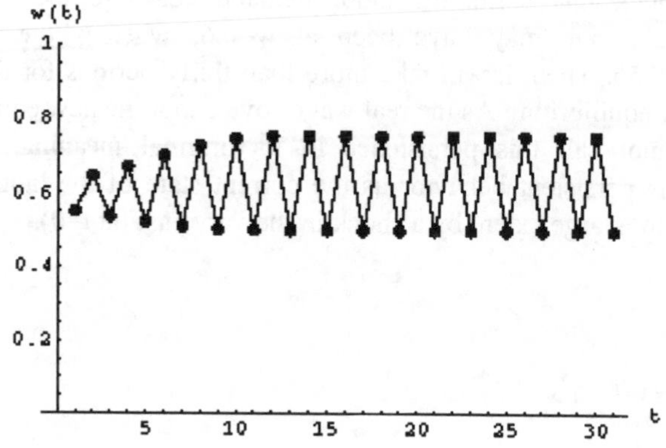

Figure 10: Period two real wage cycle, w_0=0.55, λ=0.75, α=0.5, δ=1, B=2.2, A=1.

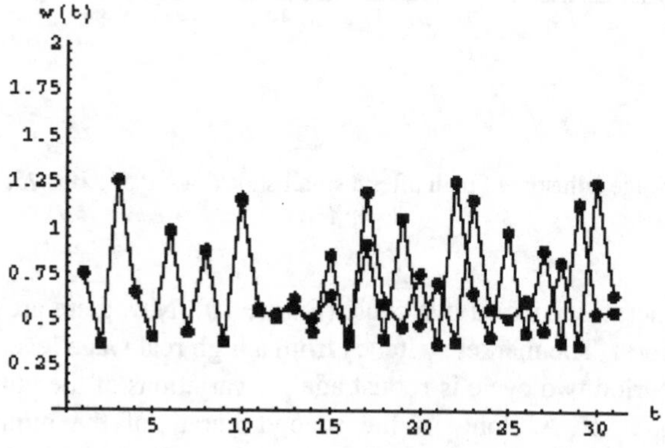

Figure 11: Real wage time series, λ=0.75, α=0.5, δ=1, A=1, B=2.7, w_0=0.75.

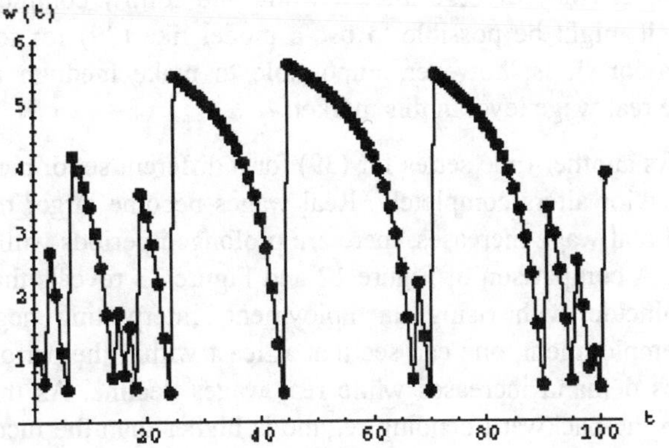

Figure 12: Real wage time series for (39), λ=5, α=0.5, δ=1, A=1, B=0.9, w_0=1.

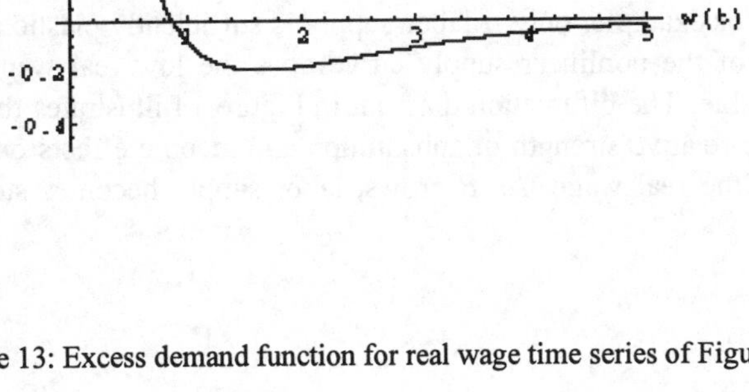

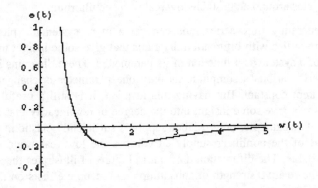

Figure 13: Excess demand function for real wage time series of Figure 12.

Sensitive dependence on initial conditions is illustrated by the second time series in Figure 11, which starts at an initial real wage level that differs only 0.1% from the initial real wage of the other time series. For the first iterations real wages coincide. However, they diverge after a while and follow completely different paths. Insofar, it might be possible to use a model like (39) for forecasting the short run behavior. It is, however, impossible to make medium and long run forecasts of the real wage level in this market.

Figure 12 shows another time series for (39) for a different set of parameters. The qualitative behavior alters completely. Real wages become larger than in Figure 11. After rapid real wage increases, there are prolonged periods within which real wages decline. A comparison of Figure 12 and Figure 13 reveals that falling real wages can coincide with rising unemployment. Interpreting negative excess demand as unemployment, one can see that at least within the periods 50 and 60 negative excess demand increases while real wages decline. As the increase in labor supply in the backward bending regime is higher than the increase in labor demand, real wages and employment are positively correlated. A smooth decline is followed by a sharp increase in the real wage level as labor demand sharply increases and labor supply is low when real wages approach the lower bound.

Prolonged periods of falling real wages and rising unemployment will also occur if a small shock that lowered the real wage level hit the economy while it was at its high and unstable real wage equilibrium. This would start a long period of real wage declines without employment gains. Finally, the labor market could get trapped at or around the low real wage (or employment) equilibrium. Former high real wage levels would never be achieved again. In addition, there might be irregular cycles around an unstable low real wage equilibrium.

Besides generating time series, one can get a more systematic picture of the dynamic properties with bifurcation diagrams that give some insight into the long run states of a system as a function of its parameters. These diagrams heavily rest on the ceteris paribus assumption, as only one parameter is changed while all others are kept constant. But having this in mind, it is still a useful tool. Such simulations can give some insight into the degree of nonlinearity that destabilizes the market. For example, only if labor supply is sufficiently elastic in the upward sloping part of the nonlinear supply curve does the low real wage equilibrium become unstable. The bifurcation diagram in Figure 14 illustrates the impact of a change in the relative strength of substitution and income effects on the long run dynamics of the real wage. As B grows, labor supply becomes steeper for real wage levels

$$w_t < \frac{1}{\delta} \tag{53}$$

as well as for the backward bending regime. A change in real wages will induce a comparably larger increase in labor supply for the upward sloping regime, and a comparably larger reduction in labor supply for the backward bending regime.

The bifurcation diagram in Figure 14 relates long run real wage levels to specific values of *B*. For every *B* in the interval [2;2.7], a time series of 200 iterations was calculated. The first 100 iterations were omitted to cancel out transitory dynamics. The second half of the time series is plotted on the vertical axis for every *B* in the interval. If there is a single stable equilibrium for *B,* all the generated real wages for the periods 101 until 200 will show up as a single point in the bifurcation diagram. As can be seen from Figure 14, there is a single stable equilibrium for B lower than approximately 2.05. Increasing *B* leads to a flip bifurcation. A stable period two cycle emerges from a stable single equilibrium. There are two long run real wage levels. With every period, the labor market switches from one real wage level to the other and back again. Increasing *B* even further causes a stable period four cycle. Now, real wages switch between four long run equilibria. Predictability is given, as with every forth period the same real wage will occur. Long run forecasts will not be possible if *B* increases further. For *B* larger than 2.55, there is a very large number of real wage levels. Although bounded, it is impossible to determine the sequence of real wages unless one knows exactly the current state of the labor market. This, however, is impossible from a practical point of view. Even small deviations in the initial conditions will cause diverging trajectories in the long run, as was illustrated in Figure 11.

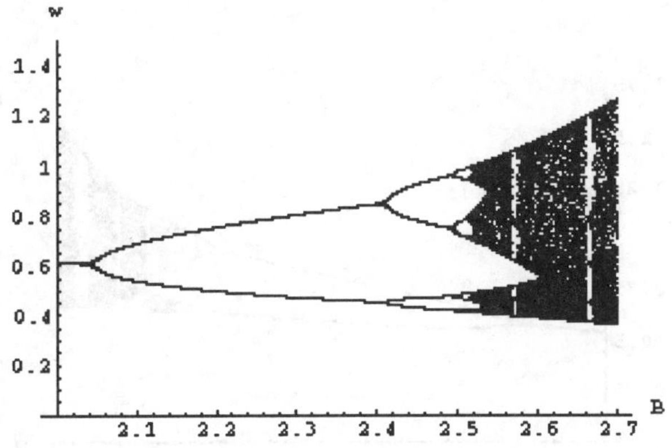

Figure 14: Bifurcation diagram for B, λ=0.75, α=0.5, δ=1, A=1.

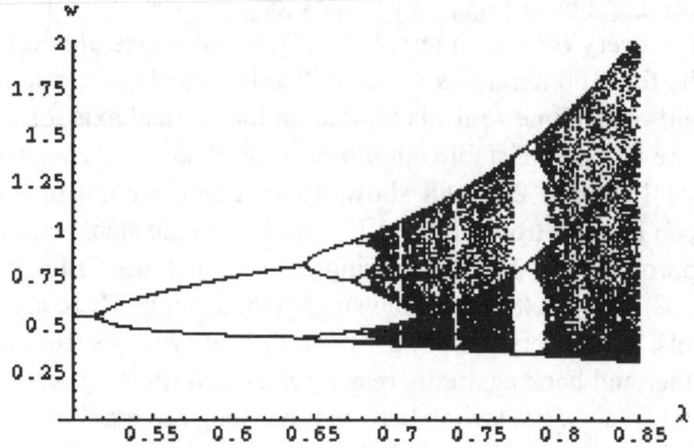

Figure 15: Bifurcation diagram for λ, α=0.5, δ=1, B=2.7, A=1.

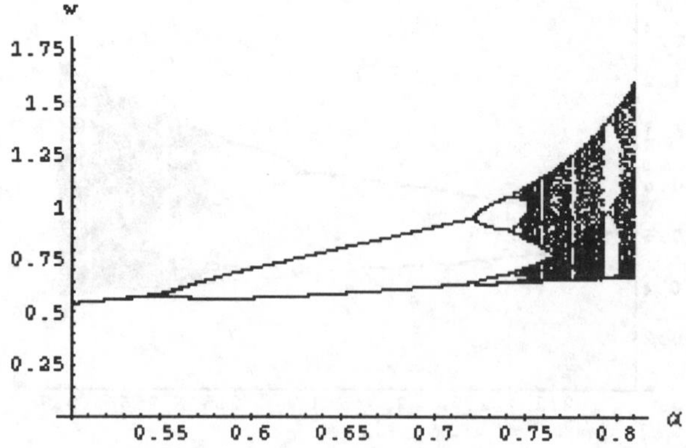

Figure 16: Bifurcation diagram for α, λ=0.5, δ=1, B=2.7, A=1.

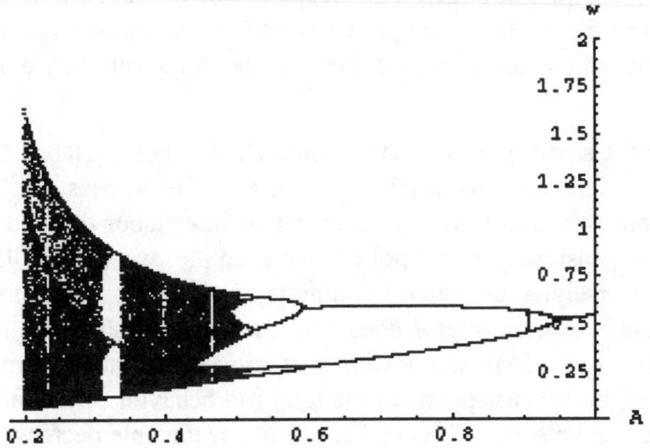

Figure 17: Bifurcation diagram for A, α=0.5, λ=0.5, δ=1, B=2.7.

Keeping B at a fixed value and varying the adjustment speed λ instead, gives some insight into the role of the auctioneer, given labor demand and supply behavior of households and firms. At an adjustment speed of λ=0.75 and B=2.7, Figure 15 implies a chaotic trajectory. Lowering the adjustment speed will stabilize the market given the same B as in Figure 14. This confirms the results of the discussion on the stability of the low real wage equilibrium. Qualitatively, the bifurcation diagram on the adjustment speed looks the same as for varying B. There is a stable regime, one with cycles of finite order, and a chaotic regime that describes the long run behavior.

Finally, Figure 16 gives some insight into the impact of the concavity of the production function. Varying the degree of decreasing returns in the production function has an ambiguous effect on the demand for labor and the slope of the labor demand curve if the latter follows (35). First, whether an increase in α leads to a higher demand depends on the real wage level. Assuming that it is sufficiently low an increase in marginal returns sparks a higher demand for labor. This shifts the demand curve outwards. At lower real wage levels, the demand for labor will be smaller. Second, with respect to the slope of the labor demand curve[12], increasing α flattens the labor demand curve at higher real wages but increases it at lower employment levels. In addition, the labor demand curve intersects the

12 A steeper labor supply or demand curve means that dL/dw is larger in absolute terms.

labor supply curve at a new equilibrium. Hence, if labor supply is nonlinear, the stability of the new equilibrium will also depend on the slope of the supply curve. Insofar, the effects of changing returns to scale are ambiguous. In Figure 16, the destabilizing forces are stronger. The steeper labor demand curve dominates the stabilizing effect from a flatter supply curve at the new equilibrium. Once more, a chaotic regime can emerge, where there is no long run single labor market equilibrium.

The effect on the stability of the market through shifts of the labor demand curve becomes even more obvious when A is varied. A is a measure for per capita productivity but serves also as a parameter that links labor demand to aggregate demand. An expansionary fiscal policy, for example, would shift labor demand outwards. Conversely, a restrictive fiscal policy would shift labor demand towards the origin. This is exactly what A does, too. Increasing A shifts the labor demand curve outwards (c.f. (35)) and lowering it moves the labor demand schedule towards the origin. What happens to the long run behavior of the labor market in the latter case can be seen in Figure 17. For a considerable decrease in aggregate demand, the labor market becomes unstable. After an aggregate demand shock, labor demand and supply curves intersect at a lower employment level. Thus, there is a higher labor supply elasticity at the new equilibrium. Households react more sensitively to any deviation from the equilibrium real wage, so the equilibrium might even become unstable if the shift in demand is sufficiently large, given that once more all other parameters are held constant.

These are just four examples of the long run dynamics of the model. As was argued, the results depend sensitively on the parameter settings and, of course, on the labor demand and supply relations that underlie the model. But irregular dynamics are robust against changes in the supply function, which will be shown in the following model where labor supply is grounded on a CES utility function and is upwards sloping.

Case 2 - An upward sloping labor supply curve with an upper bound

An upward sloping supply curve can be derived from a CES preference function where workers get utility from consumption and disutility from work

$$U(C,1-L)=(C^{\beta}+(1-L)^{\beta})^{\frac{1}{\beta}}. \tag{54}$$

The upper bound to labor supply L_{max} shall be one. Utility increases with leisure and income. β can vary between]-∞;1], yielding different supply schedules. For an upward sloping supply curve that has a positive slope in the origin of the real wage employment space, β has to be in the interval [0.5;1]. The latter is the range for β that describes the case for the following discussion. Maximizing the utility function under the restriction that consumption cannot exceed the income from work

$$C \leq L \cdot w \tag{55}$$

yields the supply of labor

$$L_S(w) = \frac{1}{1 + w^{\frac{\beta}{\beta-1}}}. \tag{56}$$

Combining (56) with the downward sloping demand of (35) gives the adjustment map

$$w_{t+1} = w_t + \lambda \cdot [(\frac{w_t}{\alpha \cdot A})^{\frac{1}{\alpha-1}} - \frac{1}{1 + w_t^{\frac{\beta}{\beta-1}}}]. \tag{57}$$

(57) has different properties than (39). Most importantly, there is always one labor market equilibrium. This can be seen from the slopes of (56) and (35). For $0<w<\infty$ labor demand is downward sloping and labor supply upward sloping. If the real wage approaches zero, (57) becomes

$$\lim_{w_t \to 0} w_{t+1} = \infty \tag{58}$$

and for w_t approaching infinity

$$\lim_{w_t \to \infty} w_{t+1} = \infty . \tag{59}$$

Together with

$$\lim_{w_t \to \infty} \frac{dw_{t+1}}{dw_t} = 1 \tag{60}$$

and

$$\lim_{w_t \to 0} \frac{dw_{t+1}}{dw_t} = -\infty \tag{61}$$

(58) and (59) imply a fish hooked adjustment map. A further look at (57) shows that by varying the parameter A one can always assure that $w_{t+1} \geq 0$. Increasing A will shift the adjustment map (Figure 20) upwards and the minimum to the right. Hence, as long as there is an equilibrium, one can find an interval

$$\underline{w} < w_t < \overline{w}$$

that maps onto itself. Should the equilibrium w^* become unstable, trajectories would be bounded from above and below.

Figure 18, Figure 19, and Figure 20 illustrate the derivation of the real wage adjustment map when labor supply is upward sloping.

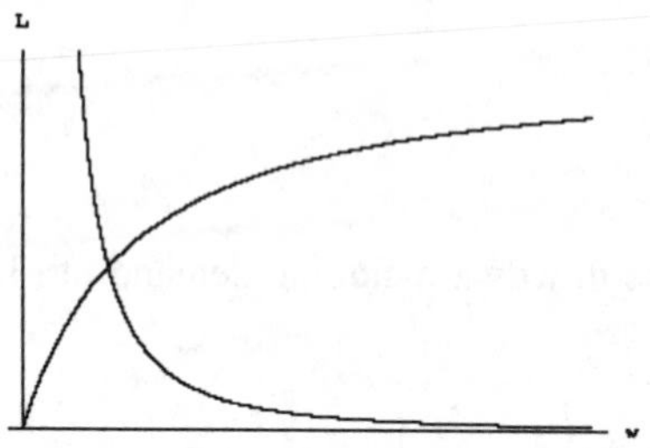

Figure 18: Labor market with an upward sloping supply and a maximal available labor force.

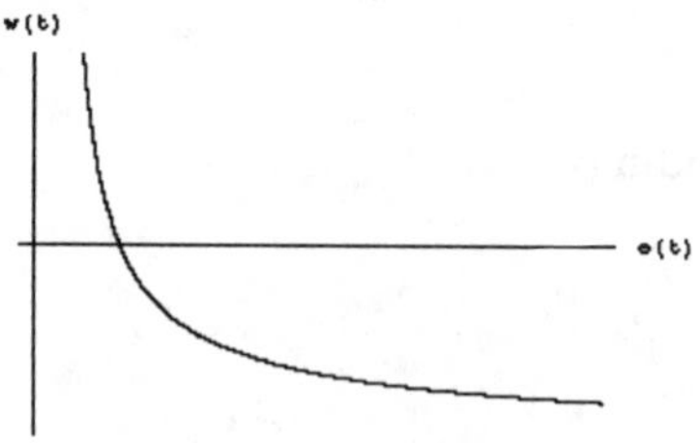

Figure 19: Excess demand function.

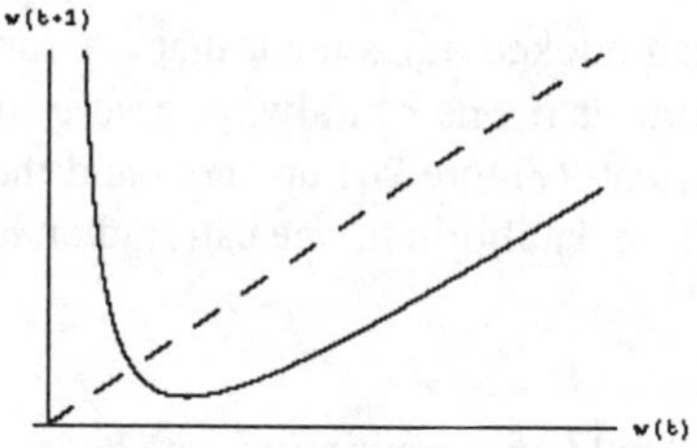

Figure 20: Real wage adjustment map.

Once more, the excess function is zero at the real wage where supply and demand curves intersect in Figure 18. At the same real wage, the adjustment map crosses the equilibrium condition in Figure 20. The real wage of the consecutive period will be higher than the current real wage level if the current real wage is to the left of the equilibrium real wage, and it will be lower if it is to the right.

Due to the highly nonlinear character of (57), it seems to be infeasible to prove a period three cycle that would imply cycles of infinite order following the theorem of Li and Yorke (1975).

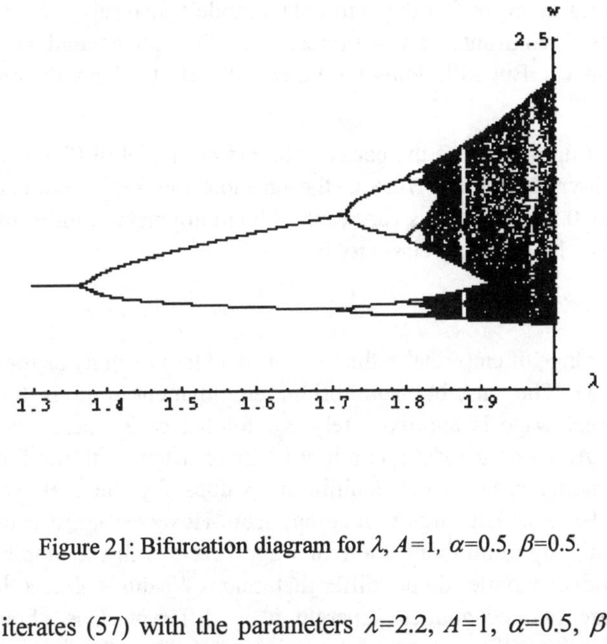

Figure 21: Bifurcation diagram for λ, A=1, α=0.5, β=0.5.

But if one iterates (57) with the parameters λ=2.2, A=1, α=0.5, β=0.5 starting with w_0=1.2, one gets a period three cycle with w_1=0.3819, w_2=3.5440, and w_3=1.8720. As a substitute for the lack of a further analytical treatment, (57) will be simulated.

The bifurcation diagram (Figure 21) for the adjustment map (57) shows that even in a labor market that has a nonlinear monotonous supply curve, real wage dynamics can become locally unstable with an infinite number of long run states. Thus, a backward bending labor supply is not a necessary condition for irregular adjustment dynamics. From Figure 21, one can also see that it takes a considerably larger adjustment speed to destabilize the labor market given the same labor demand function as in Case 1. This comes from the lower slope of the labor supply curve at the equilibrium.

3.4 How well is the calibration?

The bifurcation diagrams show that specific parameter settings are crucial for the dynamic properties of the models. Altering the slopes of labor demand, labor supply, and the adjustment speed, changes the stability conditions of the equilibria. The various long run regimes with completely different qualitative dynamic properties, from a single equilibrium to an infinite number of long run states, raise the question which one is more likely to hold on the grounds of empirical evidence that can be linked to the parameters of the models (38) or (57). This is not an empirical test and it would presumably be a futile exercise to confront these models with real time series on deflated nominal wages. They are highly stylized, and their purpose is to widen the spectrum of potential explanations for labor market dynamics. The models themselves are probably too simple to resist confrontations with real data that go beyond some of these qualitative aspects. But still, doing the latter will help to check the plausibility of the results.

The simulated time series of the backward bending model in Figure 11 coincides with an employment ratio of 70% at the unstable low real wage equilibrium of approximately 0.55. That copes very well with employment ratios of industrialized economies. The labor supply elasticity is

$$\eta_{L_S,w} = 1 - w \cdot \delta \approx 0.45 .$$

This is in the range of empirical estimates for male labor supply as reported earlier (chapter 3.1.3). The unstable equilibrium employment ratio is 0.43, and the equilibrium real wage is approximately 0.8 for the case where labor supply is monotonous. At a first glance, this might be inconsistent with the figures for the backward bending case as the equilibrium values for the real wage and the employment level deviate largely in comparison. However, constructing a simple wealth indicator by multiplying the real wage levels with the employment ratio shows that both economies do not differ that much. Wealth is almost the same, but the way these two economies generate it is different. One chooses a high employment ratio with relatively low real wages. The other prefers a smaller employment ratio at a comparably higher real wage level. The elasticity of the monotonous labor supply curve[13] is approximately 0.55. The labor demand elasticity of –2 also makes sense if compared with estimates on labor demand elasticities as summarized in Hamermesh (1993). At least it is not far beyond what is known from empirical work, although Hamermesh (1993) would narrow the range of plausible labor demand elasticities to [-0.15;-0.75]. But widening the

---

13 The labor supply elasticity for the monotonous supply function is

$$\eta_{L_S,w} = \frac{\beta}{1-\beta} \cdot \frac{1}{\frac{\beta}{w^{1-\beta}} + 1} .$$

interval is certainly supported by the many problems that the estimation of labor demand elasticities causes. An additional pitfall might arise if the measurement of labor demand elasticities grounds on time series for real wages that have an underlying system like (38) or (57). A brief look at the bifurcation diagrams reveals that if the time series are chaotic, there might be more time periods at which real wages are above the unstable equilibrium real wage. The chaotic attractor is not necessarily symmetric to the unstable equilibrium real wage. If the attractor looks like Figure 14, taking the mean of a time series such as in Figure 11 will yield an estimated equilibrium real wage level that is larger than the true equilibrium real wage. Hence, the estimated labor demand elasticity has got a bias. For example, a production function such as (34) implies a labor demand elasticity

$$\eta_{L_D,w} = \frac{1}{\alpha - 1} \tag{62}$$

A simple estimate of the labor demand elasticity would exploit the relation

$$\alpha = \frac{\omega \cdot L}{Y} \tag{63}$$

Assuming that per capita productivity is measured unbiased, a wrong estimate of the equilibrium real wage will yield a biased production coefficient on labor (63). As the bifurcation diagrams in both cases are asymmetric towards higher real wages, taking the mean of the real wage time series will introduce an upward bias on α. The estimated labor demand elasticity would be larger in absolute terms than the true one.

Taking account of what is known on the slopes of labor supply and demand curves, an unstable labor market equilibrium probably cannot be ruled out. What is left and crucial for the instability is the sensitivity with which the auctioneer reacts to disequilibrium quantities and sets the real wage for the following period. In other words, do the chaotic trajectories of the simulated model exceed a speed limit determined by empirical estimates of real wage adjustment processes? The literature sheds light onto that question from different perspectives. Unfortunately, the results vary widely.

Due to comparably high unemployment rates at the beginning of the eighties, a lot of attention was paid to real wage rigidities. The idea was that inflexible real wages could be at the heart of the European unemployment problem. Real wage gaps became a common indicator for that. Technically, real wage gaps are defined as the ratio of the difference of current real wages and the real wage consistent with full employment, to the full employment real wage. In that way, real wage gaps can give some insight into the degree to which real wages would have to fall to reach full employment. With the assumption of a Cobb Douglas production technology, the real wage is proportional to the average product of labor at full employment. Estimates of the real wage gap yielded positive and persistent deviations of current real wages from the marginal product at full employment

(Sachs 1983 and Bruno 1986). Germany, for example, had positive real wage gaps of 8.0%, 9.4%, and 12.2% in 1973, 1978, and 1981 respectively (Sachs 1983). Positive real wage gaps were also measured for the U.K. and France. The real wage gaps for Germany are even higher in Bruno (1986). In that sense, real wages would be rigid, since they did not fall despite unemployment. Indeed, real wage gaps rose. This would be strong evidence against quickly adjusting labor markets. But still, these estimates cannot make the case for very slow labor market adjustment. The evidence for excessive real wages has to be interpreted with caution. Results vary significantly with respect to authors, countries and sectors. In addition, the estimation procedure bears a lot of pitfalls. Following Schultze (1987), real wage gaps declined in the 1980's. In France, the U.K., and Italy, they were almost zero in the mid 80's for the manufacturing sector, implying larger than zero real wage adjustment speeds. Moreover, the steepest rise in unemployment in these countries was during that time, thus questioning the real wage rigidity as a major cause of unemployment[14] - maybe even as a robust indicator for real wage rigidity. In fact, the real wage gap measure rests on various assumptions that have been criticized (Kalmbach 1989). It was questioned whether the real wage at full employment can be measured correctly, alas when there really was full employment, and whether the trend of productivity growth was modeled correctly in these estimates. If, for example, labor productivity rises more than the incorporated linear trend implies, the real wage that is consistent with full employment will be higher. Consequently, the real wage gap overestimates the real wage decline that would be necessary to achieve full employment. So would an estimate of the real wage consistent with full employment that is lower than the true full employment real wage. When accounting for the income of self-employed, the wage gap boils down to almost insignificant levels (Gordon 1988). Gordon (1988) also notes that there was actually a too high real wage flexibility at the end of the 60's when real wages almost exploded.

Prachowny (1991) and Lewis and Makepeace (1984) estimate real wage adjustment speeds on the grounds of a linear dynamic model which is probably worthwhile to explain further. Opposed to real wage gaps from static models, these models give information on how responsive a market is to exogenous shocks, alas how long it will take until real wages are back at the equilibrium after a shock. Comparability of their results to the adjustment speeds in our models is limited. It was already shown that the test statistics of linear specifications can be well behaved although the underlying equations of motion are nonlinear (Blatt 1983, pp.224). Then, the coefficients of a linear stochastic type equation might imply global stability where there is actually local instability, probably biasing down real wage adjustment speeds. Hence, one should be cautious with the

14 Real wage rigidity can still be a possible explanation for European unemployment if the real wage gap induced substitution of capital for labor in the coming years.

interpretation of their results if there are strong indicators that real wages adjust in a nonlinear fashion. Besides linearity, their models differ from the models of this work with respect to the origin of the wage pressure and the lag structure. In (25) there is upward pressure on wages if the demand for labor exceeds the supply at the going real wage. Conversely, real wages decline if more people offer work than firms demand. Wage pressure is caused by disequilibrium quantities. The wage pressure in the estimated empirical models is driven by prices. Deviations from an equilibrium real wage cause real wage pressure. Furthermore, they assume that real wage changes are caused by real wage levels more than one period ahead. Under certain conditions, this might be an adequate assumption. Economies with staggered wage setting may be one example. If wages can only adjust in the sector where the contract expires and contract lengths differ, the current real wage can only partially adjust to the equilibrium. It will always be correlated with past real wage levels so that the coefficients on lagged real wages will be nonzero. Another explanation for why current wage levels might be highly correlated with past wages is that laid off worker who received comparably high wages are unwilling to take low-paying jobs. If this is true, unemployed workers would rather choose to wait for high wage job offers. Especially, if the group of workers they belong to has low employment turnover rates. Summers (1986) presents some evidence for that. Both staggered wage contracts and structural shifts against high wage sectors would cause a relatively higher serial correlation in wages. Lewis and Makepeace (1984) find a significant coefficient for the real wage lagged with one period. The coefficient on the real wage two periods back is insignificant. The estimated coefficient implies a non-oscillatory real wage adjustment path. Real wages move rather fast. 50% of a deviation from the equilibrium real wage are eliminated within half a year, and 80% after a year. They used quarterly British data from 1963 to 1980. Results for U.S. data are slightly different. In Prachowny (1991) the lag structure is more complicated. There are 13 lags that are taken into account of which up to four are significant. A simulation of the model with the estimated parameters generates an overshooting wage path. However, the adjustment speed is a bit slower than it is in Lewis and Makepeace (1984). After four quarters, 53,5% of the adjustment to the new equilibrium value is completed. It takes 7.5 quarters until the real wage has reached its new long run equilibrium value. Both estimates of the real wage adjustment speed, the one for the British and the U.S. data, imply a stable fixed point attractor. The stable equilibrium is reached rather quickly. Labor markets seem to be faster than real wage gap measures indicate but, contrary to some of our models, they have a stable long run equilibrium.

In the past years, various attempts have been made to estimate wage curves (Blanchflower and Oswald 1994, Blanchflower and Oswald 1995). Besides the highly celebrated unemployment elasticity of pay which seems to be at -0.1 across countries, those estimates may submit evidence for very high labor market adjustment speeds. This follows from a comparison of the Phillips curve with the wage curve. Whereas the Phillips curve relates wage changes to the level of unemployment, the *level* of wages is a function of the level of unemployment in the wage curve. A drop in the unemployment rate leads to an increase in wage changes on the grounds of the Phillips curve. The same drop in unemployment would lead to a higher wage *level* according to a wage curve relation. If the wage curve is what happens on labor markets, real wages might adjust very fast to a new unemployment equilibrium. This would support the idea that labor markets adjust faster to new conditions than was generally assumed. It is not difficult to come up with an empirical answer to that question within wage curve estimates. In general, estimates of wage curves regress individuals' wages on a vector of individual or work place characteristics, the industry and the regional unemployment rate, a vector of regional and industry dummies, and a vector of year dummies. To reject the notion of a Phillips curve, it suffices to include lagged wages on the right hand side of the equation. Only if the coefficient on the lagged wage is one (or close to one) is there scope for a Phillips curve. Bringing the lagged wage variable to the left hand side of the equation in that case, would yield a relationship where wage changes are dependent on unemployment. If the coefficient on the lagged wage is zero, however, the wage level relates to the level of unemployment. Current wages would be independent from past wages. Wages would adjust very fast. The estimates of Blanchflower and Oswald (1994, p.101) propose significant coefficients on the lagged wage that are not larger than 0.3. For U.S. data the estimates are close to 0.1. The coefficient is literally zero for Great Britain. Other estimates for German data support the notion of a wage curve (Baltagi and Blien 1998). If this was the end of the story, wages would adjust rather fast to changing labor market conditions. The results of Blanchflower and Oswald (1994) were, however, questioned by Blanchard and Katz (1997) mainly on the grounds of the data sets that these authors used. Blanchard and Katz (1997) claim that the very low correlation of wages in Blanchflower and Oswald (1994) is due to their use of annual earnings as the basic wage measure. These statistics would mix up the actual changes in wages with changes in hours of work so that an unchanged annual earnings value may coincide with an upward change in wages and a downward change in hours of work. If this happens, annual earnings as a basic wage measure bias down the correlation of wages. By using weekly earnings, Blanchard and Katz (1997) get a coefficient that is almost one which favors a Phillips curve specification and highly correlated wages. The evidence of Card and Hyslop (1996) heads into the same direction. They take a slightly different approach to reject the idea of a wage curve. Starting with a Phillips curve specification, they add lagged unemployment to the right hand side of the equation. If there is a wage curve, wage changes will be dependent on equal coefficients on unemployment and lagged unemployment with different signs. If not, lagged unemployment will have an insignificant effect on wage growth. They find no significant effect from lagged unemployment on wage growth for the U.S. Hence, it seems that whereas wage curves fit quite well to European data, U.S. data favors a correlation between wage changes and the level of unemployment. Interpreting these results from a point of view that starts from wage adjustment speeds, this would mean that U.S. wages respond slower to labor market conditions than European wages. This is contrary to the notion of flexible U.S. labor markets and sclerotic European markets. A different explanation was proposed by Blanchard and Katz (1999). They show that theoretical wage setting curves and a Phillips curve specification can be reconciled under two conditions. First there is no direct effect of productivity on wages given the reservation wage, and second, there is no direct effect from productivity on the reservation wage. If both conditions hold, wage curves coincide with Phillips curves. Then, the reason why wage curve specifications contrary to a Phillips curve specification fit European data quite well might be seen in the violation of one of these conditions. Blanchard and Katz (1999) argue that this might have happened for institutional reasons in Europe. Unions may be responsible for effects that run from productivity on wages. Furthermore, they speculate that a more prominent role of the underground economy may have caused significant positive effects from productivity increases on the reservation wage. But they cannot present some evidence on this topic. Hence, at this stage, a conservative judgement on labor market adjustment speeds might be that labor markets are less sluggish than it is generally supposed. Wage curve estimates especially indicate a tendency of labor markets to move toward equilibrium values rather quickly. Whether this is evidence enough to argue that chaotic trajectories will get a ticket is hard to say. Maybe, they exceed the speed limit of a stable labor market. Anyway, cautious people will keep their seat belts fastened and researchers should start thinking about the quality of their radar sets.

The bifurcation diagrams also show that the intervals within which the real wages vary are rather large and are widened if parameters change. Even the smallest interval in the chaotic regime implies an upper bound that is twice as large as the equilibrium real wage (Figure 15). The lower bound is somehow nearer to the equilibrium value, but the variance is still considerably large. Real wages do not vary to the extent that these models imply. A more realistic approach would have to cope with that. Nevertheless, the large real wage intervals do not destroy the basic results of these models: the labor market equilibrium may become unstable. This does not necessarily imply exploding real wage trajectories. The long run behavior of locally unstable labor markets may be characterized by a chaotic attractor. If so, the sequence of real wages that the auctioneer sets when trying to clear the market is irregular. This irregular behavior is furthermore endogenous. The market will never reach its equilibrium real wage. It does not clear, and there is a bounded range of an infinite number of disequilibrium real wages and employment levels.

3.5 An unstable Phillips curve and other policy implications

The backward bending supply curve implies a theoretical underpinning of the Phillips curve that differs from orthodox views (see also Chichilnisky et al. 1995). Manipulating the adjustment function (25) by setting $(L_D\text{-}L_S)$ equal to $-U_t$ and linking nominal wage changes to real wage changes[15], the model implies some kind of a Phillips curve which can be written as

$$W_{t+1} - W_t = -\lambda \cdot U_t \tag{64}$$

Nominal wage changes are a function of the level of unemployment. The faster wages adjust to new market conditions, the steeper the quasi Phillips curve is. Despite of the negative correlation between wage changes and unemployment, these results differ from the standard approach with respect to the character of the trade-off. There is no fixed trade-off here. Moreover, the model also differs from theories that deny this trade-off in the long-run because of rational or adaptive expectations. In these models, the short-run or long-run Phillips curves consist of sets of labor market equilibria. The chaotic labor market models yield a Phillips curve that consists of a set of labor market disequilibria. Combinations of wage changes and levels of unemployment erratically shift up and down the negatively sloped curve. The adjustment process does not come to a stop. Thus, the model imposes quite some restrictions to policy makers. There is no freedom of choice between wage changes and unemployment levels even in the short run, although the well-known negative relationship exists. There is a trade-off, but not a given menu which policy makers may choose from. While people order, the menu will change and it does so because of the orders. It is the cook who decides what is on the table and customers will find themselves happy or sour with what they get. Firms and households are ordering, and the cook´s decision reflects the clearing process of markets on the grounds of the interplay between demand and supply. But there is definitely no room for the management to accept or refuse orders of customers, such as in the old-fashioned orthodox policy-matters-approaches of Phillips curves. In addition, sensitive dependence on initial conditions imposes some further problem with respect to forecasts. One point on the Phillips curve at time t will not tell much about the performance of the labor market in the medium and long run as unemployment and wage changes evolve erratically. Although the system is deterministic, small errors in the analysis of the state of the labor market can imply significant forecasting failures (c.f. Figure 11). Measurement errors grow exponentially.

The inability to forecast does not imply the inability to impose policy measures. There are quite a variety of policy options at hand. But without knowing the underlying equations of motions, pursuing widely accepted policy

---

15 Maybe this is a fairly crude assumption. But one could think of indexed wage contracts like cost of living adjustment clauses (COLA).

recommendations can have detrimental effects. Lowering real wages, for example, can move an economy with a backward bending labor supply curve away from its possibly favorable high real wage equilibrium. This adds to the already existing critique of downward real wage flexibility which claims that such policies raise inequality and criminal behavior (Freeman 1995), or may just be the wrong policy if unemployment is based on a lack of demand (Bolle 1983b). Any measure that intends to lower real wages, even only transitionally, will initiate a process of further declining real wages, accompanied by rising unemployment in the model with backward bending labor supply. The economy may never again reach the high real wage equilibrium by its own. The low real wage equilibrium can become a trap with chaotic real wage cycles. Long run forecasts are impossible.

The bifurcation diagrams for λ (Figure 15 and Figure 21) show that lowering the adjustment speed yields a stable period two cycle compared to unstable cycles in the chaotic regime. It follows that imposing any kind of real wage stickiness will move a labor market out of its chaotic regime. When real wage cycles are chaotic, the auctioneer reacts very sensitively to disequilibrium quantities on the market. He varies real wages to a large extent so that the market does not find its stable equilibrium. In this sense, the labor market is too flexible and greasing the wheels will do harm. Besides the adjustment speed, any measures that increase the slopes of the labor demand and supply curve in absolute value can destabilize the market. This opens the door for tax policies. If there is, for example, a tax wedge and taxes are progressive, an increase in real wages will be coincided by a comparably lower rise in take home pay. If the take home pay is the relevant variable on which households base their decisions whether to supply labor or not, the slope of the labor supply curve will be smaller in equilibrium[16]. Demand and supply intersect at smaller angles which ceteris paribus may shift the labor market into a stable regime. A policy measure that relates to the demand side of the market could be a strategy that pursues the opening of markets. One could, for example, intend to realize welfare gains that might come from economies of scale. If opening national markets increases the marginal returns from labor, say returns from labor become constant, labor demand will become more elastic, at least for sufficiently low real wages. Any change in the real wage will induce comparably larger increases or decreases in the demand for labor. This can move the labor market towards an unstable equilibrium or longer adjustment lengths for deviations from a stable equilibrium (c.f. Figure 16). Finally, a change in the slopes of the labor demand and supply curves in the equilibrium can also arise by shifts of one or both curves. If labor demand and supply are nonlinear both curves will intersect at a different angle. That will change the stability properties of the new equilibrium as compared to the old. There are several ways to think about shifts of both curves in terms of exogenous shocks. The bifurcation diagram in Figure 17 implies that

---

16 In a labor market diagram where supply is on the vertical axis and wages are on the horizontal axis.

restrictive demand policies that shift the labor demand curve towards the origin can destabilize the market. This is due to the underlying labor supply curve that becomes steeper at lower employment levels. Hence, any deviation from the new equilibrium will cause a higher excess demand that induces comparably larger real wage changes. Conversely, a shift of the labor demand schedule to the right stabilizes the labor market (but may cause multiple equilibria if the labor supply curve changes its sign). Apart from restrictive demand policies, negative productivity shocks move the labor demand curve towards the origin. As was shown, such negative shocks do not necessarily yield chaotic behavior. One can see from Figure 17 that it would take a considerable decline in A to move the market into the chaotic regime. But, it was also made obvious that a labor market with a stable long run equilibrium may be characterized by really long adjustment paths. Hence, policy shocks, changing tastes, or any other exogenous shock can cause long lasting periods of adjusting real wages and employment even when the long run equilibrium is stable.

4 Real wage adjustment with a nonlinear labor demand

The main interest of the previous chapter was to find out about the impact of different supply schemes on labor market equilibria and the adjustment of real wages. Labor demand grounded on a production technology where capital was fixed and returns to labor were decreasing. Firms faced a competitive product market and were wage takers. The assumptions implied a downward sloping labor demand curve. It will be shown that alleviating any of those assumptions changes the slope of the labor demand curve. Labor demand might become nonlinear and real wage dynamics irregular. An example with a production technology that has partly increasing returns will illustrate the dynamic implications from a discontinuous labor demand curve.

4.1 Production functions, labor costs, and the demand for labor

Recapitulating the derivation of the labor demand curve from chapter 3.3 gives the framework of aspects that will be considered next. It was shown that in a standard approach, firms' demand for labor follows from maximizing a profit function

$$\max_{L} \Pi = p \cdot f(L) - W \cdot L \tag{65}$$

which gives the well known condition that real wages have to equal marginal costs (66).

$$w = \frac{W}{p} = f'(L). \tag{66}$$

As (66) shows, the slope of the labor demand curve is ruled by the production technology, prices, and characteristics that determine the nominal wage rate W. Three particular assumptions underlie a downward sloping labor demand curve.

Firms cannot vary prices, as they have many competitors on the product market. They are wage takers and the production technology has decreasing returns at a fully utilized capital stock. The impact of a non-competitive market on labor demand will be sketched first. Implications from alleviating the other assumptions follow.

4.1.1 Labor demand and varying mark-ups

In a competitive market, firms cannot set prices that deviate from those of their competitors. If they did, they would loose all their customers. However, there is room for price policy if only a few firms are on the market or customers are not well informed. Firms will raise prices, as this may not only compensate the loss in sales but also yield additional revenues. The firms' maximization problem changes. Profits become a function of output and of price policy. The mark up on prices that is optimal for firms will be dependent on the reduction of sales so that a higher price aggressiveness will come with a lower demand elasticity. Firms will no longer maximize profits along (65), but may choose a profit function (c.f. Carlin and Soskice 1990)

$$\max_{L} \Pi = p(f(L)) \cdot f(L) - W \cdot L \tag{67}$$

In (67) prices are a function of output and differentiating the latter gives

$$\frac{dp}{df(L)} \cdot \frac{df(L)}{dL} \cdot f(L) + p \cdot \frac{df(L)}{dL} = W \tag{68}$$

Dividing both sides of (68) with the price p and rearranging yields

$$w = \frac{W}{p} = (1 + \frac{\frac{dp}{p}}{\frac{df(L)}{dL}}) \cdot f'(L) \tag{69}$$

The right hand term in the parenthesis is the inverse of the elasticity of demand so that the real wage with imperfect competition can be written as[17]

$$w = (1 - \frac{1}{\eta}) \cdot f'(L) \tag{70}$$

(70) describes the labor demand of firms in the non-competitive case, but also includes the orthodox labor demand relation. In the competitive case any price above the market price will reduce product demand to zero. Hence, the elasticity of demand is infinite so that one has the well known case where the real wage

---

17 With the elasticity η as an absolute value.

equals the marginal product. (70) is a quasi labor demand curve often referred to as the price setting curve. It describes real wages determined by the price setting behavior of firms. From (70) follows that the quasi labor demand curve with imperfect competition lies below the labor demand curve derived from (65). The real wage of the price setting curve is always smaller than the marginal productivity, as the elasticity of demand is less than infinite in absolute value. Higher elasticities for demand shift the quasi labor demand curve towards the orthodox demand curve. Rearranging (70) to get p on the left hand side will give the mark up of prices over marginal costs.

$$p = \frac{1}{1-\frac{1}{\eta}} \cdot \frac{W}{f'(L)} \tag{71}$$

with

$$\mu = \frac{1}{1-\frac{1}{\eta}} \tag{72}$$

as the mark up. The mark up is ruled by the elasticity of demand. A higher elasticity of demand reduces the market power of each individual firm so that the difference between prices and marginal costs decreases. If the mark up in (72) was a function of the employment level, imperfect competition would not only shift the labor demand curve downwards, but turn it. The wedge

$$\frac{1}{\mu} = 1 - \frac{1}{\eta} \tag{73}$$

between the price determined real wage and the marginal productivity would increase during booms if the mark up in (70) decreases when aggregate activity takes off. The quasi labor demand curve would be flatter than the marginal product of labor curve. If mark ups are strongly counter-cyclical, the slope of the quasi labor demand curve might even become positive.

Mark ups may vary for reasons of customer loyality and collusion between oligopolistic firms. Customers develop loyalty to the products of firms - a fact that any producer will try to exploit (Bils 1989). If people who once bought a special brand will do so in the future, it might be rational for firms to lower prices during booms to gain new customers from which they will profit in the future. There are more potential new customers during booms, and even if firms lower their mark ups, it will pay in the long run due to a comparably larger stock of loyal customers during recessions. Rotemberg and Saloner 1986 argue that the incentive of an individual firm to cheat by offering lower prices than their competitors to gain a larger market share is higher during booms than when aggregate activity is low. To reduce the merits from non-cooperation, there will be more downward pressure on prices during booms. In other words, a lower mark up during booms stabilizes collusion. Again, mark ups would be counter-cyclical. Besides these theoretical considerations, there is evidence on counter-cyclical mark ups (Bils 1987, Rotemberg and Woodford 1991, Rotemberg and Woodford 1999). Insofar, it seems not out of reach that the slope of the price setting or quasi labor demand curve changes its sign (Layard, Nickell, and Jackman 1991, p. 340) just on the grounds of varying mark ups.

4.1.2 Feedback from employment on labor costs

There are several feedback mechanisms from the level of employment on labor costs that are worthwhile paying attention to as they might change labor demand through marginal labor costs . If firms are wage takers, like in the reference case (65), labor costs are a linear function of the employment level ($K(L)>0$, $dK(L)/dL>0$, and $d^2K(L)/dL^2=0$). Employment does not affect labor costs at the margin. If, however, wage costs become a function of the employment level $W=W(L)$, labor costs are $K(L)=W(L)\cdot L$. Then, the level of employment drives marginal labor costs which affects firms' demand for labor. The way in which average labor costs change depends on whether increasing employment causes upward wage pressure $dW(L)/dL>0$ or downward wage pressure $dW(L)/dL<0$. If $dW(L)/dL>0$ labor demand will still slope downwards. Increasing employment raises marginal labor costs and firms will demand less labor for a given real wage, compared to the case where labor costs are a linear function of the employment level. An additional worker does not only cost the going wage, but also an additional amount of money that comes from the higher demand for this production factor. The point where marginal costs equal marginal returns from production is reached at a lower employment level. For $dW(L)/dL<0$, the consequences are ambiguous depending on the degree of upward pressure on wages when employment falls. But generally, if marginal costs are lower than with a linear labor cost function, firms can raise their profits by expanding the labor force. Every additional worker will increase their profits as long as the marginal returns of production are higher than marginal costs. Labor demand is higher than with linear labor costs for any going real wage rate.

An example of a feedback mechanism that causes positive costs at the margin ($dW(L)/dL>0$) are monopsony labor markets. In such a market, there are a lot of workers who supply labor but will only find a single firm. Whereas this might be viewed as an unrealistic market form at a first glance, regional labor markets may be of that kind. Due to high mobility costs, workers can be cut off from other potential employers. Especially in rural areas, employment opportunities can be scarce. In a monopsony market, a higher demand for labor will generate wage pressure if reservation wages differ across workers. To attract an additional worker would mean to pay a higher wage than for the one that was employed before. Wages increase with the employment level so that labor costs rise more than linear. The demand for labor decreases compared to a fully competitive labor market for any real wage, and the labor demand curve will be steeper. Monopsony labor markets gained renewed interest in the past (Boal and Ransom 1997). Partly, because they offer an explanation for positive employment effects of minimum wages that were found in empirical studies. A monopsony labor market may also explain positive firm size effects on wages. Although empirical findings on the effects of minimum wages and firm size are in line with what monopsony labor markets would predict, empirical studies on the rate of exploitation are less compelling. Measurements of the difference between the marginal product of workers and the real wages are so far small. Another argument why labor costs rise more than linear with the level of employment is made by efficiency wage theories. These theories claim that the closer the employment level comes to the maximum labor force, the higher the costs might be from turnover or shirking. Should a worker be fired, he would very likely find a new job soon if there is almost full employment. This would spark voluntary turnover and workers would be less motivated. To economize on turnover and shirking costs, firms would be willing to pay higher wages than the market wage. Labor costs increase more than linear with the level of employment. A huge amount of literature on efficiency wage theories (Yellen 1984, Katz 1986, Stiglitz 1987) makes it hard to put these arguments aside. It seems that this approach can explain a large part of labor market performance. If for one of these reasons marginal labor costs are positive, labor demand would decrease more steeply than in the reference case (65). Labor market equilibria would be comparably more stable, and periods of adjusting prices and quantities would be shorter after exogenous shocks. But there are also some interesting mechanisms that work in the other direction, where labor costs decline at the margin as more people are employed.

When firms want to adjust their employment level, they will usually face adjustment costs of various sorts. Firing restrictions and leave payments are widespread, especially within Europe (OECD 1993, Tables 3.7 – 3.10). In many European countries advance notice is required. Employers have to consult work councils to get approval for dismissal of employees. There is legislation for severance payments, and in some countries like Germany, social closing plans were made mandatory, forcing firms to establish quitting lists before undertaking major reconstructions. Along these quitting lists, social criteria have to be obeyed so that it could happen that the most productive workers had to leave the company first. Laws on dismissal are not always clear cut. This can impose additional constraints on firms that have to adjust their workforce. If it is unclear whether a dismissal will lead to costly trials, firms will screen new applicants thoroughly and deter filling of vacancies if there are any doubts about applicants. Altogether, these shadow costs for adjusting the incumbent workforce may have reached significant levels, often blamed as 'Eurosclerosis' (Giersch 1985) and being at the heart of the European unemployment problem (Siebert 1997). The shadow costs apply for adjustments that would lower the incumbent work force, and are furthermore taken into account by firms when they intend to hire new workers.

Insofar, it is a decision of firms whether to invest in a job applicant (Bolle 1983a). The mere fact that in case of a downswing, firing costs and leave payments would have to be paid, will bias down the profitability of raising the workforce. Whereas these shadow costs are certainly given at high and low employment levels, they are probably larger for lower employment levels (Blanchard and Summers 1988). Studies on worker flows for Europe and the U.S. have shown that quit rates decline during downturns (Burda and Wyplosz, 1994, p.1295, Burgess, Lane and Stevens 1996, p.98). If this is true, firms will face relatively higher shadow costs at lower employment levels as less people will leave firms. Firms are forced to lay off workers to adjust their work force. If in addition to lower quit rates, the ratio of productive to unproductive workers who quit increases, the less productive workers are more likely to stay with the firm during recessions. This will increase firms' shadow costs even further. Social criteria for selecting workers to be laid off as sketched above head into this direction. The less productive workers stay, whereas the young, flexible and skilled ones often loose their jobs. Under these conditions, average labor cost will decline for higher employment levels. If the marginal output is larger than the marginal increase in labor costs, firms can raise their profits by employing more workers so that labor demand will slope upwards in the real wage employment space.

Marginal labor costs will also decline if there is a sufficient degree of externalities in the matching of vacancies and unemployed job searchers. In a thick market, the likelihood with which a vacancy can be filled is higher than in a thin market. To clarify the idea, one may refer to the coconut example of Diamond (1982). In this economy with some degree of fixed costs, the production of goods (coconuts) is dependent on whether these goods can be traded. If firms expect to find a trading partner for their output, they will engage in production. However, if for any reason they believe that products and customers cannot be matched, the level of production will be lower as compared to the case of optimistic expectations. Thus, the likelihood of finding a trading partner will play the key role for aggregate production. Output will be low if the perceived number of potential traders is low. An economy with a large number of potential traders will be characterized by a high production level due to the positive external effects of these traders. Matching of vacancies and unemployed workers can be discussed in the same framework (Pissarides 1986, p.523, Howitt 1988, Howitt and McAfee 1987, Mortensen 1989). Filling a vacancy will be easier for firms with a higher arrival rate of applicants. Hence, if there are more job searchers, more vacancies will be offered which in turn increases the number of people who are looking for a job as a match becomes more likely. It takes less time to fill the posted vacancy and furthermore, the likelihood of a productive match increases so that a thick market effect drives down the marginal cost of employing an additional worker. This does not yet tell why the marginal labor costs may be relatively larger for low employment levels, although there are more unemployed workers who are looking for jobs. What, however, counts is the number of unemployed workers who actually search for jobs and have the functional and extra-functional qualifications to fill the vacancies. Even though there are more unemployed workers during recessions, there might be less unemployed looking for jobs who furthermore have the required skills. Disqualification and discouraged worker effects may put a wedge between unemployed workers and those who are effectively searching. Discouraged worker effects are spurred by a considerably large fraction of long term unemployed. Lindbeck (1995, p.10) argues that during persistent recessions, habits of the unemployed change. Social norms can arise from being unemployed that have detrimental effects on the search behavior of the unemployed. People who share experiences that threaten their existence stick together. Finding a job against all odds with nearly all neighbors on a prolonged unemployment spell might violate social norms. The higher these collective customs of being on the dole are, the more disutility is attached to the individual search effort of an unemployed (Akerlof 1980). Breaking the rules is more disadvantageous to the individual than staying unemployed. Hence, he or she will be inclined to conform to the habits of the 'mass'. Once the pool of unemployed is large enough, the offer arrival rate for posted vacancies will decrease. In addition to the detrimental effects on search behavior, the skills of the unemployed will deteriorate. After long spells of unemployment, job applicants might lack the qualifications that the demand side of the market requires. This drives down the number of effective searchers even further. High ratios of long-term unemployment and bottlenecks in the supply of skilled labor on European labor markets support the view that arrival rates can be low at high unemployment.

Marginal costs will decrease if the effect from high arrival rates at low unemployment is large enough to compensate for essentially one diseconomy. As more workers come into the market the 'production' of vacancies will increase, too. There will be more productive jobs as the length of unfilled vacancies declines. It becomes less costly to fill a vacancy. Hence, more vacancies are posted. However, as more vacancies come to the market, it will be more difficult to fill these vacancies for a given arrival rate of applicants. In addition to holding a vacancy longer, now firms may consider to offer higher wages to attract more job applicants. Only if the wage effect and the increase in costs through longer vacancy duration is sufficiently small, will marginal labor costs fall with rising employment.

Estimates on the coefficients of matching functions give some hints on which externality is probably stronger. There seem to be no increasing returns for the matching of unemployed workers to vacancies in the U.K. (Pissarides 1986, pp.525), which would imply that the two diseconomies are stronger than the positive effects of thick markets. On the other hand, Blanchard and Diamond (1989), who run regressions on Cobb Douglas type matching functions, find constant or mildly increasing returns. Slightly increasing returns for the U.S. are corroborated by Anderson and Burgess (1995). They furthermore argue that earlier results of constant returns might be due to the construction of aggregate time series. This gives more strength to the latest results where individual worker -

firm match records could be used and coefficients add up to more than one. It was also found that Germany had increasing returns to scale between 1972 to 1984, but constant or decreasing returns afterwards (Gross 1997). At least, the empirical evidence does not rule out increasing returns for the matching of unemployed workers on vacancies. Again, labor costs may decrease at the margin, yielding an upward sloping labor demand curve if marginal returns are larger than marginal costs.

4.1.3 The production technology

If product markets are competitive and firms are wage takers (or marginal costs are constant $d^2K(L)/dL^2=0$), the slope of the labor demand curve is determined by the underlying production technology. In Case 1 and Case 2, labor demand followed from decreasing returns on labor. Labor demand was downward sloping. However, decreasing returns might not be an appropriate description of the underlying technology. In general, the economics of increasing returns gained renewed interest (Arrow et al. 1998, Arthur 1994, Heal 1998). They offer explanations for some market phenomena that models with concave production technologies or, generally, negative feedback mechanisms unsatisfactorily capture. An often cited example is the evolution of VCR market shares after their invention at the beginning of the eighties (see i.e. Arthur 1990). By that time two systems, Betamax and VHS, competed. Although, as some experts claim, Betamax was technically superior to VHS and both systems had equal market shares at the beginning, the latter finally captured the whole market. When video stores began to rent more videocassettes with VHS technology, there was an advantage to buying a VCR with that technology. It encouraged the video stores to fill their shelves with more movies on VHS cassettes which in turn pushed the demand for VHS recorders. The positive feedback between supply and demand for videocassettes and VCRs lead to a virtuous cycle for the VHS based technology and a vicious cycle for Beta systems. Which of the two equilibria would be achieved in the long run was not known from the beginning. A small initial deviation, and the increasing utility of sticking to the technology that was to become dominant, caused the outcome. A similar story might explain the formation of regional industrial clusters like Silicon Valley. If firms benefit from the local neighborhood of their customers because of lower transportation or transactions costs, the decision where to start a business will be in favor for areas where such industries already exist. On the grounds of increasing returns in production, one may also explain why it is difficult to trace back the emergence of certain trade patterns. If there are large set up costs due to, for example, R&D expenditures, it clearly is advantageous for both economies to produce a single good and trade, as each country only has to cover the set up costs for establishing one industry. However, which country engages in producing good A and which in good B is open. There are two possible outcomes and once more some divergence in the initial setting will be decisive for the market shares[18].

Several formal models along the lines of increasing returns have been developed that include perversely sloped labor demand curves. Blanchard and Summers (1987) derive a partly upward sloping labor demand curve on the grounds of fiscal increasing returns for an economy where the state varies the tax rate to cover a fixed budget. The basic idea is that with a concave production technology, (gross) real wages are rather high at comparably low employment levels. If the decrease in the marginal product is sufficiently low when employment takes off, the tax base increases. This allows the government to lower the tax rate without running a budget deficit. Should the reduction in the tax rate be larger than the decrease in the marginal product (gross real wages), workers` take home pay would rise. Under these conditions, labor demand is upward sloping for a range of employment levels in a net real wage employment space, even under decreasing returns to production. Lower marginal returns at comparably higher employment levels will change the slope of the demand curve again. Closing the model with some sort of a wage setting curve yields two equilibria, one of which is superior to the other. Blanchard and Summers (1987) claim that Europe may be got stuck at the less advantageous employment level. So does Manning (1990), whose price setting curve follows from a production technology with slightly increasing returns ($d^2f(L)/dL^2>0$). As in Blanchard and Summers (1987), the model is closed with a conventionally sloped wage setting curve. Estimates of the price setting equation (Manning 1992) corroborate the existence of increasing returns to scale. Increasing returns in terms of fixed costs drive the results in Weitzman (1982). He assumes that each individual firm has to commit a fixed amount of its input factors to some kind of 'overhead'. Beneath the threshold, production is not profitable due to relatively high average labor costs. Hence, firms will only start production if they expect that the overall economic activity is large enough to cover their fixed costs. If there is a coordination failure, so that some companies believe that aggregate activity will not suffice to cover their fixed expenditures, overall activity might fall below the level that is needed to induce production, as well as what aggregate demand would usually imply. Expectations are propagated as some of them will rather choose to close their plants, which in turn diminishes demand even further. In other words, Say's law is blocked. The economy will move into a recession. It will be trapped in a low employment position as long as the coordination failure holds. Hence, the demand for labor is discontinuous at the threshold level, determined by the magnitude of fixed costs in this economy[19].

The example that follows reveals how a discontinuous labor demand function can cause irregular adjustment dynamics. A production function with increasing

---

18 For more examples, see Krugman (1996).

19 Pagano (1990) closes the coordination failure model by introducing labor supply. However, the basic result of an economy with multiple equilibria remains.

returns divides the demand for labor into two regimes. One in which revenues do not cover labor costs, so that firms' demand for labor is zero, and another in which the demand for labor is downward sloping. As in Weitzman (1982), the economy may be trapped in the zero demand regime, but contrary frees itself from it endogenously.

4.2 Discontinuous labor demand and labor market equilibria

Increasing returns in production occur when enterprises face set up costs. To start running a business usually implies that money will be lost due to inefficiencies in the production process at the beginning. Learning by doing by the initially employed will eliminate these malfunctions. As the firm expands, they pass their knowledge to the entrants. Within a range of the employment levels, the firm may face a higher marginal product for every additional worker due to internal economies of scale[20]. Marginal returns will be increasing until at some employment level the firm cannot gain from the accumulated experiences of the incumbent workforce anymore. The positive impact on the productivity of entrants ceases to exist. Maybe because it becomes more difficult to ensure that all knowledge is handed over to the entrants when the workforce is already rather large. If this is what happens, the marginal product will decline once the size of the company has reached a 'critical' value. Again, the firms are constrained by the typically assumed decreasing factor profitability. The properties of a production function with increasing returns at a fixed capital stock are

$$f(L) \geq 0 \text{ with } f'(L) > 0 \tag{74}$$

and

$$f''(L) > 0 \text{ for } 0 \leq L < L_c \tag{75}$$

if returns to scale are increasing, and for the part where firms face decreasing returns

$$f''(L) \leq 0 \text{ for } L_c \leq L. \tag{76}$$

Figure 22 gives an example for a production function with these properties. As usual, labor demand follows from maximizing firms' profits

$$\max_L \Pi = f(L) - w \cdot L \tag{77}$$

This yields the well known optimality condition that real wages have to equal the marginal product of labor

20 See i.e. Arrow (1962).

$$w = \frac{df(L)}{dL}. \tag{78}$$

Contrary to the standard case of a concave production technology, firms do not always make profits if they follow (78). With increasing returns, there are real wage levels that equal marginal returns for which labor costs exceed revenues. In (74) to (76) the value of output is less than labor costs for all employment levels lower than a critical employment level L_c. That level is reached where average productivity maximizes, or, where marginal productivity equals average productivity. Since firms would have to pay a wage w to all their workers although the productivity of those who were initially employed is comparably low, output does not cover labor costs. Labor demand is zero.

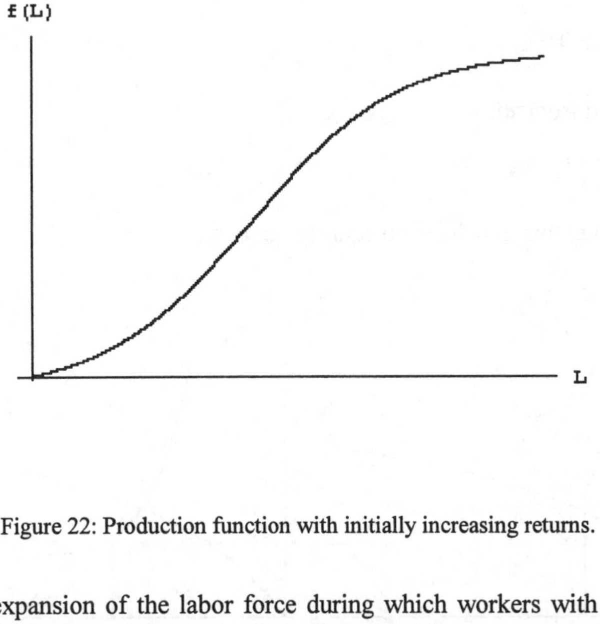

Figure 22: Production function with initially increasing returns.

It takes an expansion of the labor force during which workers with comparably higher marginal returns add to the incumbent workforce to get over the set up costs. Once workers with higher marginal products raised average productivity, revenues cover labor costs. Labor demand becomes positive. To the right of the critical employment level, firms will expand their labor force as long as the marginal product covers the cost of an additional worker. With decreasing returns in this regime, less labor will be engaged the higher the real wage is that firms have to pay. Hence, above the critical value, one has the well known downward sloping labor demand curve. The discontinuous labor demand function can be written as a piecewise map

$$L_D(w) = 0 \text{ for } w_c < w \tag{79}$$

and

$$L_D(w) > 0 \text{ for } 0 \le w \le w_c \tag{80}$$

with

$$\frac{dL_D(w)}{dw} < 0 \tag{81}$$

and

$$w_c = \left.\frac{f(L)}{L}\right|_{\max} . \tag{82}$$

Closing the model with a labor supply function that is zero for w=0, upward sloping

$$\frac{dL_S(w)}{dw} \ge 0 \tag{83}$$

and restricted from above

$$\lim_{w \to \infty} L_S(w) = L_{\max} \tag{84}$$

yields a market that may have no equilibrium at all.

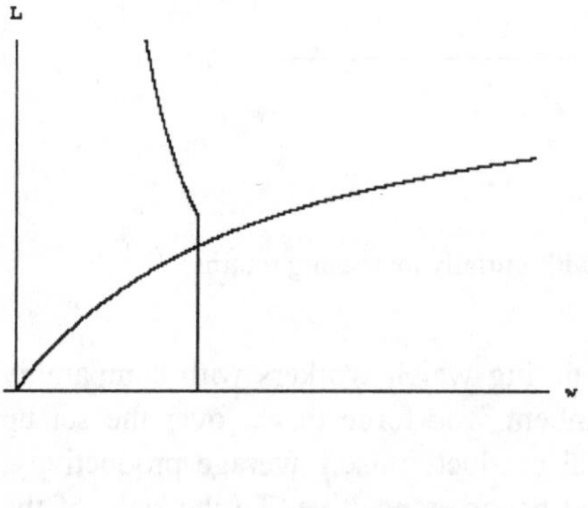

Figure 23: Labor market without an equilibrium.

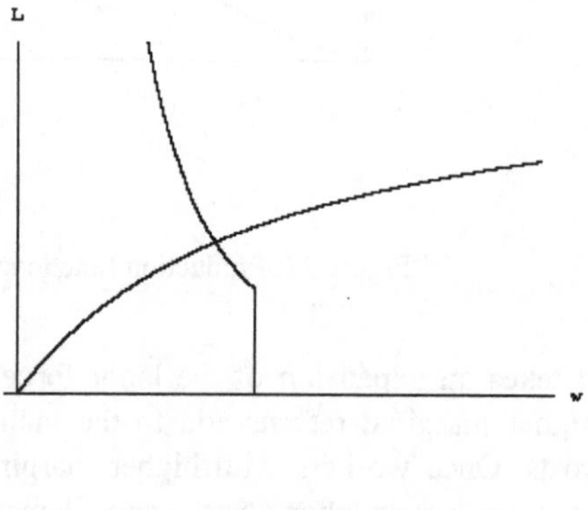

Figure 24: Labor market with an equilibrium.

With a discontinuous labor demand function, it may happen that labor demand and labor supply do not intersect. Then no real wage can be found for which households supply the amount of work that is required by firms to meet their optimal output level[21]. Although Chichilnisky et al. (1995) assumed fixed costs in production Figure 23 basically illustrates the model they analyzed. Labor demand and supply curves do not intersect. There will be no market equilibrium for a positive real wage rate, an approach that may not sound very convincing. It, however, can be shown that chaotic dynamics are possible even if an equilibrium real wage rate exists. This is the case that will be discussed here.

4.3 Adjustment dynamics

The real wage adjustment rule will be the same as for the previous labor market models. The auctioneer sets real wages according to excess demand or excess supply on the market

$$w_{t+1} - w_t = \lambda \cdot [L_D(w_t) - L_S(w_t)] \text{ and } \lambda > 0 . \tag{85}$$

As labor demand is zero for real wages above a critical value w_c, (82) is a piecewise adjustment map which can be written as

$$w_{t+1} - w_t = \lambda \cdot [L_D(w_t) - L_S(w_t)] \text{ for } w_t < w_c \tag{86}$$

and

$$w_{t+1} - w_t = -\lambda \cdot L_S(w_t) \text{ for } w_t > w_c . \tag{87}$$

It is possible to draw some general conclusions from equations (86) and (87) without specifying supply and demand curves any further.

Such a labor market may have a locally unstable equilibrium in a range of real wage levels

$$\underline{w} < w_t < \overline{w} .$$

Under certain conditions, oscillations of real wages within this range can become chaotic with a positive Lebesgue measure. An example with specific labor demand and labor supply curves follows the general discussion. It will illustrate the properties that can arise from labor market models along the lines of (86) and (87).

Given that there exists a labor market equilibrium (Figure 24 as opposed to Figure 23), it will become unstable if the condition

$$-2 < \lambda \cdot \left(\left.\frac{dL_D}{dw_t}\right|_{w^*} - \left.\frac{dL_S}{dw_t}\right|_{w^*} \right) < 0 \tag{88}$$

21 Note that quantities are on the vertical axis and real wages on the horizontal axis.

is violated. As it is assumed that labor demand and supply curves intersect, the slopes in (88) refer to the regime with positive labor demand. With an upward sloping labor supply, it follows that the term in the parenthesis is always negative. The equilibrium might become unstable for three reasons. A sufficiently high adjustment speed, a steeply downward sloping labor demand, or relatively large changes in supply when real wages increase. Then a small perturbation may drive the economy away from its equilibrium.

From the assumptions on labor demand and supply ((79) to (83)) follow the properties

$$\lim_{w_t \to 0} f(w_t) = \infty \tag{89}$$

and

$$\lim_{w_t \to \infty} f(w_t) = \infty \,. \tag{90}$$

The slopes at the borders are

$$\lim_{w_t \to 0} \frac{dw_{t+1}}{dw_t} < -\infty \tag{91}$$

and

$$\lim_{w_t \to \infty} \frac{dw_{t+1}}{dw_t} = 1 \tag{92}$$

As the adjustment map is upward sloping for $w_t > w_c$ and lies below the equilibrium condition, there is a tendency for real wages in this area to decline. Since firms would make negative profits for $w_t > w_c$, labor demand is zero and because at the same time the supply for labor is positive, the auctioneer will try to find an equilibrium by decreasing real wages. It may happen that he reacts too sensitively to an excess supply of labor and decreases the real wage below the market equilibrium w^*. This causes excess demand so that the auctioneer will set a higher real wage in the following period. In fact, all real wages below the equilibrium initiate an increase. Trajectories that are repelled from the equilibrium will be bounded if furthermore $f > 0$ holds. In that case, there would be a trapping area for real wages repelled from an unstable equilibrium. The boundaries of the trapping area

$$\underline{w} \le w_t \le \overline{w}$$

are given by the first

$$\underline{w} = f(w_{\min})$$

and second iterate

$$\overline{w} = f^2(w_{\min})$$

of the real wage w_{min} that minimizes the adjustment map.

With the possibility of an unstable equilibrium and a trapping area the question remains whether within the interval there is scope for irregular dynamics. For discontinuous maps one can show with the theorem of Lasota and Yorke (c.f. Day and Pianigiani 1991, p.142) that the adjustment map has a positive Lebesgue measure.

> *Lasota and Yorke theorem* (c.f. Day and Pianigiani 1991, p.142): Given that f is twice differentiable for both intervals, the one with decreasing returns where $w \leq w_c$ and the interval with increasing returns ($w > w_c$), there exists an absolutely continuous invariant measure for the map f, if
>
> $$|f'(w_t)| > 1$$
>
> almost everywhere.

The absolutely continuous invariant measure is stricter than the topological measure for chaos of Li and Yorke (1975). Even if a map f is chaotic in the sense of Li and Yorke (1975) it might still have a Lebesgue measure zero. In this case, there are only a few initial points within the interval that defines f from which chaos will occur. If initial conditions change slightly, or round off errors disturb the system, trajectories will converge to periodic orbits in the long run. Irregular dynamics only occur transitory. Almost all points are attracted to a periodic cycle. Contrary, a positive Lebesgue measure gives a probability with which chaos is given even for the long run. It is called absolutely continuous if it refers to subsets of the interval that defines f that are larger than single points. Hence, larger Lebesgue measures raise the probability that irregular behavior does not only hold transitory[22].

A look at the piecewise adjustment map ((86) and (87)) shows that within the regimes $w_t > w_c$ and $w_t < w_c$ the map f is a smooth function. Hence, it is twice differentiable irrespective of whether labor supply slopes upward and approaches L_{max}, or whether it is inelastic. To check if the map is expansive, the first derivative of the adjustment map is required. The first derivatives of the adjustment map are

---

22 The distinction between topological chaos and positive Lebesgue measure is probably of minor importance when applied to social systems. It is very unlikely that a system in an economic context stays the same in a longer run. Economic relationships and the behavior of agents will change and a deterministic model that is valid for a specific time period might lack an explanation when applied to different times. Hence, it is probably the short and medium run dynamics that are important so that even if chaos is topological and only transitory, it is still an important dynamic property of economic systems.

$$\frac{dw_{t+1}}{dw_t} = 1 + \lambda \cdot \left(\frac{dL_D}{dw_t} - \frac{dL_S}{dw_t}\right) \text{ for } w_t < w_c \tag{93}$$

and

$$\frac{dw_{t+1}}{dw_t} = 1 - \lambda \cdot \frac{dL_S}{dw_t} \text{ for } w_t > w_c . \tag{94}$$

Within the regime where firms cannot make profits and have zero demand for labor, it is the adjustment speed and the slope of the labor supply curve that decides whether the map is expansive (94). Assuming that labor supply is inelastic, the derivative on the supply of labor becomes zero. Then, (94) is one for every real wage larger than the critical real wage. If it was possible to show that the real wage becomes smaller than the critical real wage at least once in the real wage sequence, and the map is expansive in that regime, the derivatives would be larger than one on average. This follows from applying the chain rule to the sequence of real wages $f^k(w_t)=w_{t+k}$

$$\frac{dw_{t+k}}{dw_t} = \frac{dw_{t+k}}{dw_{t+k-1}} \cdot \frac{dw_{t+k-1}}{w_{t+k-2}} \cdot \ldots \cdot \frac{dw_{t+1}}{dw_t} . \tag{95}$$

As was already argued, there is a tendency for real wages to fall if they are larger than w_c. Eventually, there will be a real wage level that is lower than the equilibrium real wage. Whether the left hand side is expansive depends on the adjustment speed and the slopes of the labor supply and demand curves. Because labor supply is inelastic, the right term in the parenthesis of (93) is zero. If labor demand is rather elastic or the adjustment speed is high, the map becomes expansive. Then, the adjustment function is expansive in the sense of Lasota and Yorke (c.f. Day and Pianigiani 1991, p.142.) and an infinite number of real wage cycles can be observed, even in the long run.

For an upward sloping labor supply, conclusions are less straightforward. It was shown that if there is a production technology where increasing returns are an important feature, real wages have to be sufficiently low so that firms will make profits. Hence, there might be a large range of real wages in the right hand regime for which households have an upward sloping labor supply. It follows from condition (94) that the slope of the adjustment map will be smaller than one. This reduces the likelihood of an expansive map. On the other hand, if the critical real wage level is rather low, households may be sensitive to real wage increases so that labor supply is sufficiently upward sloping in the left hand regime. If, furthermore, returns to labor are sharply decreasing at the margin, (93) might become considerably smaller than –1. On average, the sequence of real wages might imply derivatives that are larger than one in absolute value. Hence, effects are ambiguous but, compared to a labor market with inelastic supply, an upward sloping supply function probably reduces the chances for chaotic cycles.

Case 3 - Real wage adjustment with a non-concave production function

As in the previous model, labor supply will ground on a CES utility function

$$U(C,1-L)=(C^{\beta}+(1-L)^{\beta})^{\frac{1}{\beta}}. \qquad (96)$$

The maximum available labor supply L_{max} shall be one. Utility increases with leisure and income. Maximizing the utility function under the restriction

$$C \leq L \cdot w \qquad (97)$$

yields the supply of labor

$$L=\frac{1}{1+w^{\frac{\beta}{\beta-1}}}. \qquad (98)$$

For $0.5<\beta<1$ (98) matches the properties of (83), alas is upward sloping and saturates at a maximum labor supply L_{max}.

There are several functions that would reasonably represent a production technology illustrated in Figure 22. One could refer to *f(L)=arctan(L)* or *f(L)=tanh(L)* and introduce some shift parameters. These functions have somehow more complicated first and second order derivatives than $f(L)=A \cdot L^{\alpha}$ and are less easy to handle. Therefore, the simulation will recur to the production function already used before, saying that

$$L_D(w)=0 \text{ for } w_c<w \qquad (99)$$

and

$$L_D(w)=(\frac{w}{A \cdot \alpha})^{\frac{1}{\alpha-1}} \text{ for } 0 \leq w \leq w_c \qquad (100)$$

with $0<\alpha<1$. The critical wage and employment levels are given where the average productivity has its maximum

$$w_c=\max\frac{f(L)}{L}. \qquad (101)$$

These functions yield a labor demand curve that has the properties of (79) to (81). Labor demand is zero for real wages larger than the critical real wage. It is positive for real wage levels below the critical real wage, and is downward sloping as marginal returns are decreasing. If, for example, increasing returns hold for employment levels up to 10% - only if firms' employment level is larger than 10% of the labor force will they make profits - the critical real wage will be

$$w_c=\alpha \cdot A \cdot L_c^{\alpha-1}=\alpha \cdot A \cdot 0.1^{\alpha-1}. \qquad (102)$$

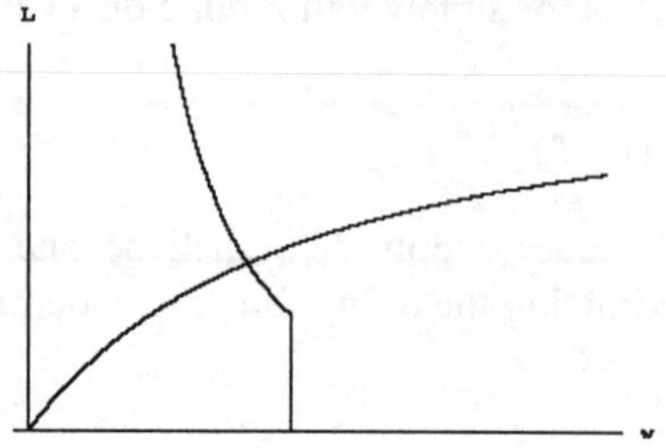

Figure 25: Labor demand and supply.

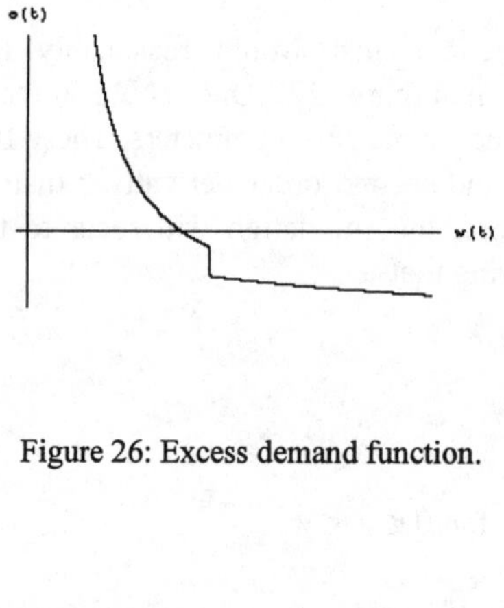

Figure 26: Excess demand function.

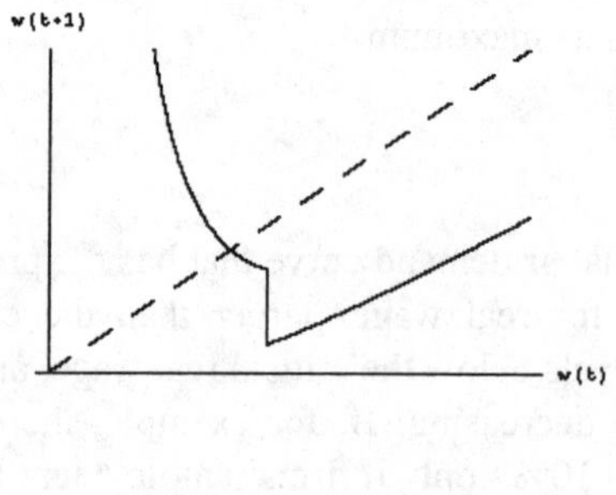

Figure 27: Real wage adjustment map.

The piecewise adjustment function can be written as

$$w_{t+1} = w_t + \lambda \cdot \left(-\frac{1}{1 + w_t^{\frac{\beta}{\beta-1}}}\right) \text{ for } w_c < w_t \tag{103}$$

and

$$w_{t+1} = w_t + \lambda \cdot \left(\left(\frac{w_t}{\alpha \cdot A}\right)^{\frac{1}{\alpha-1}} - \frac{1}{1 + w_t^{\frac{\beta}{\beta-1}}}\right) \text{ for } 0 \leq w_t \leq w_c . \tag{104}$$

Figure 25, Figure 26, and Figure 27 show the graphical derivation of the adjustment map ((103) and (104)). Excess demand is zero for the equilibrium real wage. If real wages are lower than in equilibrium, households supply less labor than is optimal for the firms and hence, there is excess demand. For real wages higher than in the equilibrium, supply exceeds demand and there is a negative excess demand. If the real wage is even higher than the critical real wage which corresponds with the maximal average labor productivity, labor demand becomes zero. At the critical wage, the excess demand function is discontinuous. Both real wage levels, the equilibrium real wage, and the critical real wage translate into the real wage adjustment map (Figure 27). The equilibrium condition, the 45-degree line, intersects the adjustment map at the equilibrium real wage. The discontinuity is at w_c.

The piecewise adjustment map in (103) and (104) fulfills the properties outlined in (89) to (92). It is positive and has a range of real wages that map onto itself for parameters which satisfy

$$\left(\frac{\lambda}{2 \cdot \alpha \cdot A}\right)^{\frac{1}{\alpha-1}} > L_c \tag{105}$$

(105) follows from comparing (103) with (104). Because the demand for labor is positive, the minimum of the adjustment map has to come with (103). Furthermore, labor supply shall be inelastic (β=0 and therefore L_S=0.5), so that the minimum of the adjustment map is given by w_{min}=w_c. Inserting (102) into (103) gives (105). There will be chaotic dynamics with positive Lebesgue measure if the piecewise adjustment map ((103) and (104)) is expansive almost everywhere. It will be shown that this is feasible under some further assumptions on the labor demand and supply curves.

Because labor supply is inelastic per assumption, the adjustment map slopes upward with

$$\frac{dw_{t+1}}{dw_t} = 1 \text{ for } w_c < w_t \tag{106}$$

in the zero profit regime. If the restrictions that arise from the boundedness condition (105) and from the assumption that supply and demand curves intersect should allow that

$$\frac{dw_{t+1}}{dw_t} \geq 1 \text{ for } w_t < w_c, \tag{107}$$

the map ((103) and (104)) would be expansive everywhere. The first derivative of (104) together with (98) and (102) gives

$$L_c > \left(\frac{2 \cdot \alpha \cdot A \cdot (1-\alpha)}{\lambda}\right)^{\frac{1}{2-\alpha}}. \tag{108}$$

Plugging in a set of parameters shows that all three conditions $w^* < w_c$, (105), and (108) can be fulfilled simultaneously. Take for example λ=1.5, α=0.8, and A=1. Setting L_c=0.3 will guarantee that there is a point at which labor supply and demand intersect, since demand is downward sloping and labor supply is 0.5 for all real wage levels. Condition (105) yields 1.38, which is larger than 0.3. Inserting the set of parameters into (108) gives 0.27, which is smaller than the critical employment level L_c=0.3. As real wages switch between both regimes, the map is expansive even though the slope in the right hand regime is one everywhere. This shows that chaos with positive Lebesgue measure is possible.

It might be interesting to note that chaos can occur for less restrictive assumptions on labor demand and supply, too. The theorem of Lasota and Yorke (c.f. Day and Pianigiani , p.142) states that the piecewise adjustment map has to be expansive almost everywhere. This means that even if real wages meet a segment where the adjustment map is not expansive, trajectories might still behave chaotic as it is the average over all iterations that counts. Hence, whether there is a positive Lebesgue measure also depends on how many times the process enters each segment. If the number of iterations in non-expansive segments is small compared to the expansive segments, the average might still be larger than one. This can be of interest with respect to the range of real wage levels

$$\underline{w} \leq w_t \leq \overline{w}$$

that the conditions for chaos imply. As the labor demand curve has to be rather steep to assure expansivity, the range of real wage levels becomes considerably large. Remember that the upper bound is the second iterate of w_{min}. If the first iterate of w_{min} is considerably smaller than w_{min}, and labor demand is very elastic, the second iterate will be very high. So one might argue that chaotic dynamics are excluded by the wide real wage range that the conditions on chaos imply. However, the range shrinks with a less elastic labor demand and real wage dynamics might still be chaotic.

Figure 28 plots a real wage time series that corresponds to the adjustment map in Figure 27. Like in (57), labor supply grounds on preferences of the CES type. It is upward sloping and restricted from above (β=0.5). The labor demand side has the same properties for the regime with positive demand, like the models in the previous chapter 3.2. Still, dynamics are completely different for the labor market with increasing returns. As can be seen from the bifurcation diagram (Figure 21), the labor market that relates to (57) had a stable period two cycle for an adjustment speed of λ=1.5. There was a real wage cycle that switched from a low level to a high level and back. There is no stable period two cycle for that set of parameters with increasing returns and a discontinuous labor demand. Trajectories that are repelled from the equilibrium do not settle at a period two cycle, but are eventually trapped in the zero demand regime (Figure 28).

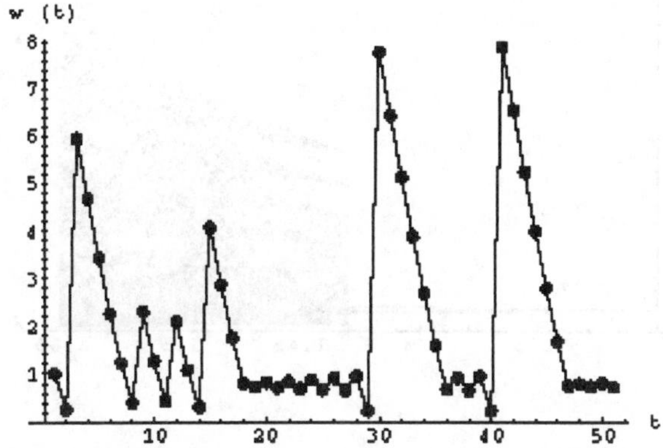

Figure 28: Real wage time series, A=1, w_0=1, β=0.5, λ=1.5, α=0.5, L_c=0.3.

This can be seen best for the sequence of real wages between period 18 and 36. Repelled from its equilibrium value, real wages begin to increase slightly. As the real wage level was too high to clear the market, the auctioneer decreased it for the following period. Being too nervous about clearing the market, he sets a real wage that is below the equilibrium real wage. Hence, demand is higher than supply and the auctioneer raises the real wage again. He once more fails to reach the equilibrium. Moreover, the current real wage deviates even more from the equilibrium than before. The process of finding the market-clearing wage goes on and the real wage variance becomes larger. In the previous model (78) it settled to a period two cycle (Figure 21). Here, however, the zero labor demand regime traps the auctioneer. The real wage sequence eventually enters the zero profit regime. Labor demand switches to zero and excess supply increases considerably so that the real wage level will be rather low in the following period. This sparks a tremendous increase in labor demand, as the elasticity is high and only a few people offer work for such a low real wage. In period 30, real wages are far above the critical real wage under which firms make profits. Labor demand is zero. Excess supply exerts downward real wage pressure. But due to rather high real wages, it still takes a considerable long time until real wages have fallen to a level below the critical real wage. As the equilibrium is unstable, future unemployment is already underway.

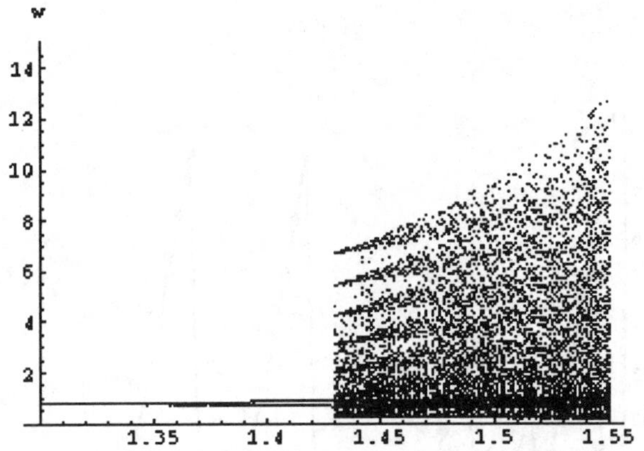

Figure 29: Bifurcation diagram for λ, A=1, β=0.5, α=0.5, L_c=0.3.

The bifurcation diagram in Figure 29 illustrates the long run properties for a labor market model with a discontinuous labor demand. The auctioneer is not warned by a period doubling of long run real wages if he increases the adjustment speed. At an adjustment speed of approximately λ=1.43, dynamics change abruptly. A period two cycle with a rather small amplitude changes into a wide range with a very high number of possible long run states. A labor market with increasing returns is already chaotic for real wage adjustment speeds that would imply stable cycles of finite order if the labor demand curve was continuous. By comparing Figure 30 with Figure 29, one can see that a smaller degree of setup costs reduces the threat of a dramatic change in the long run behavior. If the critical employment level boils down from 30% to 10%, the chaotic cycles will emerge only for higher adjustment speeds. Furthermore, the auctioneer is at least warned by a period four cycle, and if he nevertheless increases the adjustment speed, the chaotic real wage range will be smaller. No matter whether the critical employment level is at 10% or 30%, the trapping area is wider than in the models without increasing returns (c.f. Figure 21). Furthermore, the model with increasing returns emphasizes the asymmetry of the chaotic attractor. On average, real wages deviate from the equilibrium real wage to a larger extent. Interpreting negative excess demand as unemployment, this implies higher unemployment levels on average.

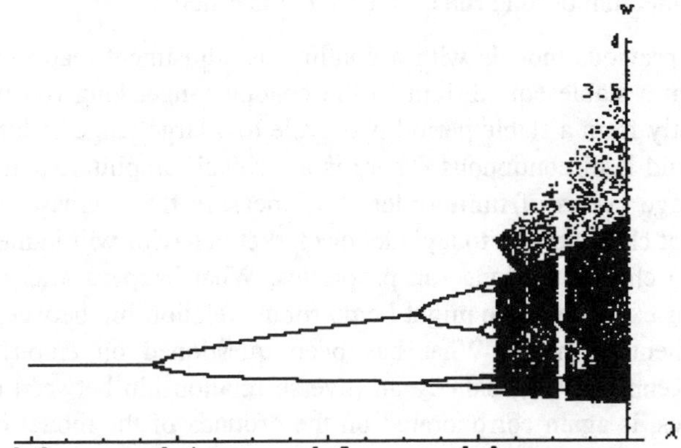

Figure 30: Bifurcation diagram for λ, A=1, β=0.5, α=0.5, L_c=0.1.

Since the calibration of the models coincides with the examples in chapter 3.3, and the unstable equilibrium is in the regime of positive labor demand, the same arguments on the plausibility, i.e. whether empirical estimates on labor supply and demand elasticities support the notion of an unstable equilibrium, hold. The real wage range is larger than in the models of the previous chapter (3.3). The simulated time series in Figure 28 shows real wage levels that are about eight times higher than the equilibrium real wage. This does not cope with real time series data on real wages, and once more emphasizes the highly stylized nature of the models.

4.4 Policy implications

Some of the policy implications derived from the previous models in chapter 3.3 also apply here. This is especially true for the downward sloping quasi Phillips curve that did not inherit a trade-off between employment and wage inflation. Again, there is a negative relationship between the level of unemployment and wage changes for the chaotic regime[23]. As long as there is unemployment, wages will fall. If there is excess demand for labor wages will increase. Unemployment may move up and down this quasi Phillips curve irregularly. If it does so, politicians cannot recur to a menu of choice, but for other reasons than within the expectations′ augmented approaches. They can order, but by the time they receive their dishes the menu has already changed. As there is probably chaos in the sense of a positive Lebesgue measure, there is no way to forecast which dish will be served in the medium or long run by the time it is ordered.

Whereas the previous models with a continuous adjustment map implied period doubling from a stable equilibrium to the chaotic range, long run behavior can change abruptly from a stable period two cycle to a large range of long run states if labor demand is discontinuous. There is a 'critical' amplitude that comes with stable real wage cycles of finite order. Any measure that increases the range of real wages that characterizes today's labor market behavior will immediately (and tremendously) change the long run properties. What happens afterwards can be confusing. For example, there might be no robust relationship between real wages and employment anymore. What has been questioned on empirical grounds (Geary and Kennan 1982), namely an inverse relationship between employment and real wages, is again corroborated on the grounds of the model described by (103) and (104). If an economy is trapped in the negative profit regime, it can take a considerably long time until the labor market clears. Should labor supply be inelastic within the zero labor demand regime, unemployment does not decline even though real wages fall. In other words, real wages and employment are not correlated. Only, if the auctioneer would cut real wages to the equilibrium level at once, could persistent unemployment be circumvented. But this auctioneer does not know the equilibrium value. He observes the excess demand and supply, and adjusts the real wage according to his proportional control rule. This might be questioned on the grounds of rational agents. But the following chapter shows that his behavior can be rational. Confronted with these irregular dynamics, it might very well be the best idea to stick to the proportional adjustment rule.

---

23 As already noted, this implies that nominal wage changes are tight to real wage changes, i.e. some kind of wage indexing.

5 A note on rationality

All the models on real wage adjustment discussed so far referred to a very simple and static market clearing rule. An auctioneer observes the current state of the labor market. If it is in disequilibrium, he decides to vary the real wage proportionately to excess demand and supply. Should labor demand be higher than supply, he will increase real wages, hoping to clear the market. If there is excess supply, the auctioneer decreases the real wage level in a determined relation to the observed disequilibrium quantities

$$w_{t+1} - w_t = \lambda \cdot [L_D(w_t) - L_S(w_t)] . \qquad (109)$$

Within the chaotic regime of the labor markets (39), (57), and (103) in combination with (104), there is no single market equilibrium. Real wages and excess employment vary within boundaries but do not settle to a specific equilibrium value. At any point in time there is a real wage that does not satisfy the optimality condition of one side of the labor market. If the real wage is above its equilibrium value, it is not profitable for firms to employ all the workers who offer labor at the going real wage. Some of the people who are willing to work for the current labor market conditions are left behind, and there is pressure that comes from the unemployed to lower real wages. More exactly, all those unemployed who would work for a real wage less than the current, but higher than the equilibrium real wage, exert the downward real wage pressure. That is what the auctioneer stands for if he decreases the real wage due to an excess supply. For a real wage lower than the equilibrium real wage, firms face a labor shortage. They cannot attract as many workers as they would need to operate at their profitable level of production. Hence, this real wage is not an optimal real wage, too. Upward real wage pressure comes from the fraction of firms who would meet their optimality conditions if real wages were higher than the current, but lower than the equilibrium. Although real wage pressure heads into the direction of the equilibrium, agents might constantly fail to find a real wage level that satisfies both sides of the market. Hence, the question arises why there is no behavioral response to chaotic market dynamics. Do agents really behave rationally by sticking to the same adjustment rule - even under constant failure at clearing the market? The answer is: The auctioneer might have tried alternative measures but did not succeed in stabilizing the market, nor in extracting useful information on how to achieve an equilibrium. If so, sticking to past behavior might be the best thing to do.

Hommes (1998) and Hommes and Sorger (1998) show that simple 'rules of thumb' can be consistent with rational behavior. Usually, one would assume that agents who do not make use of the latest information make worse forecasts than those people who try to anticipate future events. Assume for example, a situation where the monetary authority announces its money supply at the beginning of every year. Assume furthermore, that at the beginning of each period a higher growth rate is proclaimed. How would an agent with naïve or adaptive expectations predict the inflation rate as opposed to a rational agent? He would constantly underestimate the inflation rate as he only uses past information. He does not take into account that the current money supply will be even higher than the year before. The actual inflation rate will always be higher than the predicted, and in this sense, backward looking expectations are not rational because of systematic forecasting errors. This does not exclude that a rational agent is wrong with his forecast. He might even be wrong many times. But he does not make the same mistake twice as he is able to learn from his failure and adjust his forecasting algorithm (Shaw 1984, p.50). Contrary to that example, it has been shown that when price movements are chaotic, backward looking expectations can be consistent with rational behavior. Even though agents heavily base their predictions on past information, they do not perform 'badly'. Several examples of chaotic cobweb models, where backward looking behavior is consistent with rationality, have been sketched in chapter 2.1.4. In these models, predicted prices do not deviate from the actual price sequence in a systematic way. Agents do not misjudge the future. They might still be wrong in their forecast. But the distribution of their price forecasts matches the distribution of prices generated by the true underlying model. Forecasts and true market behavior do not deviate in a systematic fashion, although agents are backward looking.

Hommes (1998) proposes a measure for consistency that refers to the autocorrelation coefficients of the sequence of forecasting errors. The latter is the difference between the actual time path of the variable and the expected value. Broadly speaking, backward looking behavior is said to be consistent with rational behavior if, with means eliminated in the errors, all autocorrelation coefficients for lags $k \geq 1$ are zero. It is weakly consistent if the autocorrelation coefficients are zero for $k \geq 2$ and inconsistent otherwise. This definition of consistency runs into some problems: if there is topological chaos, varying the initial state or the parameter of a model, might change the generated time series so that it converges to a cycle with finite order in the long run. An autocorrelation function with zero coefficients for all lags might become positive for some lags under a small perturbation of the system. Consistency would not be robust. On the other hand, if the set of initial states, for which the time series is irregular even in the long run, is not a Cantor set, but has subsets of finite lengths, consistency becomes more robust to perturbations. In other words, backward looking expectations are more likely to be consistent with rational expectations if the market is chaotic with a positive Lebesgue measure. It was already argued that the notion of topological chaos suffices for economic systems as a definition for irregular behavior, since the underlying laws of motion will change in the long run anyway. A powerful model of today might be inappropriate for the future. The perspective is shorter in social systems and a positive Lebesgue measure might be a too strong concept. There is another way to circumvent the problem of positive autocorrelation coefficients from topological chaos (Hommes 1998). It is very likely that real economic systems are perturbed by exogenous shocks, even if there is a nonlinear deterministic core that mainly causes the irregularity in the data. Adding small noise levels to the generated time series of a topologically chaotic time series can reduce positive autocorrelation coefficients to values next to zero. There is an intuitive explanation to it. By the time that the exogenous shock arrives, the initial state of the model changes and a 'new' price sequence starts. This will be irregular even under topological chaos. If further exogenous shocks arrive within a reasonable time horizon (before the price sequence settles to a finite cycle), there will always be irregular behavior, even in the long run with no positive Lebesgue measure given. A small noise to signal ratio will suffice for a range of chaotic systems to get almost zero autocorrelation coefficients as the price sequence will change dramatically following an even small perturbation. This is once more due to the sensitive dependence on initial conditions in chaotic systems. Whether small exogenous shocks enable the proof of consistency still depends on the shape of the attractor. For a Lorenz attractor, one probably gets rather robust non-zero autocorrelation coefficients even under noise as the attractor basically consists of two parts. Small noise ratios will not prevent the system swaps from one 'elephant ear' of the attractor to the other.

A more fruitful way to think about consistency within chaotic systems might therefore be to build a measure that accepts positive autocorrelation coefficients, but shows that it is still impossible to extract useful information from that. Confronted with his permanent failure to equilibrate labor demand and supply, the auctioneer might decide to test the market response on different adjustment speeds. As he is confused about the labor market dynamics of the past, where there was no equilibrium, he acts cautious. He does not want to take the risk of making things even worse, and starts tuning λ in very small steps. The auctioneer, furthermore, does not know the true model. In that sense, he differs from the concept of rationality as it was proposed by Muth (1961). But he knows very well about certain forecasting techniques. Applying these techniques to what he observes will form his perception about the market properties. Hence, the auctioneer has some kind of bounded rationality in the sense outlined by Sargent (1993, p.22). He behaves like a working econometrician. In particular, he can handle autocorrelation functions very well and calculates the autocorrelation coefficients of the past real wage sequence. He is interested in the deviations from the equilibrium real wage. As he has no information about the true underlying model, he assumes that the equilibrium real wage is the mean of the real wage time series that he has been observing. Subtracting the mean real wage from every real wage level in the past gives a sequence of real wage deviations that captures his concerns about disequilibrium real wages

$$d_t = w_t - \frac{1}{N} \cdot \sum_{t=1}^{N} w_t \,. \tag{110}$$

He obtains the autocorrelation coefficients

$$\rho_k = \frac{c_k}{c_0} \tag{111}$$

with

$$c_k = \frac{1}{N} \cdot \sum_{t=1}^{N-k} d_t \cdot d_{t+k} \,. \tag{112}$$

Applying the estimator for the autocorrelation function to the chaotic real wage sequence of the labor market model with a backward bending labor supply gives Figure 31. The generated time series had a length of 100 iterations, where the first 50 values were dropped to eliminate transitory behavior. The adjustment speed is λ=0.835. With all other parameters as in Figure 15, the labor market is in its chaotic regime. All correlation coefficients are different from zero up to a lag of 11 time periods. Hence, the auctioneer should realize that there is something wrong with his real wage adjustment behavior. Starting with a negative coefficient at the first lag, whenever he observed a real wage above the market clearing level (excess supply), there would be a real wage level too low to clear the market in the following period. The market switches from excess supply to excess demand, assuming for convenience that the average real wage level is the market clearing wage[24]. The second possible interpretation starts with a real wage that is below its market clearing level. Then, the auctioneer would observe a real wage level higher than the equilibrium in the following period. In any case, the likely outcome for the consecutive period is a change in the sign on excess demand. A demand shortage will change into a supply shortage or vice versa. As the coefficient of the autocorrelation function is negative for the second lag, there is either persistence of excess demand, or excess supply, respectively. Three periods ahead, the sign on excess demand is likely to change again.

24 It is not for the labor market model investigated here. It was already mentioned that the chaotic attractor is asymmetric to the unstable equilibrium real wage. Hence, a mean value estimate of the equilibrium is likely to be biased upwards. The estimate will be higher than the actual equilibrium, and the auctioneer would still observe excess supply for a real wage that he thinks is the equilibrium value.

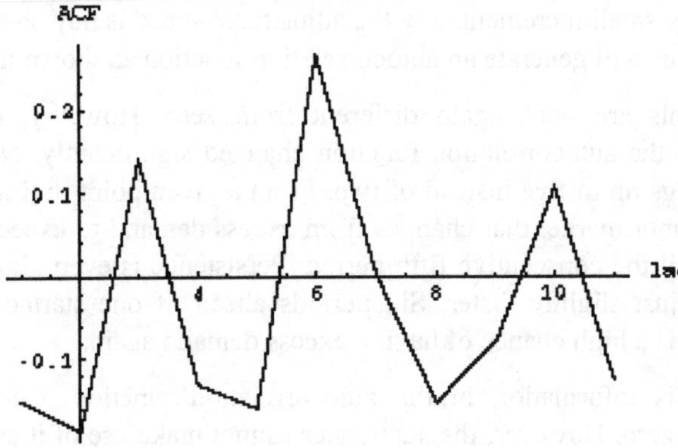

Figure 31: Autocorrelation function (ACF) for the labor market model with backward bending supply (39), λ=0.835, α=0.5, A=1, B=2.7, δ=1.

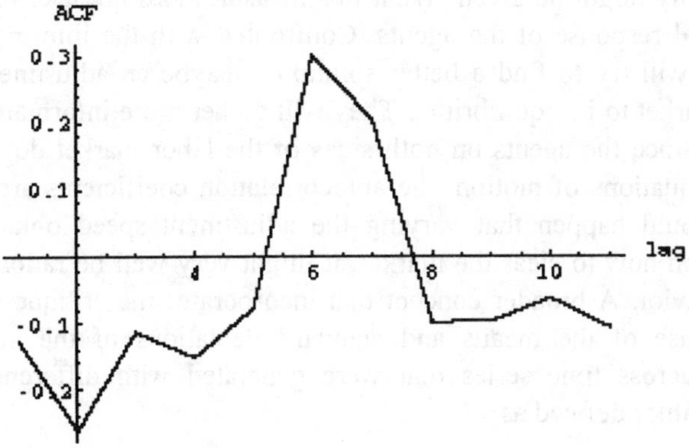

Figure 32: Autocorrelation function (ACF) for the model with backward bending labor supply (39), λ=0.840, α=0.5, A=1, B=2.7, δ=1.

Insofar, the autocorrelation function tells him that he permanently made the wrong decision, since there is a pattern for non clearing real wage levels that he should have observed. In other words, he did not act rational. To learn more about the consequences of his adjustment behavior he decides to increase the adjustment speed by a very small increment. Say the adjustment speed is now λ=0.840 instead of λ=0.835. This will generate an autocorrelation function as shown in Figure 32.

The coefficients are once again different from zero. However, the non-zero coefficients of the autocorrelation function changed significantly. Now, they are negative for lags up to five instead of two. From a given point in time, it is likely to observe a labor market that changes from excess demand to excess supply and stays there until the consecutive fifth period. Persistence is even higher, although real wages adjust slightly faster. Six periods ahead, if one started with excess demand, there is a high chance of having excess demand again.

Hence, there is information in the autocorrelation function. Coefficients are different from zero. However, the auctioneer cannot make use of it as coefficients may change significantly to every one of his actions. Varying the adjustment speed in the chaotic regime of the market generates a range of autocorrelation functions so that even if the coefficients of the autocorrelation function are different from zero, agents may behave rationally by sticking to their past behavior. They tried to learn by looking at market outcomes for different responses to a non clearing market, but could not perceive a pattern across varying adjustment speeds. Therefore, a measure that sticks to the autocorrelation coefficients of a single generated time series might be a too restrictive tool to judge whether sticking to a specific adjustment rule is consistent with rational behavior. Even if the coefficients of the autocorrelation function are different from zero, rationality might be given. What this measure does not take into account is the behavioral response of the agents. Confronted with the information on their failure, they will try to find a better solution - maybe an adjustment speed that drives the market to its equilibrium. They will gather more information by testing the system. Since the agents on both sides of the labor market do not know the underlying equations of motion, the autocorrelation coefficients are all they can get. If it should happen that varying the adjustment speed obtains no useful information on how to clear the market, it might very well be rational to stick to the past behavior. A broader concept that incorporates the critique might be one that makes use of the means and standard deviations of the autocorrelation coefficients across time series that were generated with different parameters. Then, the t-values defined as

$$\hat{t}_k = \frac{\frac{1}{M} \cdot \sum_{m=1}^{M} \rho_{k,m}}{\sqrt{\frac{1}{M} \cdot \sum_{m=1}^{M} (\rho_{k,m} - \bar{\rho}_k)^2}} \tag{113}$$

could be a convenient measure for consistency with rational behavior. *M*, which is the number of generated time series is equal to the interval of adjustment speeds

$$[\underline{\lambda};\overline{\lambda}]$$

divided by the step size $\Delta\lambda$

$$M = \frac{\overline{\lambda} - \underline{\lambda}}{\Delta\lambda}. \tag{114}$$

An alternative definition for consistency could be.

Definition: Agents behave consistent with rational behavior if for all lags k the ratio of the means to the standard deviation of the autocorrelation coefficients across different chaotic time series is smaller than a threshold

$$|\hat{t}| < \bar{t},$$

weakly consistent if this holds true for lags $k \geq 1$, and inconsistent otherwise.

Given this alternative measure, there is at least weak consistency with rational behavior in two of the three examples (Figure 33, Figure 34, and Figure 35). The models with a continuous labor demand, where supply either bends backward or saturates at a fixed supply, show relatively large negative t-values at the first lag. It seems to be a robust pattern that the labor market changes from a negative excess demand to positive excess demand in the consecutive period, or vice versa. But for all the following periods, the autocorrelation coefficients vary around their mean levels to a large extent when calculated for different adjustment speeds in the chaotic regimes. The test statistics stay below the boundaries of a significant level[25]. Hence, there is no robust pattern for lags $k \geq 1$ that would tell the auctioneer that his adjustment rule caused permanent errors in clearing the market. There is a hint on persistence in Figure 35. The t-values for the first and second lag are both positive and large. This implies that either excess demand or excess supply stay for two consecutive periods in general. Going back to Figure 28 favors the latter interpretation. The autocorrelation coefficients capture the persistence of excess supply when the labor market is trapped in its zero demand regime. This seems to be the only pattern a rational auctioneer can extract from the three examples on chaotic labor market behavior. Hence, a simple adjustment rule seems to be at least weakly consistent with rational behavior. So do the results derived from a chaotic labor market with irregular but deterministic real wage behavior.

---

[25] A threshold of

$$|\bar{t}| = 2$$

implies that the coefficients of the autocorrelation functions are significant if the standard deviation does not vary more than 50% around the mean.

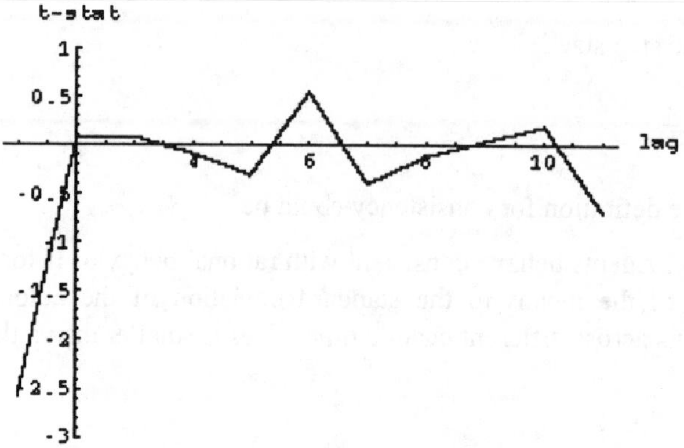

Figure 33: t-statistics for the autocorrelation coefficients of the model with backward bending labor supply, λ=[0.7;0.85] in steps of 0.005, α=0.5, A=1, B=2.7, δ=1.

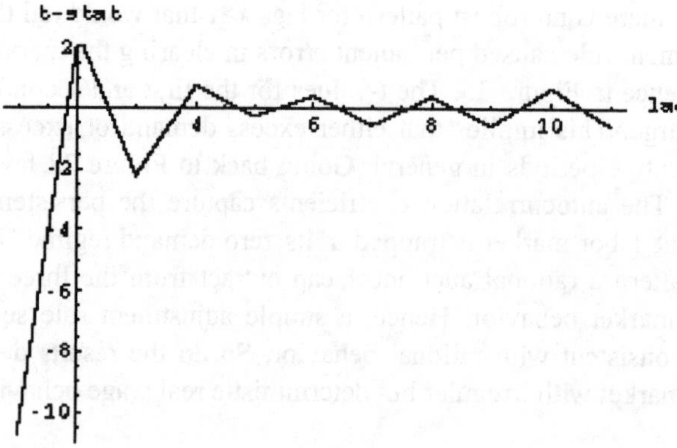

Figure 34: t-statistics for the autocorrelation coefficients of the model with an upward sloping labor supply, λ=[1.9;2] in steps of 0.005, α=0.5, A=1, β=0.5.

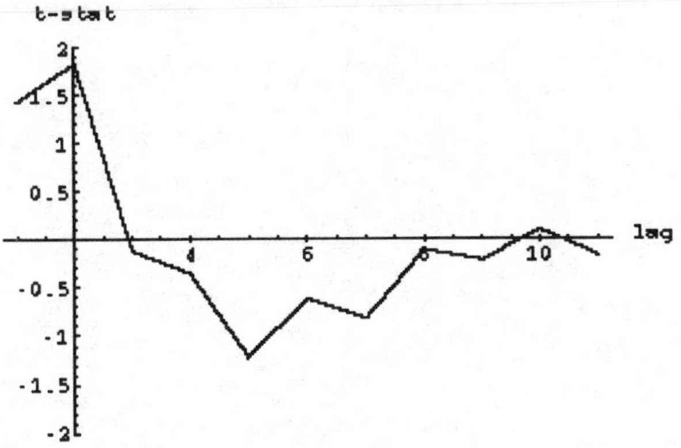

Figure 35: t-statistics for the autocorrelation coefficients of the model with upward sloping supply and discontinuous labor demand, λ=[1.44;1.54] in steps of 0.005, α=0.5, A=1, β=0.5, L_c=0.3.

6 Worker flows and the occurrence of endogenous cycles

It has been argued that merely looking at stocks of labor market variables locks away important and illuminating dynamics, because rather stable levels of unemployment can hide tremendous flows from unemployment to employment and vice versa. Should the transitions in both directions cancel out, unemployment would not vary even though it might be the case that the stock of unemployed workers completely changed. Hence, explaining variations in the level of unemployment over time, or differences across countries, may be achieved better by looking at the flows. A flow approach to labor markets (Blanchard and Diamond 1992) might be more adequate to explain the determinants of a 'natural rate of unemployment'.

What actually grounds the 'natural rate of unemployment' is controversial. Friedman (1968, p. 8) claims that structural characteristics of labor and product markets and market imperfections would cause frictions in flows from unemployment and into the pool of unemployment that determine the natural level. Since then, shifts in the 'natural rate of unemployment' have been attributed to changing demographics of the labor force, a slow down in the productivity growth coincided by a lag in the adjustment of real wage aspirations, biased technological progress, labor market rigidities or hysteresis effects (c.f. Stiglitz 1997, Blanchard and Katz 1997). All the approaches relate the dynamics of the 'natural rate' to exogenous forces. Even in theories of hysteresis where nowadays unemployment is dependent on previous unemployment, it took an exogenous force to raise unemployment in the past.

The following model will differ from those models as it highlights the role of structural relationships on the labor market itself, which can cause a varying natural level unemployment. This does not disqualify the models above. However, it is an attempt to explain variations in the natural level of unemployment endogenously by looking at worker flows. Again, this is a highly stylized model. In particular, goods and money markets are not considered, and wages are excluded. Nevertheless, it serves the purpose to sketch the idea of a natural range of unemployment at this stage. The crucial role with respect to the occurrence of endogenous cycles plays a nonlinear and decreasing outflow rate from unemployment into employment. The outflow rate is driven by the competition of employed and unemployed workers for a given number of jobs. In this sense, it is a model with heterogeneous agents. All unemployed are searching for a job. But only a fraction of the employed will do so depending on their prospects of moving to another job. The degree to which employed workers engage in search influences the level and the convexity of the outflow rate. It will be shown that downward sloping outflow rate from unemployment has important effects on the stability of the natural unemployment level. Under certain parameter settings, natural unemployment becomes unstable and a large number of bounded long run equilibria may arise. The 'natural rate of unemployment' becomes a 'natural *range* of unemployment'.

6.1 The outflow from unemployment

Inflows I and outflows O from unemployment determine the level of unemployment. A basic identity relates the changes in the unemployment level to the difference between these two flows at time t.

$$U_{t+1} - U_t = I_t - O_t \tag{115}$$

Very simple flow models assume that inflow and outflow rates (i and o respectively) are constant

$$U_{t+1} - U_t = i \cdot (L - U_t) - o \cdot U_t \tag{116}$$

This implies that outflow slopes upward and inflow slopes downward with increasing unemployment and a fixed labor force. The labor market is at its natural level of unemployment if inflows into unemployment equal outflows from unemployment. For the sum of inflow and outflow rates sufficiently small, any deviation of current unemployment from the natural level will initiate an adjustment process that moves unemployment back to the equilibrium.

On the one hand, (116) implies that quit rates are constant over the business cycle. People leave their jobs irrespective of the state of the labor market. On the other hand, with fixed outflow rates, chances for the unemployed to get a job are independent from the level of unemployment. Not only by intuition do these assumptions seem to be very crude. Pissarides (1986) claims that the change in the outflow rate measured as the ratio of outflows within a period to the stock of unemployed at the beginning of the period, explains a large fraction of rising unemployment in Britain. German outflow rates (measured as the average duration of unemployment which is the inverse of the outflow rate) show a qualitatively similar picture (Schettkat 1996). Furthermore, both Pissarides (1986) and Schettkat (1996) find rather constant inflow rates. Hence, it will be fixed in this context, though the evidence is not clear cut (Burgess 1992). However, the advantage is that it allows to focus on the importance of a nonlinear outflow rate.

A nonlinear and decreasing outflow rate may arise from competition between employed and unemployed job searchers for a given number of jobs. The specification chosen in this context follows Burgess (1994) closely. Other on-the-job search models have been developed since one of the first attempts was made by Burdett (1978). A more recent approach can be found in Pissarides (1994). He argues that higher on-the-job search during an economic upswing prohibits a decline in unemployment. As there is more congestion on the labor market, the prospects that an unemployed person finds a job do not improve significantly. Unemployment stays roughly constant. Our model is a lot simpler. In particular, it does not incorporate the effect of tenure on the job search decision of employed workers, nor are wages modeled. The main result is not persistence of unemployment, but an endogenously varying natural rate.

In our model, all the unemployed are willing to take a job offer, and in addition, there is a fraction of people who search while being employed. Several studies on employed job search emphasize the importance of on-the-job search. However, the estimates vary significantly. Partly because they relate to different groups of the labor market. Rosenfeld (1977) finds on-the-job search at 4,2% of employment, Black (1981), and Pissarides and Wadsworth (1994) at 5,5% and 5,2% of employed workers respectively. Hartog and van Ophem (1996) report on-the-job search ratios that go up to 25%. Rather high on-the-job search rates can also be found in Parsons (1991) for young men (18,9%) and young women (15,9%). Having these estimates in mind, we think that employed job search is an important feature. Hence, we model an outflow rate where in addition to the unemployed workers, employed workers are also looking for jobs. Clearly, the more job searchers there are, the harder the competition is to get one of the job offers. We assume that every contact between a vacant job and a searching worker will lead to an instantaneous filling of the position. Employers do not refuse an applicant once they got in contact with him. Hence, the model abstracts from contract probabilities saying that every contact between a vacant job and a searcher leads to a contract. This is a valid assumption as long as the main characteristics of the job searchers do not differ too much in reality. Furthermore, we assume that vacant jobs are instantaneously filled. As long as the time that it takes to fill a vacancy is relatively short compared to the time period of the model, this should be no problem. In fact, the vacancy duration is generally in weeks (van Ours 1990). If the model is calibrated on a yearly basis, a couple of weeks for an open job is relatively short. With these assumptions, we can say that the outflow rate o_t is equal to the offer arrival rate

$$o_t = \frac{M}{S_t} \tag{117}$$

with

$$S_t = S_{U,t} + S_{N,t} . \tag{118}$$

That is the rate per time unit at which an unemployed gets a job offer (that he will accept). M is the amount of job offers in this economy. There is no explicit modeling of the matching process[26] since jobs are filled once they go to the market. M is also a measure for aggregate demand. It is exogenous and reflects the decisions of firms whether posting a job is profitable. If M increases more jobs come to the market and at a given number of unemployed and employed searchers, the outflow rate increases. The outflow rate decreases if M decreases, holding the number of people who are looking for a job constant. There is more competition for the job offers in this economy, and hence the likelihood that an unemployed gets one is lower. The endogeneity of the outflow rate enters through the unemployment level that determines the amount of unemployed searchers, and the fraction of employed workers who search on-the-job. For the latter, the state of the labor market measured by the outflow rate from unemployment drives the search behavior. The employed view the outflow rate that unemployed searchers face. Comparably high outflow rates signal the employed fairly good chances for finding another job. Competition is not as hard as it would be for low outflow rates. Hence, a larger fraction of them will decide searching

$$S_t = U_t + \alpha_e(\frac{M}{S_t}) \cdot N_t \text{ with } \alpha'_e > 0 . \tag{119}$$

With more employed workers looking for a new job, the unemployed face a tougher competition for the jobs that are offered. Thus, the fraction of employed job searchers influences the transition rates of the unemployed into employment. More employed job search as a consequence of larger outflow rates partly compensates a higher outflow rate that would have been given in the absence of on-the-job search. If there was perfect crowding out, a decline in unemployment would induce an increase in the number of employed job searchers that is equal to the decline in the number of unemployed job searchers. Only in this special case would the outflow rate not change with respect to the unemployment level (c.f. (117) and (118)).

Case 4 - Unemployment dynamics with a nonlinear outflow rate

Various specifications would fit the underlying behavioral assumption of $\alpha'_e > 0$. To keep the analytical treatment as simple as possible, a proportional relationship is introduced. Hence, the equation describing the amount of searchers on the labor market becomes

---

26 As opposed to structural matching models that refer to aggregate matching functions of the Cobb-Douglas type (Blanchard and Diamond 1989).

$$S_t = U_t + b \cdot \frac{M}{S_t} \cdot N_t. \tag{120}$$

This is a quadratic function that can be solved for S_t. Since only positive values for S_t make sense, the outflow rate will be

$$o_t = \frac{M}{\frac{1}{2}(U_t + \sqrt{4 \cdot b \cdot L \cdot M - 4 \cdot b \cdot M \cdot U_t + U_t^2})}. \tag{121}$$

The outflow rate is determined at the beginning of each period on the grounds of the current unemployment level and will hold until the beginning of the next period, where if the market is not in equilibrium, the outflow rate will be a function of a new unemployment level. As unemployment cannot become negative and is restricted by the labor force from above, the outflow rate (121) is always positive. It furthermore slopes downward for higher levels of unemployment and is therefore nonlinear but monotonous. This can be seen from the derivative of the outflow rate

$$\frac{do(U_t)}{dU_t} = \frac{-M \cdot (\frac{1}{2} + \frac{1}{2} \cdot \frac{2 \cdot U_t - 4 \cdot b \cdot M}{D_t})}{(\frac{U_t + D_t}{2})^2} \tag{122}$$

with

$$D_t = \sqrt{4 \cdot b \cdot M \cdot L - 4 \cdot b \cdot M \cdot U_t + U_t^2}. \tag{123}$$

The denominator of the slope of the outflow rate is positive, and after some manipulation of the numerator, the first derivative becomes

$$\frac{do(U_t)}{dU_t} = \frac{-M \cdot \frac{D_t + 2 \cdot U_t - 4 \cdot b \cdot M}{2 \cdot D_t}}{(\frac{U_t + D_t}{2})^2}. \tag{124}$$

The slope will be negative if

$$D_t + 2 \cdot U_t - 4 \cdot b \cdot M > 0 \text{ for } 0 \le U_t < L. \tag{125}$$

As the minimum of the root in (123) is

$$U_{D,\min} = 2 \cdot b \cdot M \tag{126}$$

the inequality becomes

$$2 \cdot \sqrt{b \cdot M \cdot (L - b \cdot M)} > 0 \tag{127}$$

which is fulfilled.

As the outflow rate is downward sloping, on-the-job search will never completely crowd out the better chances of the unemployed workers for finding a job that arose from a decrease in unemployment. The change in the outflow rate that follows a change in unemployment, however, is dependent on the strength of the signaling effect b that comes from the level of the outflow rate. Inserting the outflow rate (121) into the basic identity (116) gives the nonlinear difference equation

$$U_{t+1} - U_t = i \cdot (L - U_t) - \frac{M}{\frac{1}{2}(U_t + \sqrt{4 \cdot b \cdot L \cdot M - 4 \cdot b \cdot M \cdot U_t + U_t^2})} \cdot U_t \quad (128)$$

which describes the sequence of unemployment levels over time. Figure 37 shows the map (128) for specific parameters L, M, and b.

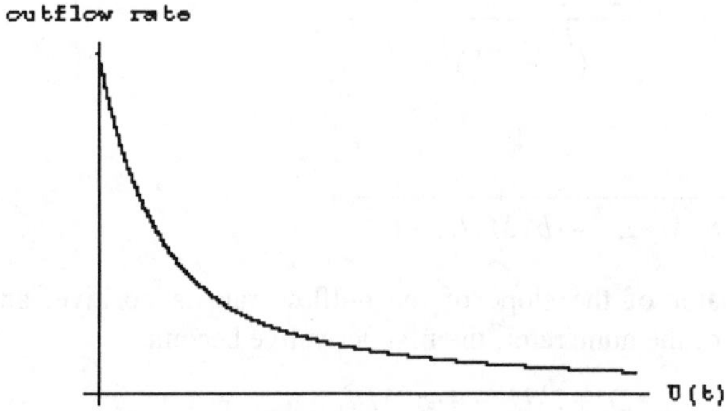

Figure 36: Outflow rate.

The discussion on the dynamics of the model will focus on three questions. First, can the worker flow model with on-the-job search become unstable? Second, if yes, is there an upper and a lower bound for the trajectories that are repelled from the equilibrium? And finally, is there a period three cycle implying chaotic behavior for the bounded oscillations?

The equilibrium condition for (128)

$$U_{t+1} - U_t = 0 \tag{129}$$

gives the equilibrium unemployment level (the natural level of unemployment)

$$U^* = L \cdot \frac{i}{i + o(U^*)} \tag{130}$$

As the outflow rate is nonlinear, there might be several equilibria. Equation (130) could hold for various U^* if there were more than one unemployment levels U^* that coincide with the same outflow rate $o(U^*)$. For this to happen, the function on the outflow rate would have to be non-invertible. However, as already argued, the outflow rate is monotonous and downward sloping so that there is always one equilibrium unemployment level that is stable if

$$\left| \frac{dU_{t+1}}{dU_t} \right|_{U*} < 1. \tag{131}$$

With

$$\frac{dU_{t+1}}{dU_t} = 1 - i - \frac{do(U_t)}{dU_t} \cdot U_t - o(U_t) \tag{132}$$

the stability condition becomes

$$0 < \left. \frac{do(U_t)}{dU_t} \right|_{U*} \cdot U * + o(U*) + i < 2. \tag{133}$$

Since

$$f(0) = i \cdot L > 0 \tag{134}$$

and

$$f(L) = L - M < L \tag{135}$$

the map $U_{t+1}=f(U_t)$ has to cross the equilibrium condition from above (Figure 37). The labor market will become unstable if the inequality (133) violates the upper bound. This will happen if the sum of the inflow rate, the outflow rate, and the change in the outflow rate weighted with the natural level of unemployment exceeds two. Both, the inflow and the outflow rate are positive. Since the outflow rate slopes downward, the first term on the left hand side of (133) is negative. Hence, the stability condition of a model with an endogenous outflow rate differs from a worker flow model with a constant outflow rate. In the latter, the equilibrium would be stable if the sum of the constant inflow and outflow rates is less than two as the first term in (133) becomes zero when the outflow rate is constant. Furthermore, the equilibrium outflow rate will be smaller when there is employed job search.

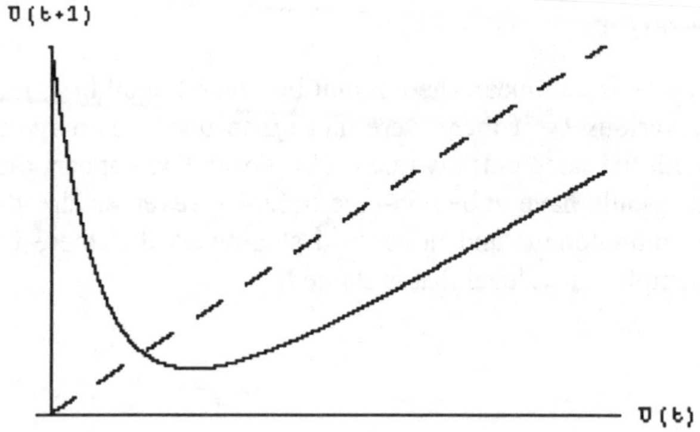

Figure 37: Adjustment map.

For any equilibrium unemployment level there will be a fraction of employed job searchers that reduces the chances for unemployed workers to find a job. An endogenous outflow rate, where employed and unemployed job searchers compete for a fixed amount of jobs, stabilizes the labor market as opposed to an economy without on-the-job search. The job search of the employed dampens the increase of the outflow rate following a reduction in unemployment (c.f. (117) and (118)). At a given degree of employed job search *b*, the outflow rate increases less than it would have if there was no crowding out of unemployed job searchers. The larger *b* is, the stronger is the stabilizing effect that comes from on-the-job search. A change in unemployment will obviously cause a larger fraction of employed workers to search for a job, and the outflow rate will be smaller. But the equilibrium can still become unstable. This happens if outflow rates are sufficiently high and deviations from the equilibrium change the outflow rate only slightly. A permanent overshooting of employment and unemployment may occur. However, there is a trapping area that restricts unemployment from above and below. As the outflow rate considerably declines for higher unemployment levels, outflows from unemployment decrease, too. Trajectories repelled from the equilibrium do not end up at unrealistic corner solutions.

It is possible to define parameters for (128) so that it maps a natural range of unemployment with an upper and lower bound onto itself. Within the natural range of unemployment, cycles can become chaotic. The conditions under which this will happen are shown next.

$f(U_{min})$ will be zero if

$$U_{\min} = L \cdot \frac{i}{i + o(U_{\min}) - 1}. \tag{136}$$

If U_{min} is chosen according to (136), the lower bound becomes zero per definition. The upper bound is

$$\overline{U} = f(0)$$

which can also be written as

$$\overline{U} = i \cdot L.$$

To guarantee that the upper bound does not exceed L, the inflow rate has to be $i \leq 1$. For such a map, all first iterates of unemployment levels that lie in the interval $[0; U^*]$ will be folded on the part of f that lies right to the unemployment equilibrium. All first iterates of unemployment levels that are larger than U_{min} will be lower than that. Hence, there is a tendency for unemployment to decline in this regime. Those unemployment levels between $[U^*; f^{-1}(U^*)]$ are iterated on the interval left to the equilibrium. Hence, there is a trapping area

$$[\underline{U}; \overline{U}]$$

which becomes for $f(U_{min})=0$, $[0; i \cdot L]$.

Within the natural range of unemployment, cycles might be of infinite order. Say, for example, that at $t=0$ unemployment is at U_{min} Then the first iterate will yield the lower bound of the natural range, which is zero. Now, all workers are employed. The outflow rate is at its highest possible level. But this cannot compensate the large inflows into unemployment that are caused by people who quit their jobs. The following period will start with an unemployment level that is at the upper bound of the natural range ($f^2(U_{min})=i \cdot L$). Inflows into unemployment are low and unemployment decreases, although the outflow rate is comparably low, too, due to the high competition for the fixed amount of jobs. If it can be shown that a period ahead from then, unemployment will be higher than U_{min}, from where the cycle started, a period three cycle would be given. This would imply unemployment cycles around the natural level of unemployment of infinite order (Li and Yorke 1975).

The derivation of the condition under which chaotic cycles in (128) may occur follows Hommes (1994) closely. The highly nonlinear nature of f impedes an explicit solution of U_{min} so that it is impossible to close the proof analytically. But it will be shown that there exists a set of parameters that generates a period three cycle. To derive the conditions, we choose a map $f(U_t)$ where $f(U_{min})=0$. The boundaries at zero and full employment are given by (134) and (135), respectively. Furthermore,

$$F(U_t) = -\mu \cdot (U_t - U_{\min}) \text{ for } 0 \le U_t \le U_{\min} \tag{137}$$

and

$$F(U_t) = \nu \cdot (U_t - U_{\min}) \text{ for } U_{\min} < U_t \le L \tag{138}$$

with

$$\mu = \frac{i \cdot L}{U_{\min}} \tag{139}$$

and

$$\nu = \frac{L - M}{L - U_{\min}} \tag{140}$$

shall be a linear version of f. Now, one can show that for F the following inequality holds

$$0 < U_{\min} < F(i \cdot L) < i \cdot L\,. \tag{141}$$

Per definition $U_{min}>0$. F was constructed in a way that $F(i{\cdot}L)<i{\cdot}L$ is always fulfilled, too. Therefore, it remains to be shown that

$$F(i \cdot L) - U_{\min} > \varepsilon \text{ for } \varepsilon > 0\,. \tag{142}$$

From (137) follows that (142) is equal to

$$\frac{L - M}{L - U_{\min}} \cdot (i \cdot L - U_{\min}) - U_{\min} > \varepsilon\,. \tag{143}$$

As L is considerably large compared to M and U_{min}, the ratio on the left hand side of (143) is almost one. Hence, (143) is fulfilled if the upper bound of the natural range of unemployment is more than two times larger than U_{min}.

Now, one has to pin down the difference of the third iterate of U_{min} between the linearized and the true model. If the difference is small enough, there is also a period three cycle in the nonlinear model. More exactly, the inequality

$$F^3(U_{\min}) - f^3(U_{\min}) < \varepsilon \tag{144}$$

must hold. Let δ_0 be an unemployment level that is slightly larger than U_{min} Then, the slope of the nonlinear model at δ_0 will be

$$\nu - \varepsilon_0 < f'(\delta_0) < \nu \text{ with } 0 < \varepsilon_0 < \nu \tag{145}$$

as it is next to the minimum of the quadratic map and the linearized map lies above f. Therefore, (144) becomes with (145)

$$F^3(U_{\min})-f^3(U_{\min})\le F(i\cdot L)-f'(\delta_0)\cdot(i\cdot L-\delta_0)\le \\ \le F(i\cdot L)-(v-\varepsilon_0)(i\cdot L-\delta_0) \quad (146)$$

The right hand side of (146) can be written as

$$F(i\cdot L)-(v-\varepsilon_0)(\delta_0-i\cdot L)=v\cdot(\delta_0-U_{\min})+\varepsilon_0\cdot(i\cdot L-\cdot\delta_0)\,. \quad (147)$$

(147) becomes equal to ε for

$$\varepsilon_0=\frac{1}{i\cdot L-\delta_0} \quad (148)$$

and

$$\delta_0=\frac{\varepsilon-1}{v}+U_{\min}\,. \quad (149)$$

(149) shows that δ_0 is larger than U_{min} if ε exceeds one. Hence, it follows from the inequality in (143) that a period three cycle will occur if the upper bound of the natural range is at least two times larger than U_{min}. As f furthermore maps onto itself, there may be cycles of infinite order within the natural range of unemployment. But as it is impossible to derive an explicit solution for U_{min}, nothing more can be said with an approach like that. However, setting, for example, L=1, M=0.125, i=0.1, and b=0.0003 one gets a sequence U_0=0.2, U_1=0.0027, U_2=0.0573, and U_3=0.0279 for f which is a period three cycle.

6.2 A calibrated version and evidence on worker flows

Simulations of (128) yield endogenous cycles that can be of finite order, like in Figure 38, or irregular order (Figure 39). Without exogenous shocks, unemployment varies around an unstable equilibrium. It is bounded from above and below. There is a 'natural range of unemployment'. The simulated time series is generated with parameters that are at least in the range of empirical estimates of labor markets. The yearly inflow rate is 0.1. That is, 10% of the employed workers are laid off or quit their jobs and enter the pool of unemployed within one year. The labor force is normalized to one. There come M=0.125 jobs to the market that are immediately filled by employed or unemployed workers. The time series show yearly rates of unemployment. There is an (unstable) 'natural rate of unemployment' of ≈1,2% in Figure 39. Now, assume the economy is at its unstable equilibrium. This exercise might look as being fruitless confronted with the large variation shown in Figure 39. But it allows some judgements on the plausibility of an unstable equilibrium. The outflow rate at the equilibrium is 9,5. This is rather high, but not far away from empirical outflow rates for economies that have low unemployment rates as it was the case in the U.K. and Western

Germany at the end of the sixties (c.f. Pissarides 1986, p.56; or Schettkat 1996, pp.257). Deviations from the natural level towards the upper bound are comparably large, too. In some periods with unemployment rates going up to 4% from levels around the natural rate in the previous period, absolute unemployment triples. Things look better for deviations to lower levels. The lower bound is at approximately 0,6%. The impact of on-the-job search on the emergence of cycles is shown in Figure 40. It shows long run states of the labor market model (128) for varying *b,* the parameter that determines the fraction of employed workers who are searching for a job. The larger *b* becomes, the more people will search while being employed. What was already discussed can be seen from the bifurcation diagram (Figure 40) again. Employed job search stabilizes the labor market.

If *b* becomes sufficiently large, there is a single long run equilibrium. However, for *b* comparably low, there is a chaotic attractor implying a very large number of long run unemployment levels that are bounded from above and below. The parameter value that was chosen in Figure 39 (b=0.0004) lies in the chaotic regime. By decreasing *b* from its stable level to the chaotic range, stable cycles of lower order will occur. There are parameters *b* for which unemployment follows a stable period two (c.f. Figure 38), period four, or period eight cycle and so forth. Values for *b* have to be bounded from below since an even lower parameter *b* would imply employment above the available labor force.

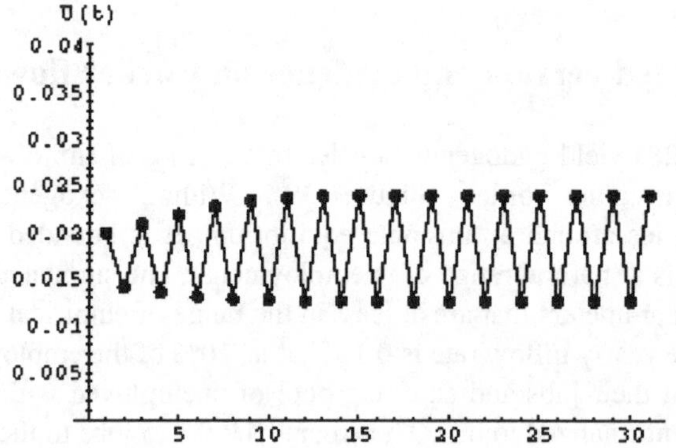

Figure 38: Time series unemployed, L=1, M=0.125, i=0.1, b=0.0008.

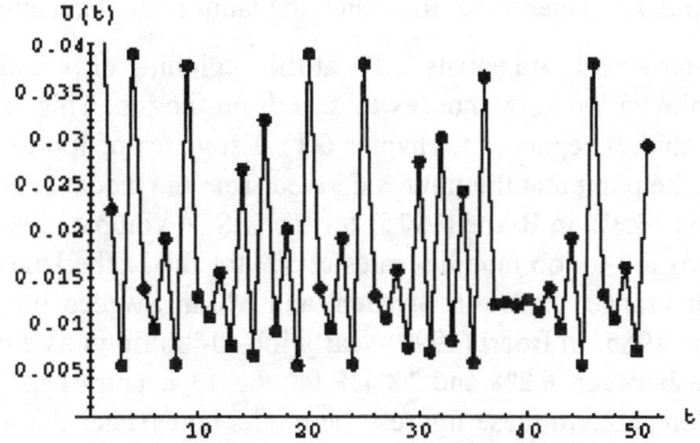

Figure 39: Time series unemployed, L=1, M=0.125, i=0.1, b=0.0004.

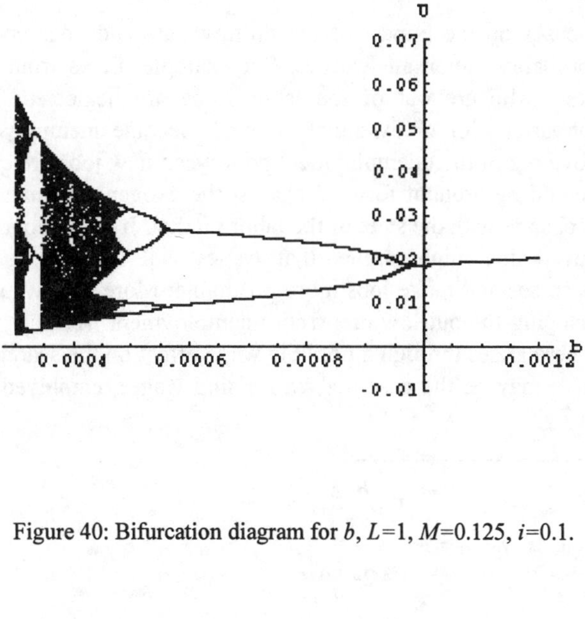

Figure 40: Bifurcation diagram for b, L=1, M=0.125, i=0.1.

Hence, endogenous dynamics occur for this specific example in a range where the magnitude of b can be approximately tripled from its lowest possible value. As before, one should keep in mind that bifurcation diagrams illustrate the long run behavior holding all other parameters constant. Insofar, it submits only limited information on the parameter space for which the labor market becomes unstable.

When the unemployment rate equals 1,2% at the beginning of period t, a fraction of 0,7% of employed workers chooses to search on-the-job. This is smaller that what empirical studies report (c.f. chapter 6.1). Estimates of job-to-job mobility rates strengthen the point that the figures derived from the model are too low. Job-to-job mobility is 14,3% in Byrne (1975) for the U.S. A comparative study of van Ours (1990) finds job-to-job mobility rates at 5% for the Netherlands, 9% for the U.K., 10,4% for France, 12,2% in Sweden, and 6% in Sweden for Labor Force Survey data from 1985. In Boeri (1999) yearly job-to-job flows as a percentage of employment are between 6,2% and 18,4% for the 13 countries that he presents estimates for. Compared to these figures, the model understates the importance of on-the-job search as the employed rather quit than search on-the-job. The results are better for estimates at the margin. Regressing on-the-job search on unemployment, Pissarides and Wadsworth (1994) find on-the-job search to decline by 40% when unemployment doubles. In Schettkat (1996) and van Ours (1990), a doubling of the unemployment rate decreases on-the-job search by 30% and 50%, respectively. Doubling unemployment in our model decreases the number of on-the-job searchers by 66%.[27] Hence, the model can cope better with changes of employed job search over the cycle, than with the stacks of people that search on-the-job and move from one job to another without spells of unemployment. At least, this is true for a calibration that yields irregular cycles.

The model focuses on the impact of the outflow rate and does not incorporate some other, probably important features. For example, flows from and into the pool of workers who are out of the labor force are neglected. Furthermore, unemployment varies with job dynamics as people become unemployed when jobs go sour, or move out of the unemployment pool when new jobs are created. Thus, an objection could be brought forward against the exogenous demand parameter M, as it might change with the state of the labor market. If unemployment is above the natural level, one might argue, that wages will fall due to some wage bargaining processes and make jobs more profitable. More jobs would come into the market changing the outflow rate from unemployment. Another problem that is not tackled here arises through a possible wage effect on the search behavior of the employed. It may be the case that with rising wages, employed workers are

---

27 The elasticity is $\eta_{S_N,U} = -\dfrac{1+\dfrac{b\cdot M}{S_N}}{1+2\cdot\dfrac{S_N}{U}}$

more inclined to search than the aggregate employment level dictates in this model. Wages may be an important variable that determines on-the-job search, although the model could cope quite well with estimates at the margin. But once more, initially sticking to one particular market feature helps highlighting the role of the latter. Eventually adding more market relations to a basic model allows discriminating between significant and less important nonlinearities. If more 'realism' enters and the basic properties do not vanish, the nonlinearity is probably worth paying attention to.

6.3 Is the natural rate a policy trap?

When employed and unemployed job searchers compete for a given number of job offers, the outflow rate from unemployment becomes downward sloping. The possible dynamic implications are an unstable 'natural rate of unemployment' and endogenous cycles within a bounded area. The parameters that generate a 'natural *range* of unemployment' are only backed by some empirical estimates. In particular, the model understates the magnitude of on-the-job search, increasing the likelihood that real labor market behavior is characterized by a stable 'natural rate of unemployment'. Endogenous cycles might thus be viewed as an exemption, and whether an outflow rate like ours is the crucial nonlinearity remains an unanswered question . But nevertheless, one should be aware of a 'natural *range* of unemployment'. In that case, the natural rate might not only vary because of exogenous factors. Movements may also be caused on the grounds of market structures themselves, raising important policy implications. An irregularly moving 'natural rate of unemployment' would be no robust tool to predict inflation. Deviations from the long run unemployment equilibrium would not indicate in which way monetary or fiscal policies should be targeted to beat inflationary or deflationary pressures. The causal relationships of a gap between actual unemployment and a falsely assumed fix 'natural rate of unemployment' and price movements would be blurred. The 'natural rate of unemployment' would become a policy trap.

7 Employment dynamics under wage setting

Wage setting curves are an alternative approach to determine labor supply behavior, as opposed to the representative agent who maximizes utility under some constraints. They might also be a more appropriate framework to explain labor market supply in markets where collective agreements play a significant role. The most important feature of wage setting curves, as opposed to the conventional labor supply curve, is that the wage curve always lies left of it and thus gives an explanation for unemployment. In this sense, the wage curve is not equal to labor supply, but describes a set of real wage employment combinations that can be interpreted as a quasi labor supply curve. It gives real wages that are consistent with certain labor market conditions, under the assumption that rents from production are divided between employers and employees in some way. More specifically, the real wage level will depend on variables like the employment level, the willingness of the unemployed to work, or unemployment benefits. Such an approach usually yields an upward sloping wage setting curve (Layard, Nickell, and Jackman 1991, Layard and Nickell 1986, Alogoskoufis and Manning 1988, Bean 1994, Franz 1996). The intuition behind this is that wage pressure rises as employment approaches the available labor force. However, an upward sloping wage setting curve is not a necessity. The quasi labor supply curve can slope downwards in the real wage employment space a case, that was also mentioned in Layard, Nickell, and Jackman (1991, p.340) and discussed in Funke (1990). And in fact, there are some good reasons to believe that the sign on employment in the wage setting curve can change. As will be shown later, this leads to endogenous adjustment dynamics in a 'right to manage model', where firms can hire and fire workers at almost zero costs. But first, a simple wage setting model will be developed. Along these lines, it will be discussed under which conditions the wage setting curve can slope downwards.

7.1 The wage setting curve

The wage setting curve is viewed as the outcome of a bargaining process between employers and workers over the rent of production. What is needed therefore, is an equation that describes the rent for a worker when being employed. Furthermore, one needs some measure for the rent of firms. The sum of both is the rent or surplus of production. Dividing the surplus between the two parties yields the wage setting curve.

Along the lines of Pissarides (1990) or Blanchard (1999) the value for a worker of being employed can be described as

$$r \cdot V_e = w + i \cdot (V_u - V_e). \tag{150}$$

The value of holding a job is the wage the worker receives, plus the difference in values from being unemployed and holding a job. Workers can loose their jobs and hence, the surplus from holding a job is weighed with the inflow rate to unemployment. Changes in the values of being employed that would usually add to the right hand side of the equation are neglected. The value of being employed on the right hand side of equation (150) must be equal to the value of an asset that could be held alternatively. The latter equalizing the value of being employed weighted with some discount factor *r*.

When the worker is unemployed, he will receive unemployment benefits *b*. In a broader interpretation, *b* would also capture the value of leisure that comes from non-working. While being unemployed, there is a chance for the worker to find a job. Ignoring the fact that the value of being unemployed might change over time, the sum of both components has to equal the value of being unemployment times the real interest rate *r*

$$r \cdot V_u = b + o \cdot (V_e - V_u). \tag{151}$$

Subtracting equation (150) from equation (151) will give the rent of a worker from having a job

$$V_e - V_u = \frac{1}{r+i+o} \cdot (w-b) \approx \frac{1}{o} \cdot (w-b). \tag{152}$$

It is positively dependent on the difference between the real wage and the reservation wage *b*. Increasing the interest rate, the inflow into unemployment, or the outflow rate from employment will decrease the value of a job. This is intuitively clear. If the probability of loosing a job rises, it is less desirable to hold this job. A higher outflow rate from unemployment means that it is easier to find a new job if unemployed. Hence, holding a job is once more comparably less desirable. If the opportunity costs of being employed are comparably high, the value of holding a job decreases, too. The ratio of one over the interest rate, the inflow rate, and the outflow rate can be approximated by the inverse of the outflow rate as the interest rate and the inflow rate are both small compared to the outflow rate from unemployment. Insofar, the value of being employed in excess of being unemployed is a function of the difference of the wage paid, and the reservation wage weighted with the inverse of the outflow rate. The latter is the average duration of unemployment. This means that the longer the expected unemployment spell is, the higher the rent is that workers attach to holding a job.

To get the rent of the firm, assume that it maximizes a profit function where labor is the only input. Of course, one can incorporate into the model some degree of market imperfection on the product market. This captures the idea that firms can set prices independently from their competitors to a certain degree. Like in the previous chapter on labor demand (chapter 4.1.1), the prices in the profit function will be a function of the output. With the profit maximizing real wage in (70), real profits per worker become

$$\frac{\Pi}{L \cdot p} = \frac{f(L)}{L} - (1 - \frac{1}{\eta}) \cdot f'(L) = y - w \,. \tag{153}$$

In a competitive market the demand elasticity on prices[28] becomes infinite. Then real profits per worker are given by the difference between average productivity and real wages. For a non-competitive market, η will be larger than one. Hence, the less competitive the product market is, the higher real profits will be per worker. Firms can take a larger rent by setting higher prices. The surplus from production is the sum of equations (152) and (153). This will be divided between both sides of the market. The firms and the workers have some degree of bargaining power, because each side will make zero rent if no wage can be found that satisfies the equations (152) and (153). Only if the real wage is above the reservation wage is the excess value of holding a job positive. For a wage that falls below b, workers do not participate in the labor market. This is the lower bound of potential real wages. The upper bound is given by the zero profit condition of firms. As w in (153) is equal to the profit maximizing real wage, any real wage that is higher than the average productivity of a worker y will lead to negative profits. Firms would rather choose to close their plants than to employ any worker in that case.

For reasons of simplicity, it is assumed that the surplus from production

$$S = \frac{1}{o} \cdot (w - b) + y - w \tag{154}$$

is divided between workers and firms in equal parts. This can be written as

$$V_e - V_u = \frac{1}{2} \cdot S \tag{155}$$

[28] η is in absolute value.

and

$$\frac{\Pi}{L} = \frac{1}{2} \cdot S . \tag{156}$$

Equalizing equation (155) and (156) will give the wage setting curve as a function of the employment level.

$$w = \frac{1}{1 + \frac{1}{o}} .(y - b) + b . \tag{157}$$

The dependency on the employment level enters the wage setting equation through the average productivity and the outflow rate from unemployment (or the average duration of unemployment)[29]. Equation (157) describes the real wage level as an outcome of bargaining over rents between firms and workers. As the bargaining power shifts with labor market conditions, it is usually argued that a higher employment level will result in a comparably higher real wage level. Workers will get a larger share of the surplus when unemployment is low. Conversely, higher unemployment would increase the bargaining power of firms. The bargained real wages would be lower, then. As already mentioned, the wage bargaining curve is bounded from above and below. The boundaries can easily be derived from equation (157) with some standard assumptions on the outflow rate from unemployment. When employment almost equals the labor force, it should be very easy for an unemployed person to find a new job. The duration of unemployment becomes infinitely small. The ratio on the right hand side of (157) becomes one and hence, the real wage will be equal to the average productivity. Firms make zero profits. The whole surplus goes to the worker. On the other extreme, when the entire labor force is unemployed, the outflow rate from unemployment becomes very small. Or, in terms of the average duration of unemployment, workers are unemployed for a really long time. The bargained real wage will be equal to the reservation wage b. Firms get the whole surplus from production.

7.1.1 Can the wage setting curve slope downwards?

A closer look at equation (157) will show that within these boundaries, the wage setting curve is not necessarily upward sloping. If one keeps the reservation wage b constant, the slope of the wage setting curve is determined by the outflow rate from unemployment and the average productivity. Like the outflow rate, as was shown in chapter 6.1, the average productivity is also unlikely to be constant over a larger range of employment levels. This is especially true for the short run. To

---

29 The wage setting curve does not explicitly depend on η, since product market in-competitiveness is already captured by the price determined real wage.

illustrate the impact on the wage setting curve that runs through a changing average productivity, assume for convenience that the production technology is Cobb Douglas with a fixed capital stock. This gives three basic cases: a constant, a decreasing, or an increasing average productivity. Average productivity will only be constant over a larger range of employment levels if the production coefficient on labor is one. In that case, average productivity equals the marginal product. For increasing returns, average productivity rises with higher employment levels. Decreasing returns ($0<\alpha<1$) yield an average productivity that declines with higher employment levels. Sure, all this holds only for the short run if firms cannot adjust their capital stock. If they could, they would no longer be subject to diminishing returns from labor. Any employment level would cause the same average productivity in the medium and long run, even under decreasing returns in the short run. But it is unlikely that the capital stock adjusts immediately due to comparably large investment lags. If this is true, average productivity will change for production technologies where one has either decreasing or increasing returns. Given the case of decreasing returns, moving toward lower employment levels coincides with an increasing average productivity, so y becomes larger on the left hand side of equation (157). With every thing else constant, the bargained real wage will be higher for the lower employment level. As there is comparably more to lose for firms with a larger average productivity, they agree on a higher wage. They concede to workers' claims. In other words, there is upward real wage pressure at lower employment levels that comes from an increase in average productivity. If the effect is strong enough, there will be a downward sloping wage setting curve.

Increasing returns have an opposite effect on the slope of the wage setting curve. Firms move towards lower average productivity levels when employment decreases. Ceteris paribus, the bargained real wage will be lower as y declines in (157). As an increase in employment will yield a higher average productivity the wage setting curve will be rather steeply upward sloping with increasing returns in production. It is obvious that the choice of the production function drives the shape of the wage setting curve. The assumption of a constant average productivity and hence, a wage setting curve that is independent from the production technology, may only be valid for a small employment range or under the specific case of constant returns to scale. Once more holding all other things constant, a production function that has initially decreasing but increasing returns to scale for employment larger than some critical level, will cause a U-shaped wage setting curve. Hence, the sign of the wage setting schedule seems to be not that clear at all.

For reasons of convenience, the outflow rate was kept constant up to now. This is surely too crude of a simplification. It is well known that chances of the unemployed for finding a new job vary with the level of employment. Hence, the exercises above can only illustrate the likely impact of various production functions on the wage setting behavior. What one furthermore needs, is an understanding of what labor market conditions drive the outflow rate from unemployment. Chapter 6 on worker flows and employment cycles proposed a framework for how to think about the outflow from unemployment into employment. Employed and unemployed job searchers competed for a fixed number of jobs. The outflow rate from unemployment was a downward sloping function in unemployment. No matter if one agrees with the notion of on-the-job search, the sign of the outflow rate seems to be clear: the unemployed have better chances at finding a job if unemployment is low. Having a look at (157) shows what this means for the wage setting curve. At high employment levels, the outflow rate from unemployment is comparably high, too. This causes upward pressure on real wages. Workers do not fear long spells of unemployment. They take a comparably large share of the surplus. Consequently, wages are rather high. The outflow rate from unemployment declines for lower employment levels. More unemployed workers compete for a given number of jobs. The chances of getting this job deteriorate. They will face a higher average duration of unemployment. As the fear of becoming unemployed is larger, workers will bargain for lower wages. Hence, if there was a constant average productivity, a varying outflow rate from unemployment would generate an upward sloping wage setting curve.

Taking account of both effects, the one that runs through the outflow rate and the one that is caused by a non-constant average productivity give the slope of a wage setting curve like (157). The slope of the wage setting curve is more likely to be positive, the stronger the outflow rate increases with employment, given a certain degree of decreasing returns. However, there will still be a downward sloping wage setting curve under decreasing returns if the effect that runs through the duration of unemployment is fairly weak. In that case, higher unemployment levels would only slightly reduce the bargaining power of workers. Though the outflow rate decreases, upward real wage pressure would still be sufficiently high so that workers take advantage of higher average productivity. Such a wage bargaining outcome is likely for an economy where workers' characteristics differ from those of the unemployed. Then, the latter do not really compete with those workers who might become unemployed due to excessive wage bargains.

7.1.2 A further look at the slope: The role of long term unemployment

The wage equation (157) was derived from a uniquely perceived outflow rate from unemployment for all workers. The assumption of a single outflow rate for all types of workers can be seen in equation (151). It gives the value that a worker attaches to being unemployed. The higher the outflow rate from unemployment is, the higher is the value of being unemployed. It is less frightening to become unemployed since the loss in wealth is considered as being small. Workers assume that they will find a new job soon. Such a unique outflow rate from unemployment for all workers might be a crude assumption. Especially, if there is no homogeneous pool of unemployed workers, or firms do not find all types of unemployed workers equally valuable. In that case, the wage setting schedule can change significantly. For the purpose of illustration, suppose that unemployment is comparably high. Furthermore, the pool of unemployed shall consist to a comparably large fraction of long term unemployed workers. If the long term unemployed are less competitive than the short term unemployed, unemployment is less frightening for those workers who still have a job. Their perceived outflow rate from unemployment is higher than the level of unemployment would usually imply. They do not fear long spells of unemployment and will bargain for a higher share of the surplus, which causes considerable wage pressure even at high levels of unemployment. The less downward real wage pressure the long term unemployed can exert, the more likely the wage setting curve will have a negative slope.

Time series studies show that exit rates from unemployment decrease with the duration of unemployment (van den Berg and van Ours 1994, Jackman and Layard 1991). Various reasons have been proposed to explain the decline in transition rates for long term unemployed. It was conjectured that as the attitude to work worsens, search intensities are lower for long term unemployed. They may become addicted to social insurance payments. Less workers would arrive for a given number of job offers. However, the detrimental impact of unemployment compensation on employment is not clear cut (c.f. Schmid 1995, Schmid and Reissert 1996). It seems that if there is any common ground that empirical studies on the impact of unemployment insurance can agree on, it is that duration matters more than replacement rates (Freeman 1998). Other candidates that might explain the decline in exit rates for long term unemployed better than unemployment insurance are deteriorating skills and adverse signals. Qualifications of long term unemployed are likely to become outdated as those people cannot participate in the technological progress. Excluded from learning on-the-job, they cannot keep track with the requirements of "nowadays" jobs. The rate of depreciation on qualifications is furthermore boosted if technological progress is skill biased. (And usually it is skill biased.) In the end, long term unemployed become less attractive to employers. Exit rates for long term unemployed would decline as firms will prefer a short term unemployed over a long term unemployed. The chances of finding a new job for an employed, should he become unemployed, are better than for a person with a protracted unemployment record. For sound reasons, he can expect a relatively short duration of unemployment even when overall unemployment is high. The chances of long term unemployed relative to short term unemployed might deteriorate, too, if employers interpret long term unemployment as an adverse signal. Under information asymmetries, firms have high costs finding out about the real productivity of applicants. To overcome these asymmetries and to economize on hiring costs, they may decide to apply hiring rules. If they think that long spells of unemployment signal a 'lemon' (Akerlof 1970), the ranking of unemployed applicants (Blanchard and Diamond 1994) with respect to the length of their unemployment spell can become a popular hiring rule. Correlating low productivity with long-term unemployment can be an efficient measure to overcome information asymmetries. Obviously, the chances of getting a job deteriorate for long-term unemployed. Firms do not consider long-term unemployed as potential employees. Once more, the perceived outflow rate of an employed worker, should he become unemployed, will be higher than under the assumption of a homogenous pool of unemployed workers.

From high perceived outflow rates, it is a short way to argue for comparably higher real wage pressure at low employment levels. It can immediately be seen from equation (157), if o is interpreted as the outflow rate of an employed worker would he become unemployed. The bargained real wage is higher than with a homogenous unemployment pool, as the expected loss from being unemployed is comparably smaller. An insider outsider argument (Lindbeck and Snower 1988) would arrive at the same result. Higher outflow rates for short term unemployed improve the bargaining power of the incumbent workforce. If insiders succeed in setting wages independent from the behavior of outsiders, they will exert comparably larger wage pressure at lower employment levels (Gregory 1986). The consequences of long term unemployment are obvious. There may be considerable upward real wage pressure at low employment levels. The wage setting curve might slope downwards, at least for a range of lower employment levels. It will be shown that a U-shaped wage setting curve can generate endogenous employment dynamics under some additional assumptions, especially low hiring and firing costs.

7.2 A tentative view: employment dynamics in a 'hire and fire' economy

It was assumed that firms and workers share the surplus of production by bargaining over real wages. The wage setting curve describes the outcome of the bargaining process. With an upward sloping wage setting curve, and a downward sloping quasi labor demand curve, there will always be one market equilibrium. This is often called the natural rate of unemployment, or the non-accelerating-inflation-rate-of-unemployment (NAIRU). At the natural rate of unemployment, real wages and employment are consistent with the share that both sides of the labor market want to capture from the surplus. At the equilibrium level, workers accept a real wage that coincides with maximum profits of firms. If employment was higher than in equilibrium, wages that workers accept would be higher, too (given an upward sloping wage setting curve). A higher real wage, however, would mean a lower demand for labor since firms move up their demand curve. Hence, neither real prices nor quantities would be in equilibrium anymore. The same holds for deviations to the left. Now, workers would accept a real wage less than in equilibrium. Firms would be willing to pay a higher real wage than in equilibrium as the marginal productivity is higher. Once more, real prices and quantities do not fit, regardless, whether employment deviates from the natural level positively or negatively. In either case, both sides of the market have diverging views on how to share the surplus from production. Hence, the question arises how the market will find its way back to the equilibrium. It will be illustrated that under specific assumptions the adjustment process can become irregular, in the sense that employment oscillates around an unstable natural rate with frequencies of infinite order.

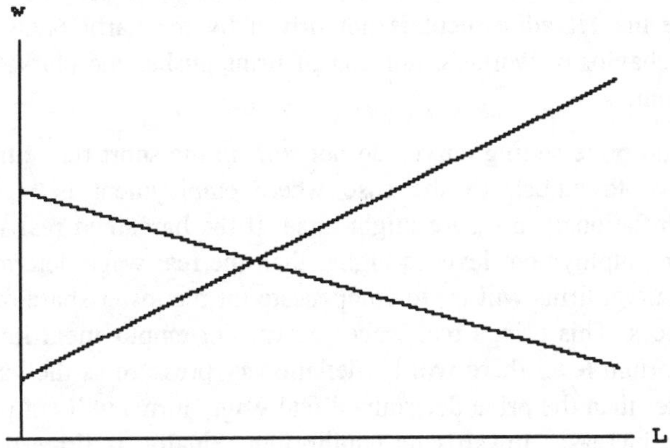

Figure 41: Market equilibrium in a wage and price setting model.

There are basically three mechanisms through which the market can equilibrate (Carlin and Soskice 1990). Suppose that unemployment is below the natural level. First, the wage or the price setting curve can shift. For employment above the natural rate, this would require an outward shift of the price setting curve or a downward shift in the wage setting curve. Such an outward shift of the quasi labor demand curve would occur if the product market becomes more competitive and the price elasticity increases (c.f. (70))[30]. A decrease in the reservation wage

[30] Another reason for an outward shift of the quasi labor demand curve would be a positive productivity shock. However, as was argued at length, the shape the wage setting curve is dependent on the production function (c.f. Franz 1995, p.6). Changes in the demand for labor due to a positive productivity shock will also shift the wage setting curve. As average productivity increases, the rent to the firm at any employment level increases, too. The wage setting curve will shift upwards. If both effects compensate each other, the natural rate will not change at all. Insofar, one has to be cautious with comparative static analysis and think about the interrelation between the wage setting schedule and the production technology.

would cause a downward shift of the wage setting curve (157). Both movements would yield a new and lower natural rate of unemployment. If the shift in the natural rate matches the original deviation from the old natural rate, claims for the surplus are consistent again. Shifts of both curves in the opposite direction would solve the problem for a deviation from the natural rate to higher unemployment. However, one would probably not observe shifts of the wage and price curves due to a disequilibrium employment level in the short run. In fact, the causes for shifts in the wage and price setting curves seem to be either long run phenomena or new market conditions imposed by exogenous factors. For example, governments may decide to fight monopolistic market structures or cut unemployment benefits. In that case, the market adjustment is not driven by the participants themselves. Neither the behavior of workers, nor that of firms pushes the market towards its new equilibrium.

If the wage and price setting curves do not shift in the short run, either prices or quantities have to adjust. In the case where employment is higher than in equilibrium, inflationary pressure might arise. If the bargained real wage for the disequilibrium employment level is higher than the real wage determined by the price setting curve, firms will try to compensate for the lower share of the surplus by raising prices. This brings real wages down. For employment lower than the natural equilibrium level there will be deflationary pressure as the bargained real wage is smaller than the price determined real wage. Firms will cut prices so that the real wage increases towards its equilibrium. Finally, if firms do not adjust prices they will vary their stock of employment. Which of the two mechanisms underlies the adjustment process depends on whether there are price or quantity rigidities. In the following, prices shall be rather sticky. This is to focus on the extreme case where the market solely adjusts through quantity changes.

Suppose both sides of the market bargain at discrete time intervals. The wage setting curve describes the bargained real wages along different employment levels. Wage contracts shall be binding. If the bargained real wage is not the equilibrium real wage, firms are not on their labor demand curve. Then, there will be pressure from the labor demand side that changes the current state of the labor market. If, as it was assumed, wage contracts are binding and prices are sticky, there is only one degree of freedom left. Firms will very likely want to adjust their labor force. Whether the labor market will nonetheless remain on the wage setting curve is a question of rigidities that may impede labor force adjustments. If firms face high employment adjustment costs implied by severance payments, or hiring costs, they might not want to adjust their workforce. Rather than hiring or firing people (or changing prices which is per assumption also costly), they accept the market real wage even though the real wage employment combination might not be on their demand curve. However, if there are only small costs for adjusting the labor force, firms will choose to hire or fire people. It pays to change the stock of the incumbent labor force and move towards the optimal labor demand. With rapid quantity adjustment, the labor market will stay on the wage setting curve for a comparably short time only. Right after the real wage contract was made, firms will choose the employment level that is consistent for them with the bargained real wage. This employment level will hold until the next bargaining round has taken place. After that, firms will adjust their work force according to the new bargained wage. Insofar, the market will always be on the demand curve when employment adjustment costs are low and real wages do not adjust due to binding wage contracts and sticky prices. Firms can choose their optimal employment level. They have the 'right to manage', and by doing so they establish a negative correlation between real wages and employment.

Consider, for example, a positive deviation from equilibrium. As the wage setting curve gives the outcome of the bargaining, the bargained real wage will be higher than the price determined real wage. As soon as the wage contract is fixed, firms will adjust their labor force. The employment level that firms will choose will be consistent with their profit maximization rule. Hence, the market will be on the quasi labor demand curve again. Employment is lower now, and after a while the wage contract of the preceding period expires. A new bargaining round starts. Confronted with rather high unemployment, workers' bargaining power decreases. They will accept lower real wages. Firms take a larger share of the surplus. After the contract is fixed, firms begin hiring. They adjust their work force to maximize profits. Relative to the contract length, it takes them only a short time to get on their labor demand curve again. Formally, such an adjustment mechanism can be written in the following way. From maximizing profits

$$\max \Pi = p(f(L)) \cdot f(L) - w \cdot L \qquad (158)$$

firms derive their quasi labor demand curve (price determined real wage schedule). The price determined real wage that maximizes profits at a given time t is (c.f. chapter 4.1)

$$w_t^D = (1 - \frac{1}{\eta}) \cdot f'(L_t)\,. \qquad (159)$$

Hence, labor demand as a function of real wages can be written as

$$L_t = f'^{-1}(\frac{\eta}{\eta - 1}) \cdot w_t^D) \qquad (160)$$

if the quasi labor demand curve is downward sloping. This will be fulfilled as long as mark ups are not strongly procyclical and the production technology has decreasing returns (c.f chapter 4.1).

When the wage setting curve is a function of the employment level only, the real wage at any time t has to be consistent with the going employment level

$$w_t^S = g(L_t)\,. \qquad (161)$$

The real wage level is the outcome of the bargaining between firms and workers and may not maximize firms' profits. As firms do not face adjustment costs, they will choose an employment level that maximizes their profits given the bargained real wage at the beginning of the period. Workers will be dismissed or hired until the optimal level of employment is reached. This is the level of employment that will hold for the following period. By the time the bargained contract expires, this will also be the employment level that determines the bargained real wage in the following round. Hence, inserting the wage setting curve (161) into the labor demand function (160) gives the employment level for the consecutive period

$$L_{t+1} = f'^{-1}\left(\frac{\eta}{\eta-1} \cdot g(L_t)\right). \tag{162}$$

Equilibrium employment is given by

$$L^* = f'^{-1}(g(L^*)). \tag{163}$$

As long as labor demand is a downward sloping function and the wage setting curve is upward sloping, there will always be a single equilibrium. With a quadratic wage setting curve, there might be more than one equilibrium or no equilibrium at all. Given there is at least one equilibrium, it will be stable if

$$\left| \frac{df'^{-1}}{dL_t} \cdot \frac{dg(L_t)}{dL_t} \right|_{L^*} < 1. \tag{164}$$

To show the possibility of complex employment dynamics under the assumption of a U-shaped wage setting curve, the latter will be approximated by a quadratic function. The price setting curve, also highly stylized, will be a linear function of the employment level. If the exercise would be beyond an illustrative purpose one would like to model both sides of the market explicitly based on the features discussed above that drive a U-shaped wage setting curve. This is not the aim at this stage.

Case 5 - Employment dynamics with a U-shaped wage setting curve

The wage setting curve is approximated with a quadratic function in L

$$w^S = b + c \cdot (L - L_c)^2. \tag{165}$$

The price setting curve is downward sloping

$$w^D = a - m \cdot L. \tag{166}$$

All parameters a, b, c, and m are positive, and $0<L_c<1$. Employment can vary between $0 \leq L \leq 1$. The quasi labor demand curve and the wage setting curve have a finite value at zero employment. This implies that there is an upper bound to average productivity when employment approaches zero. For reasons outlined in the previous chapters, the wage setting curve changes its slope. The wage setting curve slopes downward when employment is smaller than L_c. It has a positive sign for $L>L_c$.

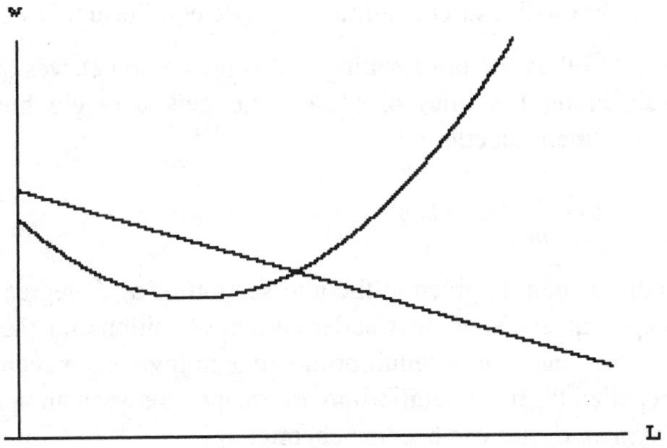

Figure 42: Short run labor market model with a downward sloping quasi-labor demand curve and a U-shaped wage setting curve.

Though the labor market has a single equilibrium in Figure 42, it is obvious that by shifting the wage setting curve upwards or the quasi labor demand curve downwards, multiple equilibria are possible. With an adjustment rule like (154), the low employment equilibrium would be unstable. A deviation from that equilibrium to the left would spark higher wage aggressiveness. The bargained real wage would be higher than the price determined real wage. After the wage contract would have been fixed, firms would begin to dismiss workers and move up the labor demand curve. A deviation from the low employment equilibrium to the right leads to a smaller bargained real wage. Now firms can profit from hiring workers. The labor market will move down the quasi labor demand curve towards the high employment equilibrium. A multiple equilibria case is particularly interesting from a perspective of efficient employment policies. If an economy sits at the unstable low employment equilibrium, it only needs a small positive aggregate demand shock and the labor market will move to the high employment equilibrium. Then real wages will be lower (if the price setting curve is downward sloping). Any deviation to the left side of the low employment equilibrium would immediately lead to zero employment with adjustment dynamics along (154)[31]. With a U-shaped wage setting curve, there may also be no equilibrium at all. If the wage setting curve sufficiently shifts upwards or the quasi labor demand curve downwards, both curves may not intersect. Nothing can be said about the labor market behavior on the grounds of (154). Only if one assumes a very high degree of stickiness in prices or quantities may it be reasonable to conclude that employment follows something like a random walk. For those reasons, the following discussion will restrict itself to the single equilibrium case.

With (158) and (159) as the price setting and wage setting curves and a dynamic adjustment rule along the lines of (154), one gets a single humped shaped employment adjustment function

$$L_{t+1} = \frac{1}{m}(a-b) - \frac{c}{m} \cdot (L_t - L_0)^2 \tag{167}$$

Equilibrium employment is given at the intersection of a 45-degree line with the adjustment map. One can show that under certain conditions for the wage setting and the price setting, curve equilibrium unemployment becomes unstable. Trajectories repelled from the equilibrium are trapped between an upper and lower bound. Employment cycles can become chaotic.

The stability condition can be derived from (154), (158), and (159), which yields

$$-1 < 2 \cdot \frac{c}{m} \cdot (L^* - L_c) < 1 \tag{168}$$

If the adjustment map crosses the equilibrium condition at a slope smaller than –1, the equilibrium will be unstable. Instability is more likely for a steeper quasi labor demand curve and a stronger U-shaped wage setting curve. Due to the single humped shape of the adjustment map, all trajectories that start within a set S will stay within this interval as long as the maximum of the adjustment map is lower than the employment level where the adjustment map crosses the X-axis. If these conditions are fulfilled all trajectories will finally be trapped in a natural range of employment

$$[\underline{L}; \overline{L}],$$

---

31 This is not to say that multiple equilibrium labor markets are less compelling. In fact, they can give interesting insights into the functioning of labor markets. Under the assumption of considerably high price and quantity adjustment costs, the economy can be stuck at the unstable low employment equilibrium for quite a while. Manning (1990), for example, models a multiple equilibria labor market where the price setting curve partly slopes upwards and the wage setting curve is downward sloping. Stability properties are discussed on the grounds of an objective function where agents face quadratic adjustment costs.

where the upper bound is the first iterate of the employment level that maximizes the adjustment map, and the lower bound is the second iterate of L_m. Applying the Li and Yorke (1975) theorem, one can show that employment cycles in the natural range can become chaotic.

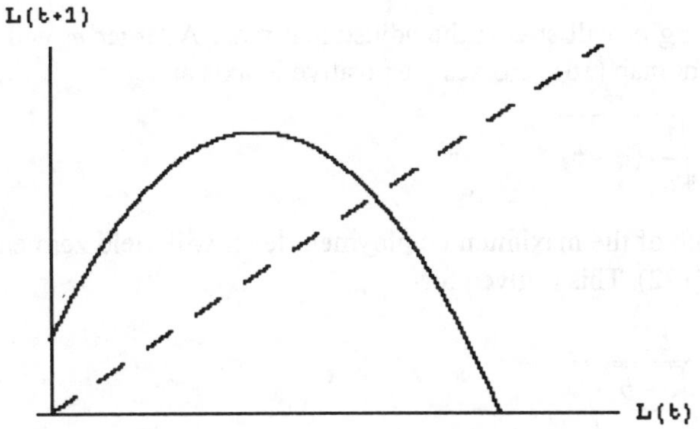

Figure 43: Employment adjustment map.

It was already shown that the iterative function

$$L_{t+1} = \frac{1}{m} \cdot (a-b) - \frac{c}{m} \cdot (L_t - L_c)^2 \qquad (169)$$

has an interval that maps onto itself. What lacks is the proof of a period three cycle

$$f(\overline{L}) \leq L_R < L_m < \overline{L} \qquad (170)$$

within this interval. The plan is to show that it is possible to stretch the quadratic function in a way that the first iteration of L_m yields the upper bound

$$\overline{L}$$

that is equal to the employment level at which the adjustment map crosses the X-axis. Then

$$f^2(L_m) = f(\overline{L}) = 0 .$$

This gives

$$f(\overline{L}) < L_m < \overline{L}.$$

Finally, it will be argued that there is an L_R, which iterated once, yields L_m.

Equation (161) has its maximum at $L_m = L_c$. The maximum employment level is

$$f(L_c) = \frac{1}{m} \cdot (a-b). \tag{171}$$

Hence, lowering m will stretch the adjustment map. A larger m will compress it. The adjustment map (161) crosses the positive X-axis at

$$\overline{L} = L_c + \sqrt{\frac{1}{c} \cdot (a-b)}. \tag{172}$$

The first iterate of the maximum employment level will yield zero employment if (171) equals (172). This is given for

$$m = \frac{a-b}{L_c + \sqrt{\frac{a-b}{c}}}. \tag{173}$$

As long as m is larger than this critical value, f will map onto itself. For m in (173), the following inequality holds

$$L_c < f(L_c) = \overline{L}.$$

As per assumption, m is chosen so that the adjustment map is zero at

$$f(\overline{L}),\ f(\overline{L}) = f^2(L_c) = 0,$$

and the inequality becomes

$$f^2(L_c) < L_c < f(L_c).$$

The last part of the proof is to show that there exists an $0 \leq L_R$ which gives $f(L_R) = L_c$. Such an L_R exists if $f(0) \leq L_c$. With

$$f(0) = \frac{1}{m} \cdot [(a-b) - c \cdot L_c^2]$$

and m taken from (173), a period three cycle

$$f(\overline{L}) \leq L_R < L_m < \overline{L}$$

follows if the feasible inequality

$$\sqrt{\frac{a-b}{c}} - \left(\frac{L_c + \sqrt{\frac{a-b}{c}}}{a-b}\right) \cdot c \cdot L_c^2 \leq 0 \tag{174}$$

is fulfilled.

Even if a labor market like (160) is not in the chaotic regime, there are interesting properties that arise from comparably flat wage setting and quasi labor demand curves. Figure 44 shows an employment adjustment path for an initial employment level that differs from the stable equilibrium by 10%. The deviation from the equilibrium might have occurred through an exogenous shock via the wage setting or quasi labor demand curve. The wage setting curve may have shifted up so that the new employment equilibrium is 10% below the old one, or labor demand may have shifted to the left causing the same effect on equilibrium employment. Even after 30 iterations, the labor market has not reached its new equilibrium. An adjustment rule like (154) delivers a propagation mechanism for exogenous shocks to labor markets that yields an economy which will suffer from this impulse for a comparably long time. Both parties of the labor market just do not bargain for the real wage that is consistent with the price determined real wage on the side of the firms. This misperception of the consequences of their bargaining behavior prevents a rapid return to the equilibrium.

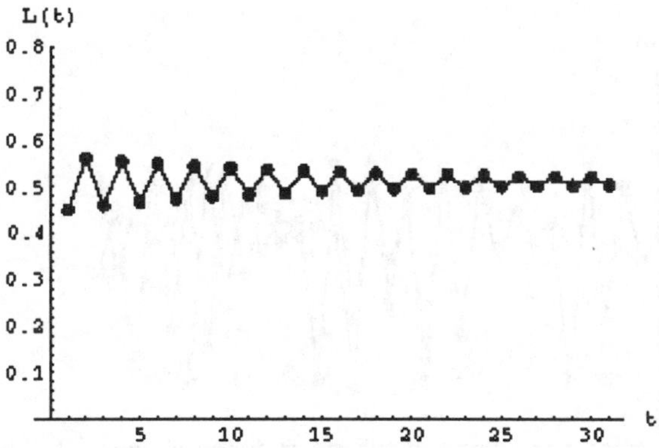

Figure 44: Time series on employment for a stable equilibrium, L_0=0.45, a=1.25, m=0.9, b=0.7, L_c=0.3, c=2.

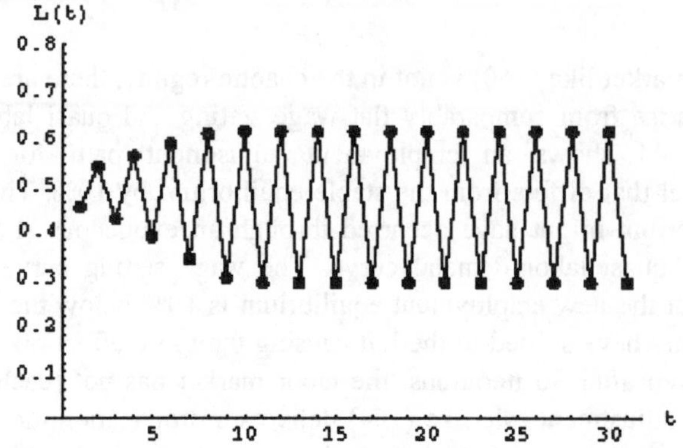

Figure 45: Period two employment cycle, L_0=0.45, a=1.25, m=0.9, b=0.7, L_c=0.3, c=3.

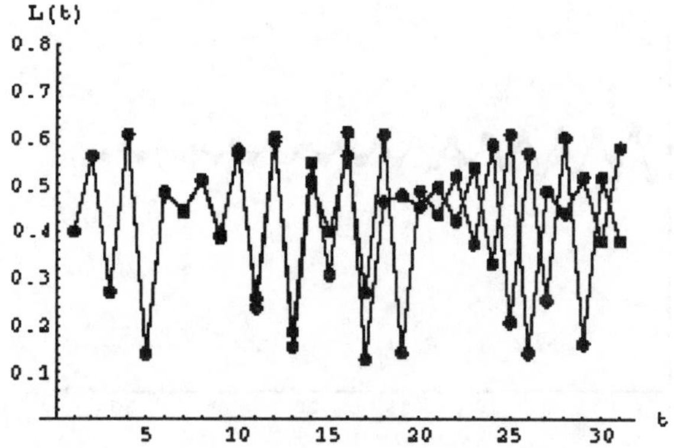

Figure 46: Time series on employment with an unstable equilibrium and bounded oscillations, parameters correspond to the labor market model in Figure 43 with L_0=0.4 and L_0=0.4004, respectively.

For a more strengthened humped shaped form of the wage setting curve, one gets stable employment cycles of finite order (Figure 45). In Figure 46 it does not take any exogenous shock to make the time series qualitatively look like real data time series. Employment varies erratically on the grounds of a deterministic model (160). One of the time series starts at an initial point L_0=0.4 that is close to the unstable equilibrium. Even after 30 iterations, it does not settle to the equilibrium. Employment shifts up and down where periods with rather large amplitudes are followed by smooth paths with only little change in the level of employment. What can also be seen in Figure 46 is that trajectories that are initially close will diverge after a while. Both time series started at an initial value that differed only with 0.1%. Nevertheless, the time paths do not show any similarity after 17 iterations, although they might come close to each other again for a while. Sensitivity on initial conditions makes long run forecasts impossible. Although one would see exactly the same employment path if the same initial point and the same parameters were chosen, this is not achievable in a real life context. There will always be measurement errors when one tries to determine the initial state of the labor market. Furthermore, it would be unrealistic to exclude any stochastic component. Although it makes sense to develop pure nonlinear deterministic models to show the dynamic implications, exogenous factors will play at least some role. If there is sensitive dependence on the initial stage of the labor market, the slightest exogenous shock will change the future tremendously.

The bifurcation diagram (Figure 47) shows the long run behavior of the labor market model given by (160). The long run employment levels result from iterating the adjustment map 200 times and dropping the first 100 values. The bifurcation diagram gives employment levels as a function of the parameter c. If c=2, the adjustment map yields a single long run employment level (L=0.51). Increasing c changes the long run behavior of the model via a flip bifurcation. At c=3, for example, there is a period two cycle. This means that even in the long run, employment changes from a high level in this period to a lower level in the consecutive period and back. Increasing c even further paves the way for additional flip bifurcations. Each of which doubles the possible long run employment levels. Finally, the chaotic regime is reached where there is an infinite number of long run states. Within a bounded range, the natural range of employment, all kinds of long run states are possible. As increasing c strengthens the U-shaped nature of the wage setting curve, this parameter shows the consequences for employment dynamics if such effects like high ratios of long term unemployment or strongly decreasing returns shift the bargaining power towards the employed workers. Then, a downward sloping wage setting curve folds back trajectories that are repelled from an unstable equilibrium. Should employment fall below the equilibrium, higher wage pressure will cause a real wage that is above the one that would be bargained for if the wage setting curve was linear or monotonous. This dampens the employment adjustment of firms. As the real wage is higher compared to the linear case, firms will hire less workers. Employment expands to a smaller degree so that the amplitudes of the employment path cannot increase infinitely. Hence, a nonlinear wage setting curve can explain why employment does not explode, even if the wage setting curve is steeper than the quasi labor demand curve which is probably the more likely case in equilibrium. Some empirical evidences on this topic will be discussed later on (c.f. chapter 7.3).

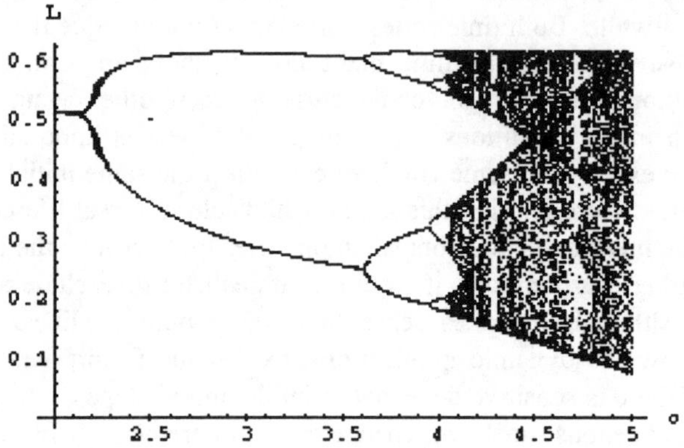

Figure 47: Bifurcation diagram for the labor market model (167) when parameter c changes, a=1.25, m=0.9, b=0.7, L_c=0.3.

As within the other models in the previous chapters, the question arises why this should happen in a context of rational agents. In a world where workers and firms know the right model, no such behavior would occur. They would probably change their bargaining mechanism if they see that it takes such a long time for the labor market to settle down at its equilibrium level. Maybe, workers would anticipate that a bargained real wage above the price determined real wage will force firms to downsize their workforce. The fear of a job loss would probably moderate upward real wage pressure when actual employment is to the right of the equilibrium employment level. In the case of excess unemployment, real wage pressure would rise under the assumption of forward looking agents as workers can expect that firms will hire right after the wage contract was settled. In both cases, there would be a stronger tendency to return to the equilibrium. But, what is true for regular dynamics, which cause consistent patterns in the autocorrelation function, allowing both sides of the market to draw firm conclusions on the consequences of their behavior - is at least partly wrong for the chaotic regime. As was argued in chapter 5, agents can draw only limited information on the system's behavior if they do not know the exact model, but apply some simple empirical tools to learn about the underlying economic mechanisms. It was shown that under chaotic dynamics, the coefficients of an autocorrelation function may have no robust pattern when the parameters of the model are slightly changed. The same argument applies here, too. In the chaotic regime, a 'right-to-manage' model can be consistent with rational behavior.

7.3 Evidence on the parameters of the model

It would certainly be a futile exercise to confront a model like (162) with data on real wage and employment cycles. The functional forms of the wage setting and price setting curves capture the underlying economic relationships in a highly stylized fashion. Any quantitative validity beyond the qualitative properties of the model would certainly be very surprising. But still, one may want to confront some of the assumptions with evidence on coefficients of wage and price setting curves, employment adjustment, and bargaining arrangements.

Of particular interest are the signs and magnitudes of the slopes of the wage and price setting curves, since equilibrium employment will become unstable (162) if the slope of the wage setting curve exceeds the absolute value of the slope of the quasi labor demand curve. In fact, the evidence on the slopes of wage setting and the short run price setting curves suggests that this cannot be excluded. Layard, Nickell and Jackman (1991, p.449-496) present their own estimates together with a summary of estimates of Newell and Symons (1985), Alogoskoufis and Manning (1988a), Bean, Layard, and Nickell (1986), and Grubb (1986). Layard, Nickell, and Jackman themselves estimated price setting and wage setting curves for 19 countries. The parameters on unemployment in the price setting equation are negative in four out of 19 cases. In other words, in most countries the price setting curve seems to slope downwards at the equilibrium. The coefficients on unemployment in the wage setting curve equations are negative for all countries, indicating that the wage setting curve slopes upward in the real wage employment space. For those countries where the parameter on unemployment in the price setting curve is not negative, one finds 10 cases where the slope of the wage setting curve is steeper than the slope of the price setting curve. This would imply an unstable equilibrium with exploding trajectories, if wage and price setting curves were linear and the market would adjust according to (154). Using Layard, Nickell and Jackman's (1991) estimates for α, a parameter that links unemployment and a demand index, one can calculate the coefficients for the unemployment variable for the wage and price setting equation based on the estimates of Bean, Layard, and Nickell (1986). Then, 10 out of 14 countries have a short run upward sloping quasi labor demand curve. In one country that has a downward sloping price setting curve, the wage setting curve is steeper in absolute terms. Layard, Nickell and Jackman (1991) get a flat price setting curve for that country. Besides that the coefficients differ across countries, they also vary from author to author. For example, Layard, Nickell and Jackman (1991) estimate the coefficient on unemployment in the wage setting equation at -0.32 for Germany. Grubb (1986) estimates that same coefficient at -1.07, Alogoskoufis and Manning (1988a) get -1.36, Newell and Symons (1985) arrive at -0.36, and Bean, Layard, and Nickell (1986) get -3.02. What seems to hold on empirical grounds is that in equilibrium the wage setting curve is upward sloping. However, the slope varies significantly. The sign on the price setting curve is not that clear. At least, all this does not contradict the assumptions on which the model generates endogenous employment cycles. The simulated models (Figure 46 and Figure 44) ground on a coefficient on unemployment[32] in the quasi labor demand curve that is in the range reported by Layard, Nickell, and Jackman (1991). The coefficient on unemployment in the wage setting curve is -2 in Figure 46 and -0.8 in Figure 44. Again, both values of the simulated model are covered by the empirical estimates.

The employment dynamics ground on the assumptions that firms can easily hire and fire workers after a wage contract was settled between a single union and firms' representatives. This idea fits only to strongly centralized bargaining arrangements where there is one union that represents all workers and firms are collectively organized, too. Any form of staggered wage contracts will probably decrease the degree of wage responsiveness (c.f. Taylor 1992) to labor market conditions and dampen employment cycles, since a positive wage gap will only cause a downsizing of the work force for that specific sector. Unemployment will rise to a minor extent compared to an economy wide agreement. In the next period, when the other parties bargain for a new wage contract, bargained wages will be comparably higher due to lower aggregate unemployment (at least when the wage setting curve is monotonous and upward sloping). Firms will hire less workers. A period ahead from then, the former parties will agree on a comparably lower real wage so that the cycle is dampened. Whether firms can easily adjust the work force in that way is debatable. It was cited earlier on (c.f. chapter 4.1) that European labor markets may have suffered from high employment adjustment costs in the eighties. If this is true, firms would rather choose to stay on the wage setting curve than to adjust employment until they are on the quasi labor demand curve again. Employment adjustment costs would cause frictions in the labor market. An adjustment process along the lines of chapter 7.2 would not be an adequate description. If labor markets are, however, flexible and firms can downsize the incumbent workforce when bargained wages are above the marginal product (or price determined real wage), and vice versa hire new workers at low costs, bargaining over real wages may spark employment cycles. Again, this is a highly stylized version of labor market dynamics. It excludes per assumption that prices change. Such an asymmetry between price stickiness and flexible quantity adjustment is a strong simplification. Usually, one would expect that the market

32 The coefficient is equal to *m*.

adjusts through movements in both variables. But still the model can show how the adjustment behavior of firms can propagate bargained real wages that are inconsistent with the price determined real wage which firms are willing to pay. Under such assumptions, a non-sclerotic labor market with a high degree of centralization in wage bargaining is more likely to generate endogenous employment cycles than a decentralized labor market with rather high adjustment costs.

7.4 Some consequences from flexible labor markets

Like the approaches before, this model, too, should be viewed as an example to show how complex dynamics can arise in almost textbook like settings. Therefore, drawing policy conclusions is probably as difficult as to get some empirical validity out of such a model. But still there are some implications that are worth to be mentioned. It is interesting to see that low adjustment costs may have a detrimental impact on labor market behavior. Fighting labor market sclerosis and boiling down job security arrangements can at least cause rather long adjustment paths. If quantity adjustments are more feasible than price adjustments, employment can vary around an unstable equilibrium.

If prices are sticky, as was assumed above, employment varies irrespectively of any price movements in the chaotic regime. It was argued that in an extreme case, the market adjusts solely through changing quantities. If this is true, there can be a natural range of unemployment instead of a natural rate of unemployment, like in the model on worker flows (c.f. chapter 6). Various employment levels would coincide with one inflation rate. Again, this would make the natural rate a policy trap. Forecasting inflationary or deflationary pressure from movements of the actual rate of unemployment would become more difficult. If there is no stable natural rate, one cannot distinguish movements in the actual unemployment level from variations in the natural rate. A delta of both rates does not tell anything anymore. It may cause inflationary pressure, but it also may not. It depends on the directions of movements of the underlying natural rate compared to actual unemployment. If both rates shift into the same direction, the delta does not change and there will be no inflationary pressure, although actual unemployment may have declined significantly.

8 Testing for chaos in German labor market data

The highly stylized nature of the models does not allow direct tests. But it is possible to test time series for a nonlinear deterministic core and chaotic behavior, although there are quite a range of pitfalls (c.f. chapter 2.2.3). The methods were described earlier in chapter 2.2.1. Now, these tools are applied to (West-) German labor market data on employment, the labor cost ratio in the manufacturing sector, monthly hours worked in the mining, manufacturing sector, and overall registered unemployment.

8.1 Filtering the data

The time series are taken from the International Statistical Yearbook[33]. All time series consist of monthly observations starting at the beginning of the sixties. Compared to the studies on nonlinearities in labor market data already done for Canada, the U.K or the U.S.[34] the time series are rather long. They are all in the range of the small sample size generated by Barnett et al. (1997) for their competition of tests for nonlinearity and chaos that still showed reasonable results.

33 International Statistical Yearbook:

Data	Data Set No.
Employment, manufacturing, in thousands of persons, West Germany	12427708; (1994)
Labor cost, manufacturing, ratio, West Germany	1240302; (1996)
Working hours, mining and manufacturing, in millions, West Germany	12428908; (1994)
Registered unemployment, in thousands of persons, West Germany	12428208; (1994)

34 Alogoskoufis and Stengos (1991), Brock and Sayers (1987), Frank and Stengos (1988).

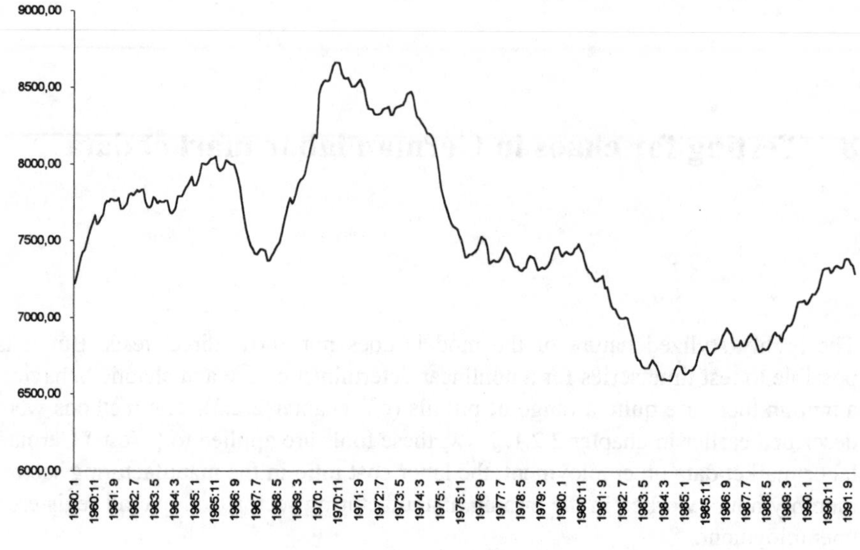

Figure 48: Employment for the manufacturing sector; in thousands of persons from 1960.01-1991.12, West Germany.

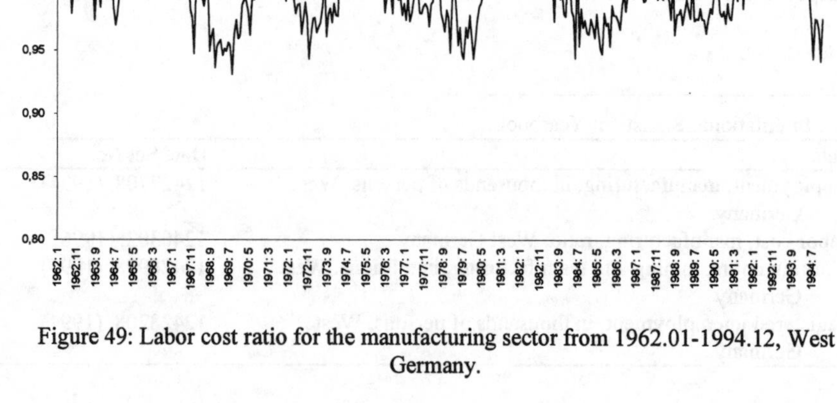

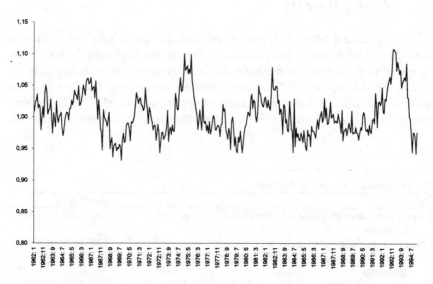

Figure 49: Labor cost ratio for the manufacturing sector from 1962.01-1994.12, West Germany.

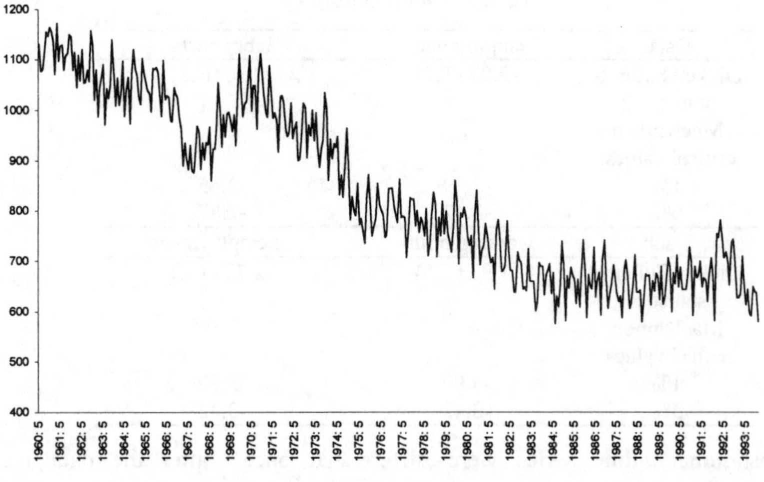

Figure 50: Monthly hours worked; in millions from 1960.05-1993.12, West Germany.

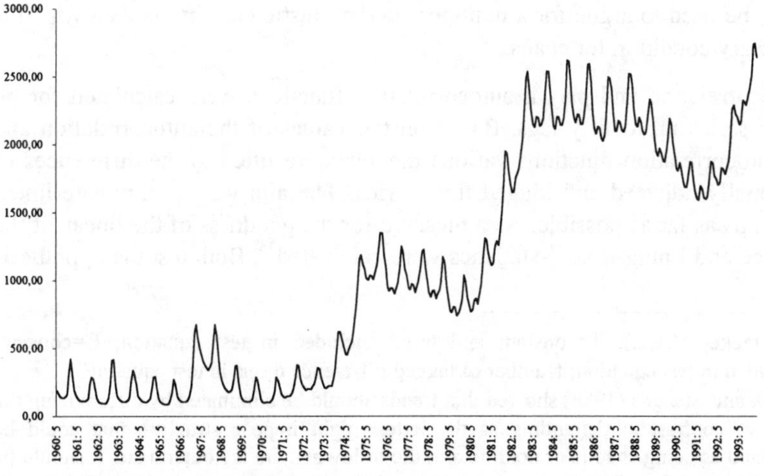

Figure 51: Registered unemployment, in thousands of persons from 1960.05-1994.03, West Germany.

The time series were searched for unit roots, as the tests for nonlinearity require stationary data. Except for the labor cost data, unit roots could not be rejected (Table 1).

Table 1: Unit root tests

Data:	employment	labor costs
Dickey Fuller t-statistic[35]:	-2.09 (T,2)	-3.36 (C,2)
MacKinnon critical values:		
1%	-3.99	-3.45
5%	-3.42	-2.87
Data:	working hours	unemployment
Dickey Fuller t-statistic:	-1.91 (T,5)	-2.72 (T,2)
MacKinnon critical values:		
1%	-3.99	-3.99
5%	-3.42	-3.42

The nonstationary time series were differenced once[36] after the data was seasonally adjusted with a moving average process[37] and logs were taken. With nonstationarities and seasonalities eliminated, stochastic linear and nonlinear underlying systems had to be removed before the BDS test could be applied. This is to be sure that a rejection of the null hypothesis of the BDS test is due to deterministic nonlinear relationships. Otherwise, comparably large test values could not be used to argue for a nonlinear deterministic core in the data which is the necessary condition for chaos.

The autocorrelation and partial autocorrelation functions were calculated for all four time series up to fifty lags. Based on the values of the autocorrelation and partial autocorrelation functions various models were fitted to the differences of the seasonally adjusted and logged time series. The aim was to eliminate linear relationships as far as possible. As a measure for the goodness of the linear fit the Box-Pierce and Ljung-Box Q-statistics were calculated[38]. Both test the hypothesis

---

35 In brackets (...,...): T=constant and trend included in test equation; C=constant included in test equation; Number of lagged difference terms in test equation.

36 Frank and Stengos (1988) showed that trends should be eliminated by differencing the data in contrast to detrending as the latter might impose structure that could be detected as being chaotic or nonlinear in the following. On the other hand, it should be kept in mind that differencing the data amplifies high frequency noise in relation to low frequencies and deteriorates the signal to noise ratio.

37 The moving average process covered a whole year and was centered around the current observation. The seasonal factors with which the time series were adjusted had been achieved by taking the mean of the ratios of the moving average process for every month.

38 The specifications of the linear fits are available on request.

that all autocorrelations are zero. Values of more than *90%* for the employment, the labor cost, and the working hours data imply little serial correlation. The results on the residuals of the unemployment data are less straight forward but still acceptable. Hence, it was assumed that linear relationships were removed successfully.

Table 2: Tests for linearity in the residuals

Data	employment	labor costs
Box-Pierce:	0.95	0.94
Ljung-Box:	0.90	0.89
Data	working hours	unemployment
Box-Pierce:	0.99	0.33
Ljung-Box:	0.98	0.22

8.2 Testing for nonlinearity and chaos

The BDS-test rejected[39] the null hypothesis for the filtered and unfiltered employment series for embedding dimensions from m=2...10, although the BDS values are lower for the residuals than for the unfiltered time series. This implies that a linear specification cannot capture all the employment dynamics. The residuals hide more information. The same holds true for the dynamics of the working hours and unemployment series. Linear specifications do not satisfactorily explain movements of both of these variables. The logged labor cost ratio makes an exemption. Here, linear dynamics are given. Hence, we skip labor costs for the tests on chaos as the necessary condition (deterministic nonlinearity) is not fulfilled.

Table 3: BDS tests for employment data

m	Unfiltered data $\sigma = 0.0038$		Residuals of linear fit $\sigma = 0.0029$	
	$r = \sigma$	$r = 2*\sigma$	$r = \sigma$	$r = 2*\sigma$
2	15.05	11.44	6.31	7.27
3	15.98	11.61	6.61	7.03
4	17.68	11.97	7.01	6.96
5	17.48	11.66	6.94	6.72
6	19.49	11.33	6.74	6.55
7	21.72	11.24	6.72	6.49
8	24.54	11.08	6.53	6.38
9	27.80	10.86	6.46	6.24
10	31.76	10.66	6.44	6.19

[39] The BDS software is at: http://www.ssc.wisc.edu/~blebaron/software/index.html.

Table 4: BDS tests for working hours data

m	Unfiltered data $\sigma = 0.0485$		Residuals of linear fit $\sigma = 0.0315$	
	$r = \sigma$	$r = 2*\sigma$	$r = \sigma$	$r = 2*\sigma$
2	11.10	11.22	4.49	5.04
3	12.47	9.90	5.16	5.06
4	12.72	9.20	5.44	5.20
5	12.61	8.39	5.61	5.23
6	12.97	7.68	5.42	5.14
7	13.33	7.12	5.24	4.92
8	14.01	6.78	4.66	4.68
9	15.11	6.47	4.02	4.48
10	18.07	6.47	4.00	4.45

Table 5: BDS tests for unemployment data

m	Unfiltered data $\sigma = 0.1074$		Residuals of linear fit $\sigma = 0.0662$	
	$r = \sigma$	$r = 2*\sigma$	$r = \sigma$	$r = 2*\sigma$
2	12.29	8.30	10.88	4.86
3	13.73	8.10	12.25	5.78
4	14.00	7.40	13.88	6.50
5	14.13	7.17	15.38	6.95
6	14.74	6.68	17.18	7.25
7	15.30	6.02	19.24	7.42
8	15.89	5.63	22.19	7.56
9	17.05	5.61	26.69	7.87
10	20.74	5.73	32.33	8.34

Table 6: BDS tests for labor cost data

m	Unfiltered data $\sigma = 0.0336$		Residuals of linear fit $\sigma = 0.0166$	
	$r = \sigma$	$r = 2*\sigma$	$r = \sigma$	$r = 2*\sigma$
2	40.85	30.97	1.51	2.27
3	46.08	31.24	1.28	1.89
4	52.19	30.95	0.94	1.37
5	60.99	30.76	1.08	1.27
6	73.00	30.83	0.90	1.22
7	89.82	31.16	0.69	1.18
8	111.91	31.66	0.48	1.11
9	142.53	32.36	0.15	1.13
10	184.91	33.22	-0.30	1.07

As was already indicated, the rejection of the null hypothesis could also be due to nonlinear stochastic processes. Tests on the squared residuals of the linear fits implied conditional heteroscedasticity (ARCH test). However, fits of ARCH and GARCH models to the residuals were not successful. Thus, changing variances were not the stochastic nonlinearities that caused the rejection of the null.

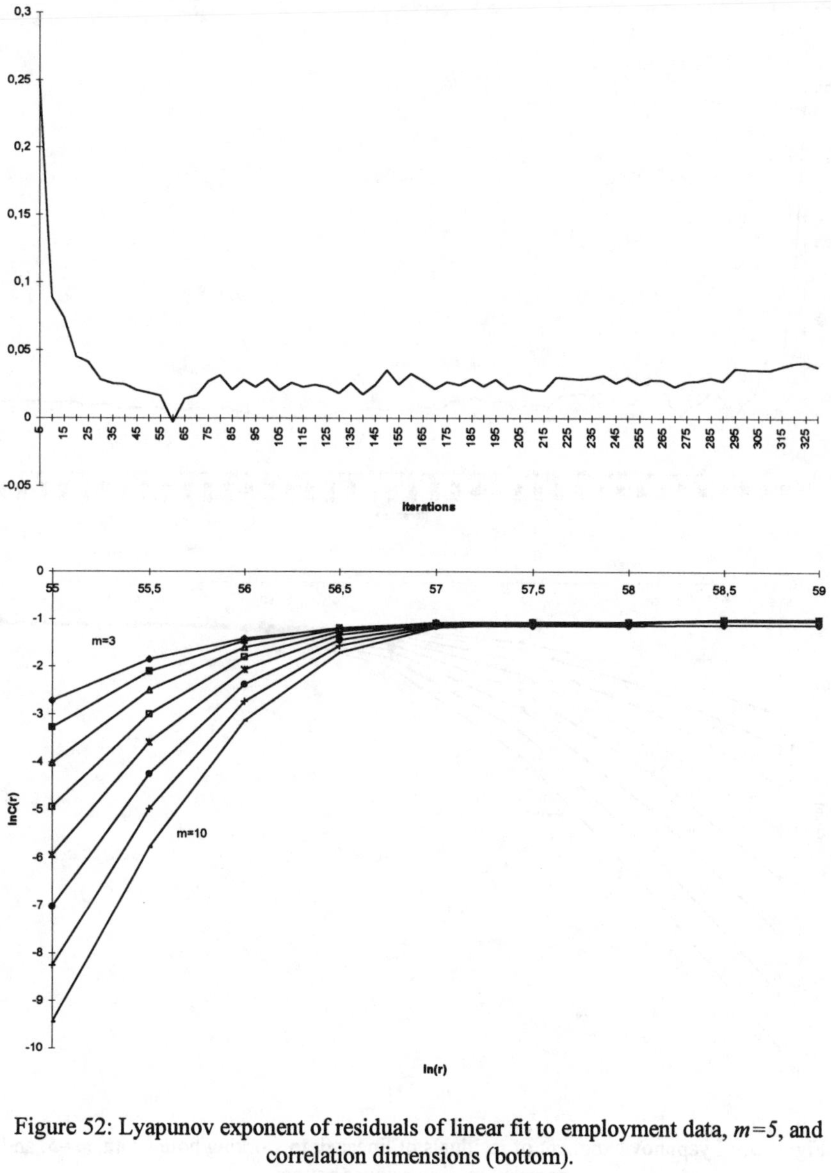

Figure 52: Lyapunov exponent of residuals of linear fit to employment data, $m=5$, and correlation dimensions (bottom).

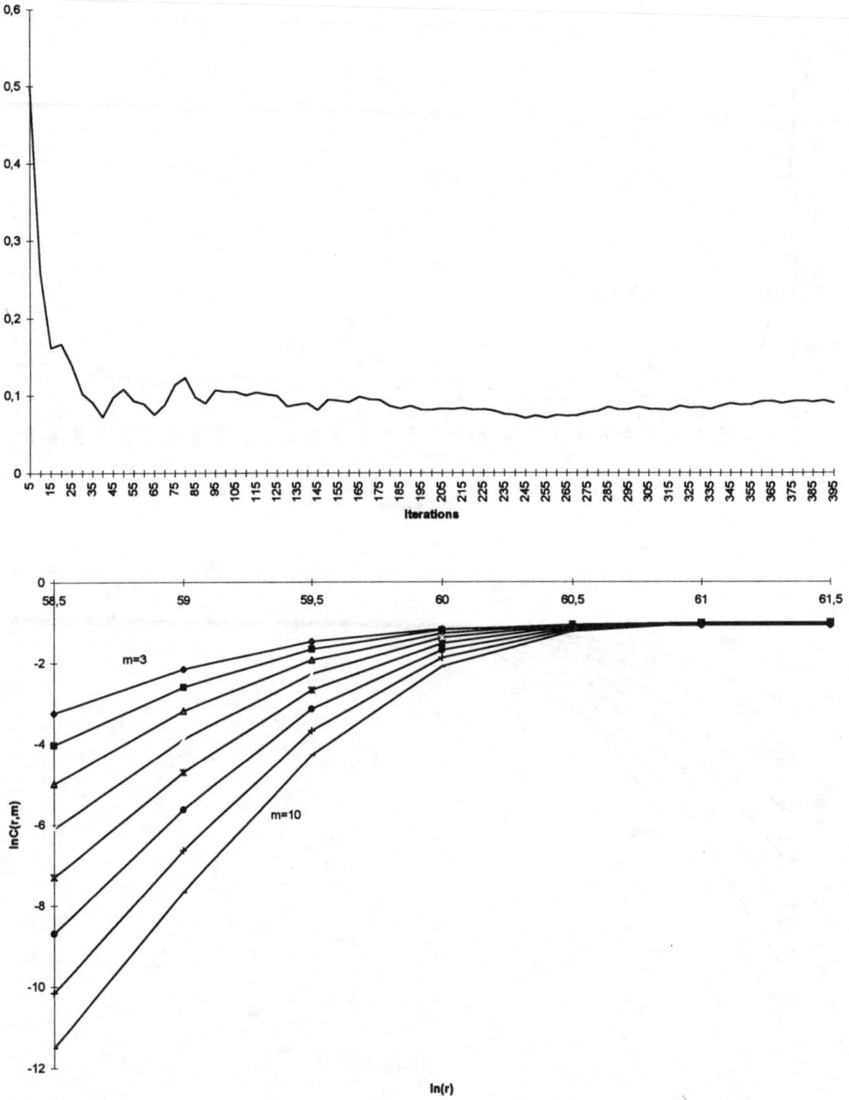

Figure 53: Lyapunov exponent of residuals of linear fit to working hours data, $m=5$, and correlation dimensions (bottom).

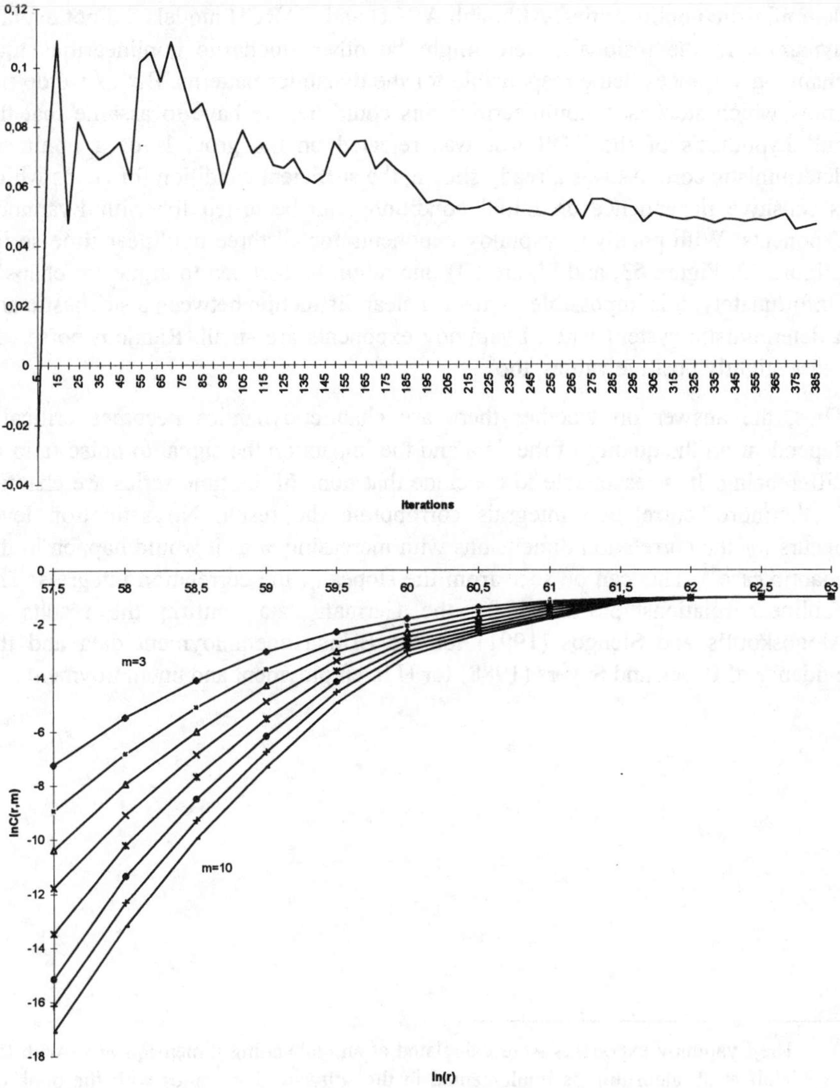

Figure 54: Lyapunov exponent of residuals of linear fit to unemployment data, m=5, and correlation dimensions (bottom).

For the time series where the BDS test rejected the null hypothesis the necessary condition for chaos was fulfilled. Of course, one could argue that the rejection of the null hypothesis for the BDS test does not necessarily imply underlying deterministic nonlinearities. Although ARCH and GARCH models did not explain dynamics in the residuals there might be other stochastic nonlinearities than changing variances being responsible for the dynamics patterns. But as we do not know which stochastic nonlinearities this could be, we have to assume that the null hypothesis of the BDS test was rejected on the grounds of a nonlinear deterministic core. As was already shown, the sufficient condition for chaos which is sensitive dependence on initial conditions can be tested for with Lyapunov exponents. With positive Lyapunov exponents for all three nonlinear time series (Figure 52, Figure 53, and Figure 54) one might be inclined to argue for chaos[40]. Unfortunately, it is impossible to make a clear distinction between a stochastic and a deterministic system when Lyapunov exponents are small. Random noise can cause slightly positive values, too[41].

Thus, the answer on whether there are chaotic dynamics becomes critically dependent on the quality of the data and the impact on the signal to noise ratio of differencing. It is reasonable to conclude that none of the time series are chaotic. Furthermore, correlation integrals corroborate the result. No saturation level occurs for the correlation dimensions with increasing *m* as it would happen in the chaotic case[42]. This can be seen from the slopes of the correlation integrals. The nonlinear relationships found for the German data confirm the results of Alogoskoufis and Stengos (1991) for the British unemployment data and the evidence of Brock and Sayers (1988) for U.S. employment and unemployment.

---

40 The Lyapunov exponents were calculated at an embedding dimension $m=5$ with the Wolf et al. algorithm as implemented in the software that comes with the book on chaotic dynamics of Medio (1992). The minimum distance and the threshold value were taken as *2%* and *10%* of the range of the data values, respectively. The propagation step size was set to five, so that at every fifth iteration the length of the separation from the fiducial trajectory was measured.

41 C.f. Chen (1993), p. 222.

42 Actually the correlation integral is supposed to become zero. However, as r is not chosen big enough to capture all points in phase space, the correlation integral reaches the theoretical value only approximately.

9 Summary and concluding remarks

One can find many economic models embedded in well accepted frameworks such as utility maximizing agents in overlapping generations models, neoclassical growth models, or IS/LM models that generate irregular behavior. Variables like the GDP, the stock of capital, or the level of employment undergo persistent cycles that look as if they were random, but are grounded on fixed equations of motion that do not have a stochastic component. These models strongly indicate the possibility of nonlinear deterministic and chaotic dynamics in economics. The models that are discussed above try to widen the spectrum of endogenous and irregular dynamics to labor markets. Various models are developed that sketch the impact of nonlinearities on labor market dynamics. It is shown that by incorporating nonlinear relationships into standard models of the labor market, dynamic properties arise that include long lasting adjustment periods and locally or globally unstable equilibria. Variables such as real wages and employment may undergo persistent cycles of finite and infinite order. Although these models are highly stylized, and would not perform satisfactorily when confronted with real data, they can make an important contribution to the understanding of labor market dynamics. They shift attention to endogenous explanations of labor market dynamics that linear stochastic approaches are not able to provide. In particular, we develop models where real wages adjust to disequilibrium quantities assuming a backward bending labor supply, a nonlinear but monotonous supply curve, or a discontinuous demand curve that arises from increasing returns in the underlying production technology. Two further approaches focus on the adjustment dynamics in the level of unemployment, either driven by diverging flows into and from unemployment, or by the hiring and firing behavior of firms in a 'right to manage model' that has a U-shaped wage setting curve.

When labor supply is backward bending, and labor demand slopes downwards, the labor market can have a single, two, or no equilibrium at all. If demand and supply curves do not intersect and real wages behave according to a proportional adjustment rule, real wage trajectories will explode. If labor demand and supply curves cross twice, the equilibrium with a high real wage is always unstable. Movements from this equilibrium towards the equilibrium with a low real wage can be accompanied by rising unemployment. Real wages and unemployment are then negatively correlated. At the equilibrium where real wages are low, labor supply and demand may be rather elastic so that small deviations from the equilibrium are followed by long adjustment periods. Real wages overshoot until they settle to a stable equilibrium. The low real wage equilibrium can become locally unstable. Real wage and employment cycles of finite order follow. Increasing the speed of real wage adjustment or the elasticity of supply or demand yields chaotic cycles, which implies an infinite number of long run states on a, however, finite attractor. If one interprets excess supply as unemployment and ties real wage changes to nominal wage changes, it is possible to derive a negatively sloped quasi Phillips curve that has no trade off, neither in the short run nor in the long run. In the standard approaches, the Phillips curve has a negative slope with adaptive expectations in the short run and becomes vertical in the long run, or is vertical at any time, if rational expectations are given. With a vertical Phillips curve there is no menu of choice in these models, but there is a trade off with a negatively sloped curve. Here, the chaotic models imply a negatively sloped Phillips curve that does not offer a menu of choice. In the chaotic regime, the labor market moves the quasi Phillips curve up and down erratically. Although the Phillips curve is downward sloping, there is no stable relation between the level of unemployment and wage changes, even in the short run. Due to sensitive dependence on initial conditions, it is impossible to make forecasts for the long run. Only if the exact state of the labor market could be determined would it be possible to describe the path of combinations of wages changes and unemployment even for the long run. For practical reasons, however, it is impossible to pin down the initial conditions exactly. Locally unstable and chaotic labor markets are robust against variations in the supply schedule. Even if labor supply is derived from the maximization of a CES utility function under the usual constraints, and is nonlinear and upward sloping, real wage dynamics can become chaotic. A quasi Phillips curve shows up once more. In both cases, the flat labor demand and supply curves rely on parameters that are in the range of empirical estimates of labor supply and labor demand elasticities. The high degree of real wage flexibility that is necessary for irregular dynamics is probably not backed by empirical estimates, although labor markets seem to adjust faster to new conditions than is generally assumed.

If the underlying production technology has increasing returns for low employment levels, and marginal productivity decreases at higher employment, real wages have to undercut a threshold so that firms make profits. If real wages exceed the threshold, there is no demand for labor. Labor demand becomes a discontinuous function of the real wage. The labor market has no equilibrium if labor supply lies in the zero labor demand regime. Contrary to that, the case is discussed where labor demand and supply intersect. As before, real wage adjustment is driven by a proportional adjustment rule. By comparing this model with the model that has a continuous labor demand function, we find that real wage trajectories are chaotic where they described a period two cycle with a continuous labor demand function. The discontinuous labor demand function causes abrupt changes in the long run behavior of the labor market. There may be no period doubling if the adjustment speed is increased. The market can switch from a period two cycle to chaotic dynamics immediately. If trajectories that are repelled from the equilibrium get trapped in the zero demand regime, there may be unemployment for a considerably long time, although real wages decline. If labor supply is inelastic, falling real wages are accompanied by a constant negative excess demand. Real wages and unemployment are not correlated in this case. As in the models with a nonlinear labor supply, the chaotic regime implies a quasi Phillips curve where there is no trade off in the short run, although the Phillips curve is downward sloping.

One may conjecture that rational agents who constantly fail to clear the market would revise their behavior. If the auctioneer does not know the exact labor supply and demand schedules, but is informed about econometric techniques that allow him to distill information out of the real wage time series, the conjecture may be wrong for chaotic time series. Under the proposed concept - the auctioneer looks at the coefficients of the autocorrelation function while tuning the speed of adjustment - sticking to the proportional control rule is weakly consistent with rational behavior. The autocorrelation coefficients do not deliver robust information for lags larger than one, from which the auctioneer could learn that he is applying an inappropriate market clearing rule. It follows that the market participants are wrong in what they do - but always in a different way. They do not make systematic errors. Therefore, they act rationally.

Unemployment varies if total inflows from employment to unemployment differ from total outflows from unemployment to employment. Total inflows into unemployment are the inflow rate times employment. The outflow rate times the number of workers who are unemployed gives total outflows. That is the basic identity that links worker flows to the path of unemployment levels. The outflow rate becomes a nonlinear decreasing function in unemployment when unemployed workers, and a fraction of employed workers that is dependent on the transition rate from unemployment to employment itself, compete for a given number of jobs. It is shown that workers who search on-the-job as a reaction to their perceived chances to finding a new job stabilizes the labor market equilibrium. Nevertheless, the natural level of unemployment can become locally unstable. Trajectories repelled from the equilibrium will be bounded from above and below. The natural rate becomes a natural range of unemployment. Unemployment cycles within the natural range can be of finite as well as infinite order. On-the-job search characteristics for an unstable equilibrium with irregular cycles cope quite well with estimates at the margin but not with findings on hirings from the stock of employed or stocks of workers who search on-the-job.

The last nonlinear labor market model refers to wage and price setting curves. It is shown that the wage setting curve can change its sign if average productivity follows some U-shaped function, or a large fraction of unemployed workers cannot exert sufficient downward real wage pressure when unemployment is high. Then, the wage setting curve can be downward sloping for low employment levels and upward sloping as is usually assumed elsewhere. With sticky prices and low hiring and firing costs, firms may decide to adjust employment if the bargained real wage does not allow an efficient production. In other words, firms will try to get on the quasi labor demand curve while the wage contract holds. Under such an adjustment mechanism, the natural rate becomes locally unstable if the wage setting curve slopes upwards more steeply than the quasi labor demand curve slopes downwards in equilibrium. A review of coefficients in estimated price setting and wage setting curves shows that this cannot be ruled out. Once more, the natural rate becomes a natural range of unemployment.

The models sketch the impact of various kinds of nonlinearities that may generate complex behavior. All of them are highly stylized which impedes direct empirical tests. Nevertheless, it was attempted to confront the most important assumptions that underlie the dynamic implications, with results from empirical work on labor markets such as estimates of labor supply and demand elasticities, real wage flexibility, or on the slopes of wage and price setting curves. There are other roads to approach nonlinear and chaotic dynamics from an empirical starting point. Such an attempt is made in the last chapter. A test of monthly German labor market time series that cover the last 30 years reveals a nonlinear deterministic core in three out of four cases. Although Lyapunov exponents are slightly positive for the time series with an underlying nonlinear deterministic core, chaotic behavior is rejected, as small positive Lyapunov exponents might also be due to noisy data. Furthermore, it is not possible to find a correlation dimension that settles to a finite value. Generally, the tests for chaos in economic data have to surpass a range of obstacles that may explain why chaos is so elusive in economic data. To arrive at robust results, the tests require, for economic standards, rather large data sets which are usually only given for financial time series. Other data, such as on labor markets, has to cover more than thirty years, if it is monthly, to arrive at the lower bound that will still give reliable test statistics. In addition, no direct tests for chaos exist. Time series have to be filtered before tests for nonlinear deterministic processes can be applied. Apart from distinct cases, it is pretty unclear how these filters change the test statistics.

It is the aim of this work to look at endogenous labor market dynamics. We start from distinct approaches that have a common feature. All models incorporate some degree of nonlinearity. On these grounds, it is possible to derive irregular labor market dynamics in such variables as real wages or unemployment. The problem about such an approach is that it can only deliver partial knowledge on what determines complex labor market dynamics. Of course, it is possible to pin down exactly the assumptions that underlie the dynamic properties in each of the models. But still, the models are more like a patchwork than a coherent picture, which would give advice on when to expect endogenous labor market dynamics. One is tempted to ask for an exact map from which economic theorists and policy advisors could read when there is chaos ahead. It would enable them to fasten their seat belts whenever necessary. But unfortunately this cannot be achieved, here. All one can say at this stage is, that you better keep your seat belts fastened to be prepared for the irregular dynamics that may be around the corner.

Figures

Tables

References

Adelman, I., Adelman, F.L. (1959): The dynamic properties of the Klein-Goldberger model. Econometrica 27, 4, 596-625

Akerlof, G. (1970): The market for lemons: Quality uncertainty and the market mechanism. Quarterly Journal of Economics 84, 488-500

Akerlof, G. (1980): A theory of social customs, of which unemployment may be one consequence. Quarterly Journal of Economics 94, 4, 749-775

Alogoskoufis, G. (1987): On intertemporal substitution and aggregate labor supply. Journal of Political Economy 95, 938-960

Alogoskoufis, G., Manning, A. (1988): On the persistence of unemployment. Economic Policy 7, 427-469

Alogoskoufis, G.S., Stengos, T. (1991): Testing for nonlinear dynamics in historical unemployment series. EUI Working Paper, ECO No. 91/38

Anderson, P.M., Burgess, S.M. (1995): Empirical matching functions: estimation and interpretation using disaggregated data. NBER Working Paper, No. 5001

Arrow, K.J. (1962): The economic implications of learning-by-doing. Review of Economic Studies 29, 155-173

Arrow, K.J. et al. (Eds.) (1998): Increasing returns and economic analysis. MacMillan Press

Arthur, B.W. (1990): Positive feedbacks in the economy. Scientific American, February, 92-99

Arthur, B.W. (Ed.) (1994): Increasing returns and path dependence in economics. University of Michigan Press, Ann Arbor

Artstein, Z. (1983): Irregular cobweb dynamics. Economic Letters 11, 15-17

Ball, L. (1990): Intertemporal substitution and constraints on labor supply, evidence from panel data. Economic Inquiry 28, 706-724

Baltagi, B.H., Blien, U. (1998): The German wage curve: evidence from the IAB employment sample. Economics Letters 61, 135-142

Barnett, W.A., Chen, P. (1988): The aggregation-theoretic monetary aggregates are chaotic and have strange attractors: an economic application of mathematical chaos. In: Barnett, W.A., Berndt, E.R., White, H. (Eds.): Dynamic Econometric Modeling. Cambridge University Press, Cambridge, 199-245

Barnett, W.A., Gallant, R.A. Hinich, M.J. Jungeilges, J.A., Kaplan, D.T., Jensen, M.J. (1997): A single blind controlled competition among tests for nonlinearity and chaos. Journal of Econometrics 82, 157-192

Barzel, Y., McDonald, R. (1973): Assets, subsistence and the supply curve of labor. American Economic Review 63, 621-633

Baumol, W., Benhabib, J. (1989): Chaos, significance, mechanism, and economic applications. Journal of Economic Perspectives 3, 77-105

Bean, C. (1994): European unemployment: A survey. Journal of Economic Literature 32, 573-619

Bean, C., Layard, R., Nickell, S. (1986): The rise in unemployment: a multi-country study. Economica 51, S21-S22

Becker, G.S., Murphy, K.M. (1988): A theory of rational addiction. Journal of Political Economy 96, 675-700

Benhabib, J. (1996): On cycles and chaos in economics. Studies in Nonlinear Dynamics and Econometrics 1, 1-2

Benhabib, J., Day, R.H. (1980): Erratic accumulation. Economics Letters 6, 113-117

Benhabib, J., Day, R.H. (1982): A characterization of erratic dynamics in the overlapping generations model. Journal of Economic Dynamics and Control 4, 37-55

Bertola, G. (1990): Job security, employment and wages. European Economic Review 34, 851-886

Bils, M. (1987): The cyclical behavior of marginal cost and price. American Economic Review 77, 838-855

Bils, M. (1989): Pricing in a customer market. Quarterly Journal of Economics 104, 699-718

Black, M. (1981): An empirical test of the theory of on-the-job search. The Journal of Human Resources 16, Winter, 129-140

Blanchard, O.J. (1999): Unemployment. (unpublished lecture notes at http://web.mit.edu/blanchar/www/books.html)

Blanchard, O.J., Diamond, P. (1994): Ranking, unemployment duration, and wages. Review of Economic Studies 61, 417-434

Blanchard, O.J., Diamond, P. (1989): The Beveridge curve. Brookings Papers on Economic Activity 1, 1-76

Blanchard, O.J., Diamond, P. (1992): The flow approach to labor markets. American Economic Review 82, Papers and Proceedings, 354-359

Blanchard, O.J., Fischer, S. (1989): Lectures on macroeconomics. The MIT Press, Cambridge Massachusetts, London England

Blanchard, O.J., Katz, L. (1997): What we know and do not know about the natural rate of unemployment. Journal of Economic Perspectives 11, 51-72

Blanchard, O.J., Katz, L. (1999): Wage dynamics: reconciling theory and evidence. NBER Working Paper 6924

Blanchard, O.J., Summers, L.H. (1987): Hysteresis in unemployment. European Economic Review 31, 288-295

Blanchard, O.J., Summers, L.H. (1988): Beyond the natural rate hypothesis. American Economic Review. Papers and Proceedings 78, 182 -187

Blanchard, O.J., Summers, L.H. (1986): Hysteresis and the European unemployment problem. In: Fischer, S. (Ed.), NBER Macroeconomics Annual 1, 15-78

Blanchflower, D.G., Oswald, A.J. (1994): The wage curve. The MIT Press, Cambridge Massachusetts, London England

Blanchflower, D.G., Oswald, A.J. (1995): International wage curves. In: Freeman, R., Katz, L. (Eds): Differences and changes in wage structures. NBER comparative labor market studies, 145-174

Blatt, J.M. (1983): Dynamic economic systems - A Post-Keynesian approach. M.E. Sharpe, Armonk, New York

Boal, W.M., Ransom, M.R. (1997): Monopsony in the labor market. Journal of Economic Literature 35, 86-112

Boeri, T. (1999): Enforcement of employment security regulations, on-the-job search and unemployment duration. European Economic Review 43, 65-89

Boldrin, M., Deneckere, R.J. (1990): Sources of complex dynamics in two sector growth models. Journal of Economic Dynamics an Control 14, 627-653

Boldrin, M., Montrucchio, L. (1986): On the indeterminancy of capital accumulation paths. Journal of Economic Theory 40, 26-39

Boldrin, M., Woodford, M. (1990): Equilibrium models displaying endogenous fluctuations and chaos. Journal of Monetary Economics 25, 189-222

Bolle, M. (1971): Kurz- und langfristige Analyse ungleichgewichtiger makroökonomischer Angebot-Nachfrage-Systeme. Duncker & Humblot, Berlin

Bolle, M. (1973): Geld, Wachstum und Beschäftigung. Zeitschrift für die gesamten Staatswissenschaften 129, 1-22

Bolle, M. (1975): Simulation eines ökonomischen Makrosystems auf dem Digitalcompter. In: Baetge, J. (Ed.): Grundlagen der Wirtschafts- und Sozialkybernetik. Duncker & Humblot. Berlin, 283-295

Bolle, M. (1983a): Anpassungsprozesse auf Arbeitsmärkten bei Gütermarktimpulsen, In: Bolle, M., Gabriel, J. (Eds.): Die Dynamik der Arbeitsmärkte aus der Sicht der Forschung. Minerva Publikation, München, 132-148

Bolle, M. (1983b): Die eiskalte Hand des Marktes und angemessene Möglichkeiten, In: Bolle, M., Grottian, P. (Eds.): Arbeit schaffen - jetzt! Rowohlt, Reinbek bei Hamburg, 20-36

Brock, W.A., Dechert, W.D., Scheinkman, J.A., LeBaron, B. (1996): A test for independence based on the correlation dimension. Econometric Reviews 15, 197-235

Brock, W.A., Hommes, C.H. (1997): A rational route to randomness. Econometrica 65, 5, 1059-1095

Brock, W.A., Sayers C.L. (1987): Is the business cycle characterized by deterministic chaos? Working Paper 87 - 15, Department of Economics, University of North Carolina

Brooks, C. (1998): Chaos in foreign exchange markets: a sceptical view. Computational Economics 11, 265-281

Bruno, M. (1986): Aggregate supply and demand factors in OECD unemployment: an update. Economica 53, S35-S52

Burda, M., Wyplosz, C. (1994): Gross worker and job flows in Europe. European Economic Review 38, 1287-1315

Burdett, K. (1978): A theory of employee job search and quit rates. American Economic Review 68, 212-220

Burgess, S. (1992): The flow into unemployment in Britain. Economic Journal 102, 888-895

Burgess, S. (1994): Matching models and labour market flows. European Economic Review 38, 809-816

Burgess, S., Lane, J., Stevens, D. (1996): Job flows and worker flows: issues, and evidence from a panel of US firms. In: Schettkat, R. (Ed.): The flow analysis of labour markets. Routledge, London New York, 96-114

Burgess, S.M. (1993): Nonlinear dynamics in a structural model of employment. In: Pesaran, M.H., Potter, S.M. (Eds.): Nonlinear dynamics, chaos and econometrics. John Wiley & Sons, Chichester New York Brisbane Toronto Singapore, 93-110

Byrne, J.J. (1975): Occupational mobility of workers. Monthly Labor Review 98, February, 53-57

Card, D. (1991): Intertemporal labor substitution: an assessment. NBER Working Paper No. 3602

Card, D., Hyslop, D. (1996): Does inflation "grease the wheels of the labor market". NBER Working Paper No. 5538

Carlin, W., Soskice, D. (1990): Macroeconomics and the wage bargain, a modern approach to employment, inflation and the exchange rate. Oxford University Press, Oxford New York

Cecen, A.A., Erkal, C. (1996): Distinguishing between stochastic and deterministic behavior in high frequency foreign exchange rate returns: can non-linear dynamics help forecasting? International Journal of Forecasting 12, 465 - 473

Chen, P. (1993): Searching for economic chaos: a challenge to econometric practice and nonlinear tests. In: Day, R.H., Chen, P. (Eds.): Nonlinear dynamics and evolutionary economics. Oxford University Press, Oxford New York, 217-253

Chiarella, C. (1988): The cobweb model, its instability and the onset of chaos. Economic Modelling, October, 377-384

Chichilnisky, G., Heal, G., Lin, Y. (1995): Chaotic price dynamics, increasing returns and the Phillips curve. Journal of Economic Behavior and Organization 27, 279-291

Day, R.H. (1982): Irregular Growth Cycles. American Economic Review 72, 406-414

Day, R.H. (1983): The emergence of chaos from classical economic growth, Quarterly Journal of Economics 98, 201-213

Day, R.H., Pianigiani, G. (1991): Statistical dynamics and economics. Journal of Economic Behavior and Organization 16, 37-83

Day, R.H., Shafer, W. (1985): Keynesian chaos. Journal of Macroeconomics 7, 277-295

Deneckere, R., Pelikan, S. (1986): Competitive chaos. Journal of Economic Theory 40, 1-25

Diamond, P. (1982): Aggregate demand in search equilibrium. Journal of Political Economy 90, 881-894

Dockner, E.J., Feichtinger, G. (1993): Cyclical consumption patterns and rational addiction. American Economic Review 83, 256-263

Finegan, T.A. (1962): Communication: the backward-sloping supply curve. Industrial and Labor Relations Review 15, 230-234

Finkenstädt, B. (1995): Nonlinear dynamics in economics, a theoretical and statistical approach to agricultural markets. Springer-Verlag, Berlin Heidelberg New York

Finkenstädt, B., Kuhbier, P. (1992): Chaotic dynamics in agricultural markets. Annals of Operations Research 37, 73-96

Flaschel, P., Franke, R., Semmler, W. (1997): Dynamic macroeconomics. The MIT Press, Cambridge Massachusetts

Frank, M.Z., Gencay, R., Stengos, T. (1988): International Chaos? European Economic Review 32, 1569-1584

Frank, M.Z., Stengos, T. (1988): Some evidence concerning macroeconomic chaos. Journal of Monetary Economics 22, 423-438

Franz, W. (1991): Arbeitsmarktökonomik. Springer-Verlag, Berlin Heidelberg New York

Franz, W. (1996): Theoretische Ansätze zur Erklärung der Arbeitslosigkeit: Wo stehen wir 1995? In: Gahlen, B., Hesse, H., Ramser, H.J. (Eds.): Arbeitslosigkeit und Möglichkeiten ihrer Überwindung. Mohr, Tübingen, 3-45

Freeman, R. (1976): A cobweb model of the supply and starting salary of new engineers. Industrial and Labor Relations Review, 236-248

Freeman, R. (1995): The limits of wage flexibility to curing unemployment. Oxford Review of Economic Policy 11, 63-72

Freeman, R. (1998): Which labor market institutions for the 21st century? Labour Economics 5, 1-24

Friedman, M. (1968): The role of monetary policy. American Economic Review 58, 1-17

Funke, M. (1990): Das Hysteresis-Phänomen. Zeitschrift für Wirtschafts- und Sozialwissenschaften 111, 527-551

Gärtner, W. (1986): Zyklische Konsummuster, Jahrbuch für Nationalökonomie und Statistik 201, 55-65

Gärtner, W., Jungeilges, J. (1988): A non-linear model of interdependent consumer behavior. Economic Letters 27, 145-150

Giersch, H. (1985): Eurosclerosis. Kiel Discussion Papers No. 112

Goodwin, R.M. (1967): A growth cycle. In: Feinstein, C.H. (Ed.): Socialism, capitalism and economic growth, 54-58

Goodwin, R.M., Pacini, P.M. (1992): Nonlinear economic dynamics and chaos: An introduction. In: Vercelli, A., Dimitri, N. (Eds.): Macroeconomics, a survey of research strategies. Oxford University Press, Oxford, 236-291

Gordon, R.J. (1988): Wage gaps versus output gaps: Is there a common story for all of Europe? In: Giersch, H. (Ed.): Macro and micro policies for more growth and employment. Oxford University Press, Oxford, 97-151

Grandmont, J.-M. (1985): On endogenous competitve business cycles. Econometrica 22, 995-1037

Granovetter, M., Soong, R. (1986): Threshold models of interpersonal effects in consumer demand. Journal of Economic Behavior and Organization 7, 83-99

Grassberger, P., Procaccia, I. (1983): Measuring the strangeness of strange attractors. Physica D 9, 189-208

Gregory, R. (1986): Wage policy and unemployment in Australia. Economica 53, S53-S74

Gross, D.M. (1997): Aggregate job matching and returns to scale in Germany. Economics Letters 56, 243-248

Grubb, D. (1986): Topics in the OECD Phillips Curve. Economic Journal 96, 55-79

Ham, J.C. (1986): Testing whether unemployment represents intertemporal labour supply behaviour. Review of Economic Studies LIII, 559-578

Hamermesh, D.S. (1993): Labor demand. Princeton University Press, Princeton

Hartog van Ophem (1996): On-the-job-search, mobility and wages in the Netherlands: what do we know? In: Schettkat, R. (Ed.): The flow analysis of labour markets. Routledge, London New York, 229-255

Heal, G.M. (1998): The economics of increasing returns. Paine Webber Working Paper Series in Money, Economics and Finance PW-97-20

Heckman, J. (1993): What has been learned about labor supply in the past twenty years. American Economic Review 83, 116-121

Hicks, J.R. (1950): A contribution to the theory of the trade cycle. Oxford University Press, Oxford

Holmes, J.M., Manning, R. (1988): Memory and market stability, The case of the cobweb. Economics Letters 28, 1-7

Hommes, C. (1994): Dynamics of the cobweb model with adaptive expectations and nonlinear supply and demand. Journal of Economic Behavior and Organization 24, 315-335

Hommes, C.H. (1991): Chaotic dynamics in economic models, some simple case-studies. Wolters-Noordhoff, Groningen

Hommes, C.H. (1998): On the consistency of backward-looking expectations: the case of the cobweb. Journal of Economic Behavior and Organization 33, 333-362

Hommes, C.H., Sorger, G. (1998): Consistent expectations equilibria. Macroeconomic Dynamics 2, 287-321

Howitt, P. (1988): Business cycles with costly search and recruiting. Quarterly Journal of Economics 103, 147-165

Howitt, P., McAfee, R.P. (1987): Costly search and recruiting. International Economic Review 28, 89-107

Hsieh, D. (1989): Testing for non-linear dependence in foreign exchange rates. Journal of Business 62, 339 - 368

Hsieh, D. (1991): Chaos and nonlinear dynamics: application to financial markets. Journal of Finance 46, 1839-1877

Huang, Y. (1976): Backward-bending supply curves and behaviour of subsistence farmers. Journal of Development Studies 12, 191-211

Jackman, R., Layard, R. (1991): Does long-term unemployment reduce a persons chance of a job? A time series test. Economica 58, 93-106

Jullien, M. (1988): Competitive business cycles in an overlapping generations economy with productive investment. Journal of Economic Theory 46, 45-65

Kaldor, N. (1940): A model of the trade cycle. Economic Journal 50, 78-92

Kalmbach, P. (1989): Reallohnsatz und Beschäftigung, Zur Theorie und Empirie eines umstrittenen Zusammenhangs. In: Emmerich, K. et al. (Eds.): Einzel- und gesamtwirtschaftliche Aspekte des Lohnes. Nürnberg, 157-175

Katz, L.F. (1986): Efficiency wage theories, A partial evaluation. In: Fisher, S. (Ed.): NBER Macroeconomic Annuals 1986. 235-276

Kelsey, D. (1988): The economics of chaos or the chaos of economics. Oxford Economic Papers 40, 1-31

Killingsworth, M.R. (1983). Labor supply. Cambridge University Press, Cambridge London New York

Kimmel,, J., Kniesner, T.J. (1998): New evidence on labor supply: employment versus hours elasticity by sex and marital status. Journal of Monetary Economics 42, 289-301

Krugman, P. (1996): The self-organizing economy. Blackwell, Cambridge Massachusetts

Kugler, P., Lenz, C. (1990): Sind Wechselkursfluktuationen zufällig oder chaotisch. Schweizerische Zeitschrift für Volkswirtschaft und Statistik 2, 113-128

Layard, R., Nickell, S., Jackman, R. (1991): Unemployment, macroeconomic performance and the labour market. Oxford University Press, Oxford, New York

Layard, R., Nickell, S. (1986): Unemployment in Britain. Economica 53, S121-S170

Lewis, P., Makepeace, G. (1984): The estimation of a disequilibrium real wage equation for Britain. Journal of Macroeconmics 6, 399-410

Li, T.Y., Yorke, J.A. (1975): Period three implies chaos. American Mathematical Monthly 82, 985-992

Lindbeck, A. (1995): Hazardous welfare-state dynamics. American Economic Review 85, Papers and Proceedings, 9-15

Lindbeck, A., Snower, D. (1988): The insider-outsider theory of employment and unemployment. MIT Press, Cambridge Massachusetts

Lorenz, H.-W. (1987a): Goodwin´s nonlinear accelerator and chaotic motion. Zeitschrift für Nationalökonomie 47, 413-418

Lorenz, H.-W. (1987b): International trade and the possible occurrence of chaos. Economics Letters 23, 135-138

Lorenz, H.-W. (1987c): Strange attractors in a multisector business cycle model. Journal of Economic Behavior an Organization 8, 397-411

Lorenz, H.-W. (1993): Nonlinear dynamical economics and chaotic motion, 2nd edition. Springer-Verlag, Berlin Heidelberg New York

Lucas, R.E., Rapping, L.A. (1969): Real wages, employment and inflation. Journal of Political Economy 77, 721-754

Mankiw, G.N. et al. (1985): Intertemporal substitution in macroeconomics. Quarterly Journal of Economics 100, 225-251

Manning, A. (1990): Imperfect competition, multiple equilibria and unemployment policy. Economic Journal, Conference Papers 100, 151-162

Manning, A. (1992): Multiple equilibria in the British labour market, some empirical evidence. European Economic Review 36, 1333-1365

Medio, A. (1992): Chaotic dynamics, theory and applications to economics. Cambridge University Press, Cambridge

Medio, A., Negroni, G. (1996): Chaotic dynamics in overlapping generations models with production. In: Barnett, W.A., Kirman, A.P., Salmon, M.S. (Eds.): Nonlinear dynamics and economics: proceedings of the tenth international symposium in economic theory and econometrics. Cambridge University Press, Cambridge, 3-44

Meissner, W. (1971): Ökonometrische Modelle, Rekursivität und Interdependenz aus der Sicht der Kybernetik. Duncker & Humblot, Berlin

Mizrach, B. (1996): Determining delay times for phase space reconstruction with application to the FF/DM exchange rate. Journal of Economic Behavior and Organization 30, 369-381

Mortensen, D.T. (1989): The persistence and indeterminancy of unemployment in search equilibrium. Scandinavian Journal of Economics 91, 347-370

Muth, J.F. (1961): Rational expectations and the theory of price movements. Econometrica 29, 315-335

Neugart, M. (1999): Is there chaos on the German labor market? Jahrbücher für Nationalökonomie und Statistik 218, 5+6, 658-673

Neumann, M. (1991): Theoretische Volkswirtschaftslehre II, Produktion, Nachfrage und Allokation, 3.Auflage. Verlag Franz Vahlen, München

Newell, A., Symons, J.S.V. (1985): Wages and unemployment in OECD countries. London School of Economics, Centre for Labour Economics, Discussion Paper No. 219

Nickell, S. (1997): Unemployment and labor market rigidities: Europe versus North America. Journal of Economic Perspectives 11, 55-74

Nishimura, K., Sorger, G. (1996): Optimal cycles and chaos, a survey. Studies in Nonlinear Dynamics and Econometrics 1, 11-28

Nishimura, K., Yano, M. (1995): Nonlinear dynamics and chaos in optimal growth: an example. Econometrica 63, 981-1001

OECD (1993): Employment outlook

Pagano, M. (1990): Imperfect competition, underemployment equilibria and fiscal policy. Economic Journal 100, 440-463

Parsons, D.O. (1991): The job search behavior of employed youth. The Review of Economics and Statistics 73, 597-604

Pencavel, J. (1986): Labor supply of men: a survey. In: Ashenfelter, O., Layard, R. (Eds.): Handbook of Labor Economics. North-Holland, Amsterdam, 3-102

Pissarides, C. (1986): Unemployment and Vacancies in Britain. Economic Policy 3, 499-559

Pissarides, C. (1990): Equilibrium unemployment theory. Basil Blackwell, Cambridge Massachusetts

Pissarides, C. (1994): Search unemployment with on-the-job search. Review of Economic Studies 61, 457-475

Pissarides, C., Wadsworth, J. (1994): On-the-job-search, some empirical evidence from Britain. European Economic Review 38, 385-401

Prachowny, M. (1991): What is the speed limit along the U.S. Phillips curve? Journal of Macroeconomics 13, 417-434

Puu, T. (1989): Nonlinear economic dynamics. Springer-Verlag, Berlin Heidelberg New York

Ramsey, J.B., Sayers, C.L., Rothman, P. (1990): The statistical properties of dimension calculations using small data sets: some economic applications. International Economic Review 31, 991-1020

Reichlin, P. (1986): Equilibrium cycles in an overlapping generations model with production. Journal of Economic Theory 40, 89-102

Reichlin, P. (1997): Endogenous cycles in competitive models: an overview. Studies in Nonlinear Dynamics and Econometrics 1, 175-185

Rosenfeld, C. (1977): Job search of the unemployed. Monthly Labor Review 100, 39-43

Rotemberg, J.J., Saloner, G. (1986): A supergame-theoretic model of price wars during booms. American Economic Review 76, 390-407

Rotemberg, J.J., Woodford, M. (1991): Markups and the business cycle. NBER Macroeconomic Annual 6, 63-129

Rotemberg, J.J., Woodford, M. (1999): The cyclical behavior of prices and costs. NBER Working Paper 6909

Sachs, J. (1983): Real wages and unemployment in the OECD countries. Brooking Papers on Economic Activity 1, 255-289

Sargent, T.J. (1993): Bounded rationality in macroeconomics. The Arne Ryde memorial lectures. Clarendon Press, Oxford

Scheinkman, J.A., LeBaron, B. (1989a): Nonlinear dynamics and GNP data. In: Barnett, W.A., Geweke, J., Shell, K. (Eds.): Economic complexity: chaos, suspots, bubbles, and nonlinearity. Cambridge University Press, Cambridge, 213-227

Scheinkman, J.A., LeBaron, B. (1989b): Nonlinear dynamics and stock returns. Journal of Business 62, 311-337

Schettkat, R. (1996): Labor market dynamics in Germany. In: Schettkat, R. (Ed.): The flow analysis of labour markets. Routledge, London New York, 256-271

Schmid, G. (1995): Institutional incentives to prevent unemployment: unemployment insurance and active labor market policy in a comparative perspective. Journal of Socio-Economics 24, 51-103

Schmid, G., Reissert, B. (1996): Unemployment compensation and labour market transitions. In: Schmid, G., O'Reilly, J., Schömann, K. (Eds.): International handbook of labour market policy and evaluation. Edward Elgar, Cheltenham Brookfield, 235-276

Semmler, W. (1986): On nonlinear theories of economic cycles and the persistence of business cycles. Mathematical Social Sciences 12, 47-76

Shaffer, S. (1984): Chaos, naivete, and consistent conjectures. Economics Letters 14, 155-162

Shaw, G.K. (1984): Rational expectations. Wheatsheaf Books, Brighton Sussex

Siebert, H. (1997): Labor market rigidities: at the root of unemployment in Europe. Journal of Economic Perspectives 11, 37-54

Stiglitz, J. (1987): The causes and consequences of the dependence of quality on price. Journal of Economic Literature 25, 1-48

Stiglitz, J. (1997): Reflections on the natural rate hypothesis. Journal of Economic Perspectives 11, 3-10

Stutzer, M. (1980): Chaotic dynamics and bifurcation in a macro-model. Journal of Economic Dynamics and Control 2, 253-276

Summers, L.H. (1986): Why is unemployment so very high near full employment? Brookings Papers on Economic Activity 2, 339-383

Taylor, J.B. (1992): Synchronized wage determination and macroeconomic performance in seven large countries. In: Vercelli, A, Dimitri, N. (Eds.): Macroeconomics, a survey of research strategies, 321-334

Van den Berg, G.J., van Ours, J. (1994): Unemployment dynamics and duration dependence in France, the Netherlands, and United Kingdom. Economic Journal 104, 432-443

Van Ours, J. (1990): An international comparative study on job mobility. Labour 4, 33-55

Vatter, H.G. (1961): On the folklore of the backward-sloping supply curve. Industrial and Labor Relations Review 14, 578-586

Vendrik, M. (1993): Collective habit formation and norms in labour supply. Journal of Economic Behavior and Organization 20, 353-372

Vendrik, M. (1998): Unstable bandwagon and habit effects on labor supply. Journal of Economic Behavior and Organization 36, 235-255

Weitzman, M.L. (1982): Increasing returns and the foundations of unemployment theory. Economic Journal 92, 787-804

Wolf, A., Swift, J.B., Swinney, H.L., Vastano, J.A. (1985): Determining Lyapunov exponents from a time series. Physica D 16, 285-317

Yellen, J. (1984): Efficiency wage models of unemployment. American Economic Review 74, Papers and Proceedings, 200-205

Zabel, J.E. (1997): Estimating wage elasticity for life-cycle models of labour supply behavior. Labour Economics 4, 223-244

Software: Mathematica 3.0, DMC Software by Giampaolo Gallo, BDS algorithm as implemented by Blake LeBaron, Microsoft Word 7.0, Microsoft Excel 5.0

[illegible] (19[illegible]) "Reflections on the 'natural' rate hypothesis", Journal of Economic Perspectives [illegible]

[illegible] (19[illegible]) [illegible] dynamics and [illegible] Journal of Economic Dynamics and Control [illegible]

[illegible] (19[illegible]) "Why is unemployment so [illegible] high [illegible] full employment?" Brookings Papers on Economic Activity 2, [illegible]

[illegible] (1972) [illegible] fixed [illegible] performance in [illegible] large countries. In: [illegible] (ed.) [illegible] of [illegible] strategies, [illegible]

Van den Berg, G.J., Van Ours, J.C. (19[illegible]) [illegible] and [illegible] dependence in France, the Netherlands, and the United Kingdom. Economic Journal [illegible] 4[illegible]

[illegible] (19[illegible]) [illegible] national comparative study of job [illegible]. Labour [illegible]

[illegible] (19[illegible]) On the effects of the [illegible] bending supply curve. [illegible] Labor Relations Review [illegible]

[illegible] (19[illegible]) [illegible] labour supply. Journal of Economic Behavior and Organization [illegible]

[illegible] (19[illegible]) [illegible] effects [illegible] labour supply. Journal of Economic Behavior and Organization [illegible]

[illegible] M. (19[illegible]) [illegible] Economic Journal [illegible]

Wolf, A., [illegible], J., Swinney, [illegible], Vastano, J.A. (1985) Determining Lyapunov exponents from a time series. Physica D 16, [illegible]

[illegible] (19[illegible]) [illegible] models of unemployment. American Economic Review 74 Papers and Proceedings, [illegible]

[illegible] (19[illegible]) [illegible] labour supply behavior. Labour Economics [illegible]

Software: [illegible] (19[illegible]) [illegible] (Version [illegible]) [illegible]

Printing: Weihert-Druck GmbH, Darmstadt
Binding: Buchbinderei Schäffer, Grünstadt

Lecture Notes in Economics and Mathematical Systems

For information about Vols. 1–295
please contact your bookseller or Springer-Verlag

Vol. 300: U. Derigs, Programming in Networks and Graphs. XI, 315 pages. 1988.

Vol. 301: J. Kacprzyk, M. Roubens (Eds.), Non-Conventional Preference Relations in Decision Making. VII, 155 pages. 1988.

Vol. 302: H.A. Eiselt, G. Pederzoli (Eds.), Advances in Optimization and Control. Proceedings, 1986. VIII, 372 pages. 1988.

Vol. 303: F.X. Diebold, Empirical Modeling of Exchange Rate Dynamics. VII, 143 pages. 1988.

Vol. 304: A. Kurzhanski, K. Neumann, D. Pallaschke (Eds.), Optimization, Parallel Processing and Applications. Proceedings, 1987. VI, 292 pages. 1988.

Vol. 305: G.-J.C.Th. van Schijndel, Dynamic Firm and Investor Behaviour under Progressive Personal Taxation. X, 215 pages.1988.

Vol. 306: Ch. Klein, A Static Microeconomic Model of Pure Competition. VIII, 139 pages. 1988.

Vol. 307: T.K. Dijkstra (Ed.), On Model Uncertainty and its Statistical Implications. VII, 138 pages. 1988.

Vol. 308: J.R. Daduna, A. Wren (Eds.), Computer-Aided Transit Scheduling. VIII, 339 pages. 1988.

Vol. 309: G. Ricci, K. Velupillai (Eds.), Growth Cycles and Multisectoral Economics: The Goodwin Tradition. III, 126 pages. 1988.

Vol. 310: J. Kacprzyk, M. Fedrizzi (Eds.), Combining Fuzzy Imprecision with Probabilistic Uncertainty in Decision Making. IX, 399 pages. 1988.

Vol. 311: R. Färe, Fundamentals of Production Theory. IX, 163 pages. 1988.

Vol. 312: J. Krishnakumar, Estimation of Simultaneous Equation Models with Error Components Structure. X, 357 pages. 1988.

Vol. 313: W. Jammernegg, Sequential Binary Investment Decisions. VI, 156 pages. 1988.

Vol. 314: R. Tietz, W. Albers, R. Selten (Eds.), Bounded Rational Behavior in Experimental Games and Markets. VI, 368 pages. 1988.

Vol. 315: I. Orishimo, G.J.D. Hewings, P. Nijkamp (Eds), Information Technology: Social and Spatial Perspectives. Proceedings 1986. VI, 268 pages. 1988.

Vol. 316: R.L. Basmann, D.J. Slottje, K. Hayes, J.D. Johnson, D.J. Molina, The Generalized Fechner-Thurstone Direct Utility Function and Some of its Uses. VIII, 159 pages. 1988.

Vol. 317: L. Bianco, A. La Bella (Eds.), Freight Transport Planning and Logistics. Proceedings, 1987. X, 568 pages. 1988.

Vol. 318: T. Doup, Simplicial Algorithms on the Simplotope. VIII, 262 pages. 1988.

Vol. 319: D.T. Luc, Theory of Vector Optimization. VIII, 173 pages. 1989.

Vol. 320: D. van der Wijst, Financial Structure in Small Business. VII, 181 pages. 1989.

Vol. 321: M. Di Matteo, R.M. Goodwin, A. Vercelli (Eds.), Technological and Social Factors in Long Term Fluctuations. Proceedings. IX, 442 pages. 1989.

Vol. 322: T. Kollintzas (Ed.), The Rational Expectations Equilibrium Inventory Model. XI, 269 pages. 1989.

Vol. 323: M.B.M. de Koster, Capacity Oriented Analysis and Design of Production Systems. XII, 245 pages. 1989.

Vol. 324: I.M. Bomze, B.M. Pötscher, Game Theoretical Foundations of Evolutionary Stability. VI, 145 pages. 1989.

Vol. 325: P. Ferri, E. Greenberg, The Labor Market and Business Cycle Theories. X, 183 pages. 1989.

Vol. 326: Ch. Sauer, Alternative Theories of Output, Unemployment, and Inflation in Germany: 1960–1985. XIII, 206 pages. 1989.

Vol. 327: M. Tawada, Production Structure and International Trade. V, 132 pages. 1989.

Vol. 328: W. Güth, B. Kalkofen, Unique Solutions for Strategic Games. VII, 200 pages. 1989.

Vol. 329: G. Tillmann, Equity, Incentives, and Taxation. VI, 132 pages. 1989.

Vol. 330: P.M. Kort, Optimal Dynamic Investment Policies of a Value Maximizing Firm. VII, 185 pages. 1989.

Vol. 331: A. Lewandowski, A.P. Wierzbicki (Eds.), Aspiration Based Decision Support Systems. X, 400 pages. 1989.

Vol. 332: T.R. Gulledge, Jr., L.A. Litteral (Eds.), Cost Analysis Applications of Economics and Operations Research. Proceedings. VII, 422 pages. 1989.

Vol. 333: N. Dellaert, Production to Order. VII, 158 pages. 1989.

Vol. 334: H.-W. Lorenz, Nonlinear Dynamical Economics and Chaotic Motion. XI, 248 pages. 1989.

Vol. 335: A.G. Lockett, G. Islei (Eds.), Improving Decision Making in Organisations. Proceedings. IX, 606 pages. 1989.

Vol. 336: T. Puu, Nonlinear Economic Dynamics. VII, 119 pages. 1989.

Vol. 337: A. Lewandowski, I. Stanchev (Eds.), Methodology and Software for Interactive Decision Support. VIII, 309 pages. 1989.

Vol. 338: J.K. Ho, R.P. Sundarraj, DECOMP: An Implementation of Dantzig-Wolfe Decomposition for Linear Programming. VI, 206 pages.

Vol. 339: J. Terceiro Lomba, Estimation of Dynamic Econometric Models with Errors in Variables. VIII, 116 pages. 1990.

Vol. 340: T. Vasko, R. Ayres, L. Fontvieille (Eds.), Life Cycles and Long Waves. XIV, 293 pages. 1990.

Vol. 341: G.R. Uhlich, Descriptive Theories of Bargaining. IX, 165 pages. 1990.

Vol. 342: K. Okuguchi, F. Szidarovszky, The Theory of Oligopoly with Multi-Product Firms. V, 167 pages. 1990.

Vol. 343: C. Chiarella, The Elements of a Nonlinear Theory of Economic Dynamics. IX, 149 pages. 1990.

Vol. 344: K. Neumann, Stochastic Project Networks. XI, 237 pages. 1990.

Vol. 345: A. Cambini, E. Castagnoli, L. Martein, P Mazzoleni, S. Schaible (Eds.), Generalized Convexity and Fractional Programming with Economic Applications. Proceedings, 1988. VII, 361 pages. 1990.

Vol. 346: R. von Randow (Ed.), Integer Programming and Related Areas. A Classified Bibliography 1984–1987. XIII, 514 pages. 1990.

Vol. 347: D. Ríos Insua, Sensitivity Analysis in Multi-objective Decision Making. XI, 193 pages. 1990.

Vol. 348: H. Störmer, Binary Functions and their Applications. VIII, 151 pages. 1990.

Vol. 349: G.A. Pfann, Dynamic Modelling of Stochastic Demand for Manufacturing Employment. VI, 158 pages. 1990.

Vol. 350: W.-B. Zhang, Economic Dynamics. X, 232 pages. 1990.

Vol. 351: A. Lewandowski, V. Volkovich (Eds.), Multiobjective Problems of Mathematical Programming. Proceedings, 1988. VII, 315 pages. 1991.

Vol. 352: O. van Hilten, Optimal Firm Behaviour in the Context of Technological Progress and a Business Cycle. XII, 229 pages. 1991.

Vol. 353: G. Ricci (Ed.), Decision Processes in Economics. Proceedings, 1989. III, 209 pages 1991.

Vol. 354: M. Ivaldi, A Structural Analysis of Expectation Formation. XII, 230 pages. 1991.

Vol. 355: M. Salomon. Deterministic Lotsizing Models for Production Planning. VII, 158 pages. 1991.

Vol. 356: P. Korhonen, A. Lewandowski, J . Wallenius (Eds.), Multiple Criteria Decision Support. Proceedings, 1989. XII, 393 pages. 1991.

Vol. 357: P. Zörnig, Degeneracy Graphs and Simplex Cycling. XV, 194 pages. 1991.

Vol. 358: P. Knottnerus, Linear Models with Correlated Disturbances. VIII, 196 pages. 1991.

Vol. 359: E. de Jong, Exchange Rate Determination and Optimal Economic Policy Under Various Exchange Rate Regimes. VII, 270 pages. 1991.

Vol. 360: P. Stalder, Regime Translations, Spillovers and Buffer Stocks. VI, 193 pages . 1991.

Vol. 361: C. F. Daganzo, Logistics Systems Analysis. X, 321 pages. 1991.

Vol. 362: F. Gehrels, Essays in Macroeconomics of an Open Economy. VII, 183 pages. 1991.

Vol. 363: C. Puppe, Distorted Probabilities and Choice under Risk. VIII, 100 pages . 1991

Vol. 364: B. Horvath, Are Policy Variables Exogenous? XII, 162 pages. 1991.

Vol. 365: G. A. Heuer, U. Leopold-Wildburger. Balanced Silverman Games on General Discrete Sets. V, 140 pages. 1991.

Vol. 366: J. Gruber (Ed.), Econometric Decision Models. Proceedings, 1989. VIII, 636 pages. 1991.

Vol. 367: M. Grauer, D. B. Pressmar (Eds.), Parallel Computing and Mathematical Optimization. Proceedings. V, 208 pages. 1991.

Vol. 368: M. Fedrizzi, J. Kacprzyk, M. Roubens (Eds.), Interactive Fuzzy Optimization. VII, 216 pages. 1991.

Vol. 369: R. Koblo, The Visible Hand. VIII, 131 pages.1991.

Vol. 370: M. J. Beckmann, M. N. Gopalan, R. Subramanian (Eds.), Stochastic Processes and their Applications. Proceedings, 1990. XLI, 292 pages. 1991.

Vol. 371: A. Schmutzler, Flexibility and Adjustment to Information in Sequential Decision Problems. VIII, 198 pages. 1991.

Vol. 372: J. Esteban, The Social Viability of Money. X, 202 pages. 1991.

Vol. 373: A. Billot, Economic Theory of Fuzzy Equilibria. XIII, 164 pages. 1992.

Vol. 374: G. Pflug, U. Dieter (Eds.), Simulation and Optimization. Proceedings, 1990. X, 162 pages. 1992.

Vol. 375: S.-J. Chen, Ch.-L. Hwang, Fuzzy Multiple Attribute Decision Making. XII, 536 pages. 1992.

Vol. 376: K.-H. Jöckel, G. Rothe, W. Sendler (Eds.), Bootstrapping and Related Techniques. Proceedings, 1990. VIII, 247 pages. 1992.

Vol. 377: A. Villar, Operator Theorems with Applications to Distributive Problems and Equilibrium Models. XVI, 160 pages. 1992.

Vol. 378: W. Krabs, J. Zowe (Eds.), Modern Methods of Optimization. Proceedings, 1990. VIII, 348 pages. 1992.

Vol. 379: K. Marti (Ed.), Stochastic Optimization. Proceedings, 1990. VII, 182 pages. 1992.

Vol. 380: J. Odelstad, Invariance and Structural Dependence. XII, 245 pages. 1992.

Vol. 381: C. Giannini, Topics in Structural VAR Econometrics. XI, 131 pages. 1992.

Vol. 382: W. Oettli, D. Pallaschke (Eds.), Advances in Optimization. Proceedings, 1991. X, 527 pages. 1992.

Vol. 383: J. Vartiainen, Capital Accumulation in a Corporatist Economy. VII, 177 pages. 1992.

Vol. 384: A. Martina, Lectures on the Economic Theory of Taxation. XII, 313 pages. 1992.

Vol. 385: J. Gardeazabal, M. Regúlez, The Monetary Model of Exchange Rates and Cointegration. X, 194 pages. 1992.

Vol. 386: M. Desrochers, J.-M. Rousseau (Eds.), Computer-Aided Transit Scheduling. Proceedings, 1990. XIII, 432 pages. 1992.

Vol. 387: W. Gaertner, M. Klemisch-Ahlert, Social Choice and Bargaining Perspectives on Distributive Justice. VIII, 131 pages. 1992.

Vol. 388: D. Bartmann, M. J. Beckmann, Inventory Control. XV, 252 pages. 1992.

Vol. 389: B. Dutta, D. Mookherjee, T. Parthasarathy, T. Raghavan, D. Ray, S. Tijs (Eds.), Game Theory and Economic Applications. Proceedings, 1990. IX, 454 pages. 1992.

Vol. 390: G. Sorger, Minimum Impatience Theorem for Recursive Economic Models. X, 162 pages. 1992.

Vol. 391: C. Keser, Experimental Duopoly Markets with Demand Inertia. X, 150 pages. 1992.

Vol. 392: K. Frauendorfer, Stochastic Two-Stage Programming. VIII, 228 pages. 1992.

Vol. 393: B. Lucke, Price Stabilization on World Agricultural Markets. XI, 274 pages. 1992.

Vol. 394: Y.-J. Lai, C.-L. Hwang, Fuzzy Mathematical Programming. XIII, 301 pages. 1992.

Vol. 395: G. Haag, U. Mueller, K. G. Troitzsch (Eds.), Economic Evolution and Demographic Change. XVI, 409 pages. 1992.

Vol. 396: R. V. V. Vidal (Ed.), Applied Simulated Annealing. VIII, 358 pages. 1992.

Vol. 397: J. Wessels, A. P. Wierzbicki (Eds.), User-Oriented Methodology and Techniques of Decision Analysis and Support. Proceedings, 1991. XII, 295 pages. 1993.

Vol. 398: J.-P. Urbain, Exogeneity in Error Correction Models. XI, 189 pages. 1993.

Vol. 399: F. Gori, L. Geronazzo, M. Galeotti (Eds.), Nonlinear Dynamics in Economics and Social Sciences. Proceedings, 1991. VIII, 367 pages. 1993.

Vol. 400: H. Tanizaki, Nonlinear Filters. XII, 203 pages. 1993.

Vol. 401: K. Mosler, M. Scarsini, Stochastic Orders and Applications. V, 379 pages. 1993.

Vol. 402: A. van den Elzen, Adjustment Processes for Exchange Economies and Noncooperative Games. VII, 146 pages. 1993.

Vol. 403: G. Brennscheidt, Predictive Behavior. VI, 227 pages. 1993.

Vol. 404: Y.-J. Lai, Ch.-L. Hwang, Fuzzy Multiple Objective Decision Making. XIV, 475 pages. 1994.

Vol. 405: S. Komlósi, T. Rapcsák, S. Schaible (Eds.), Generalized Convexity. Proceedings, 1992. VIII, 404 pages. 1994.

Vol. 406: N. M. Hung, N. V. Quyen, Dynamic Timing Decisions Under Uncertainty. X, 194 pages. 1994.

Vol. 407: M. Ooms, Empirical Vector Autoregressive Modeling. XIII, 380 pages. 1994.

Vol. 408: K. Haase, Lotsizing and Scheduling for Production Planning. VIII, 118 pages. 1994.

Vol. 409: A. Sprecher, Resource-Constrained Project Scheduling. XII, 142 pages. 1994.

Vol. 410: R. Winkelmann, Count Data Models. XI, 213 pages. 1994.

Vol. 411: S. Dauzère-Péres, J.-B. Lasserre, An Integrated Approach in Production Planning and Scheduling. XVI, 137 pages. 1994.

Vol. 412: B. Kuon, Two-Person Bargaining Experiments with Incomplete Information. IX, 293 pages. 1994.

Vol. 413: R. Fiorito (Ed.), Inventory, Business Cycles and Monetary Transmission. VI, 287 pages. 1994.

Vol. 414: Y. Crama, A. Oerlemans, F. Spieksma, Production Planning in Automated Manufacturing. X, 210 pages. 1994.

Vol. 415: P. C. Nicola, Imperfect General Equilibrium. XI, 167 pages. 1994.

Vol. 416: H. S. J. Cesar, Control and Game Models of the Greenhouse Effect. XI, 225 pages. 1994.

Vol. 417: B. Ran, D. E. Boyce, Dynamic Urban Transportation Network Models. XV, 391 pages. 1994.

Vol. 418: P. Bogetoft, Non-Cooperative Planning Theory. XI, 309 pages. 1994.

Vol. 419: T. Maruyama, W. Takahashi (Eds.), Nonlinear and Convex Analysis in Economic Theory. VIII, 306 pages. 1995.

Vol. 420: M. Peeters, Time-To-Build. Interrelated Investment and Labour Demand Modelling. With Applications to Six OECD Countries. IX, 204 pages. 1995.

Vol. 421: C. Dang, Triangulations and Simplicial Methods. IX, 196 pages. 1995.

Vol. 422: D. S. Bridges, G. B. Mehta, Representations of Preference Orderings. X, 165 pages. 1995.

Vol. 423: K. Marti, P. Kall (Eds.), Stochastic Programming. Numerical Techniques and Engineering Applications. VIII, 351 pages. 1995.

Vol. 424: G. A. Heuer, U. Leopold-Wildburger, Silverman's Game. X, 283 pages. 1995.

Vol. 425: J. Kohlas, P.-A. Monney, A Mathematical Theory of Hints. XIII, 419 pages, 1995.

Vol. 426: B. Finkenstädt, Nonlinear Dynamics in Economics. IX, 156 pages. 1995.

Vol. 427: F. W. van Tongeren, Microsimulation Modelling of the Corporate Firm. XVII, 275 pages. 1995.

Vol. 428: A. A. Powell, Ch. W. Murphy, Inside a Modern Macroeconometric Model. XVIII, 424 pages. 1995.

Vol. 429: R. Durier, C. Michelot, Recent Developments in Optimization. VIII, 356 pages. 1995.

Vol. 430: J. R. Daduna, I. Branco, J. M. Pinto Paixão (Eds.), Computer-Aided Transit Scheduling. XIV, 374 pages. 1995.

Vol. 431: A. Aulin, Causal and Stochastic Elements in Business Cycles. XI, 116 pages. 1996.

Vol. 432: M. Tamiz (Ed.), Multi-Objective Programming and Goal Programming. VI, 359 pages. 1996.

Vol. 433: J. Menon, Exchange Rates and Prices. XIV, 313 pages. 1996.

Vol. 434: M. W. J. Blok, Dynamic Models of the Firm. VII, 193 pages. 1996.

Vol. 435: L. Chen, Interest Rate Dynamics, Derivatives Pricing, and Risk Management. XII, 149 pages. 1996.

Vol. 436: M. Klemisch-Ahlert, Bargaining in Economic and Ethical Environments. IX, 155 pages. 1996.

Vol. 437: C. Jordan, Batching and Scheduling. IX, 178 pages. 1996.

Vol. 438: A. Villar, General Equilibrium with Increasing Returns. XIII, 164 pages. 1996.

Vol. 439: M. Zenner, Learning to Become Rational. VII, 201 pages. 1996.

Vol. 440: W. Ryll, Litigation and Settlement in a Game with Incomplete Information. VIII, 174 pages. 1996.

Vol. 441: H. Dawid, Adaptive Learning by Genetic Algorithms. IX, 166 pages.1996.

Vol. 442: L. Corchón, Theories of Imperfectly Competitive Markets. XIII, 163 pages. 1996.

Vol. 443: G. Lang, On Overlapping Generations Models with Productive Capital. X, 98 pages. 1996.

Vol. 444: S. Jørgensen, G. Zaccour (Eds.), Dynamic Competitive Analysis in Marketing. X, 285 pages. 1996.

Vol. 445: A. H. Christer, S. Osaki, L. C. Thomas (Eds.), Stochastic Modelling in Innovative Manufactoring. X, 361 pages. 1997.

Vol. 446: G. Dhaene, Encompassing. X, 160 pages. 1997.

Vol. 447: A. Artale, Rings in Auctions. X, 172 pages. 1997.

Vol. 448: G. Fandel, T. Gal (Eds.), Multiple Criteria Decision Making. XII, 678 pages. 1997.

Vol. 449: F. Fang, M. Sanglier (Eds.), Complexity and Self-Organization in Social and Economic Systems. IX, 317 pages, 1997.

Vol. 450: P. M. Pardalos, D. W. Hearn, W. W. Hager, (Eds.), Network Optimization. VIII, 485 pages, 1997.

Vol. 451: M. Salge, Rational Bubbles. Theoretical Basis, Economic Relevance, and Empirical Evidence with a Special Emphasis on the German Stock Market.IX, 265 pages. 1997.

Vol. 452: P. Gritzmann, R. Horst, E. Sachs, R. Tichatschke (Eds.), Recent Advances in Optimization. VIII, 379 pages. 1997.

Vol. 453: A. S. Tangian, J. Gruber (Eds.), Constructing Scalar-Valued Objective Functions. VIII, 298 pages. 1997.

Vol. 454: H.-M. Krolzig, Markov-Switching Vector Autoregressions. XIV, 358 pages. 1997.

Vol. 455: R. Caballero, F. Ruiz, R. E. Steuer (Eds.), Advances in Multiple Objective and Goal Programming. VIII, 391 pages. 1997.

Vol. 456: R. Conte, R. Hegselmann, P. Terna (Eds.), Simulating Social Phenomena. VIII, 536 pages. 1997.

Vol. 457: C. Hsu, Volume and the Nonlinear Dynamics of Stock Returns. VIII, 133 pages. 1998.

Vol. 458: K. Marti, P. Kall (Eds.), Stochastic Programming Methods and Technical Applications. X, 437 pages. 1998.

Vol. 459: H. K. Ryu, D. J. Slottje, Measuring Trends in U.S. Income Inequality. XI, 195 pages. 1998.

Vol. 460: B. Fleischmann, J. A. E. E. van Nunen, M. G. Speranza, P. Stähly, Advances in Distribution Logistic. XI, 535 pages. 1998.

Vol. 461: U. Schmidt, Axiomatic Utility Theory under Risk. XV, 201 pages. 1998.

Vol. 462: L. von Auer, Dynamic Preferences, Choice Mechanisms, and Welfare. XII, 226 pages. 1998.

Vol. 463: G. Abraham-Frois (Ed.), Non-Linear Dynamics and Endogenous Cycles. VI, 204 pages. 1998.

Vol. 464: A. Aulin, The Impact of Science on Economic Growth and its Cycles. IX, 204 pages. 1998.

Vol. 465: T. J. Stewart, R. C. van den Honert (Eds.), Trends in Multicriteria Decision Making. X, 448 pages. 1998.

Vol. 466: A. Sadrieh, The Alternating Double Auction Market. VII, 350 pages. 1998.

Vol. 467: H. Hennig-Schmidt, Bargaining in a Video Experiment. Determinants of Boundedly Rational Behavior. XII, 221 pages. 1999.

Vol. 468: A. Ziegler, A Game Theory Analysis of Options. XIV, 145 pages. 1999.

Vol. 469: M. P. Vogel, Environmental Kuznets Curves. XIII, 197 pages. 1999.

Vol. 470: M. Ammann, Pricing Derivative Credit Risk. XII, 228 pages. 1999.

Vol. 471: N. H. M. Wilson (Ed.), Computer-Aided Transit Scheduling. XI, 444 pages. 1999.

Vol. 472: J.-R. Tyran, Money Illusion and Strategic Complementarity as Causes of Monetary Non-Neutrality. X, 228 pages. 1999.

Vol. 473: S. Helber, Performance Analysis of Flow Lines with Non-Linear Flow of Material. IX, 280 pages. 1999.

Vol. 474: U. Schwalbe, The Core of Economies with Asymmetric Information. IX, 141 pages. 1999.

Vol. 475: L. Kaas, Dynamic Macroelectronics with Imperfect Competition. XI, 155 pages. 1999.

Vol. 476: R. Demel, Fiscal Policy, Public Debt and the Term Structure of Interest Rates. X, 279 pages. 1999.

Vol. 477: M. Théra, R. Tichatschke (Eds.), Ill-posed Variational Problems and Regularization Techniques. VIII, 274 pages. 1999.

Vol. 478: S. Hartmann, Project Scheduling under Limited Resources. XII, 221 pages. 1999.

Vol. 479: L. v. Thadden, Money, Inflation, and Capital Formation. IX, 192 pages. 1999.

Vol. 480: M. Grazia Speranza, P. Stähly (Eds.), New Trends in Distribution Logistics. X, 336 pages. 1999.

Vol. 481: V. H. Nguyen, J. J. Strodiot, P. Tossings (Eds.). Optimations. IX, 498 pages. 2000.

Vol. 482: W. B. Zhang, A Theory of International Trade. XI, 192 pages. 2000.

Vol. 483: M. Königstein, Equity, Efficiency and Evolutionary Stability in Bargaining Games with Joint Production. XII, 197 pages. 2000.

Vol. 484: D. D. Gatti, M. Gallegati, A. Kirman, Interaction and Market Structure. VI, 298 pages. 2000.

Vol. 485: A. Garnaev, Search Games and Other Applications of Game Theory. VIII, 145 pages. 2000.

Vol. 486: M. Neugart, Nonlinear Labor Market Dynamics. X, 175 pages. 2000.